Harry Hopkins

and the Grand Alliance
of the Second World War

Harry Hopkins

and the Grand Alliance
of the Second World War

June Hopkins

FOREWARD

During WWII, Harry Hopkins acted as liaison between U.S. President Franklin Roosevelt and British Prime Minister Winston Churchill, leaders whose clashing temperaments and divergent policy goals required his agile diplomacy. The wartime alliance between the U.S. and Britain was critical to victory in war being waged against fascism. As the president's personal envoy to Great Britain and the Soviet Union, Hopkins became a cornerstone for Allied success.

This monograph investigates the complex interrelationships of Churchill, Roosevelt, and Stalin from the perspective of Hopkins' career and demonstrated how he influenced wartime strategy. In addition, Hopkins' commitment to social justice as federal relief administrator during the Great Depression profoundly informed his work on the international stage.

Arguing against the commonly held notion that Hopkins had two separate careers, I demonstrate that Hopkins saw the defeat of fascism as the ultimate attainment of social justice. Such attention to the historical connections between the local and the global is relevant today, and could stimulate new ways of thinking about such issues as global climate change and the proper role of government.

Drawing on a meticulous investigation into the newly digitized Winston Churchill Papers archived at The George Washington University as well as personal Hopkins family papers, this study offers a nuanced analysis of the Grand Alliance, with particular attention to Roosevelt's use of personal diplomacy. Such an approach not only revises current considerations of Hopkins' larger career, but also offers a fuller understanding of the largely overlooked yet crucial relationship between Churchill and Hopkins.

TABLE OF CONTENTS

Introduction

At 2:00 on Friday afternoon, February 2, 1946, 2,000 mourners sat quietly in St. Bartholomew's Episcopal Church on the corner of Park Avenue and 51st Street in New York City for a funeral service. It was crowded with mourners. Some were unable find a seat inside and had to stand in the back of the beautiful cruciform church. Harry Hopkins, President Franklin Roosevelt's close friend and advisor, had died three days before. Family members, friends, and notables from all over the world had come to pay their last respects to this man, a much admired and much vilified public servant.[1] Despite the frigid temperature, the curious packed the sidewalk on the west side of Park Avenue, hoping to catch sight of a celebrity.

During the funeral service, Rev. George Paul T. Sargent reflected on Hopkins' service to his country and to his President when he offered an original prayer:

> We thank Thee, O God for all the loyalty and courage which have passed from the life of this Thy servant into the lives of others and have left the world richer for his presence: for a life's task faithfully discharged; for loyalty to country and duty; for friendship and helpfulness; for sadness met without surrender and weakness endured without defeat; for these blessings we thank Thee, O God.

At the conclusion of the service, as the African mahogany casket, draped with flowers, was slowly carried out of the church, the walls resounded with the church's magnificent pipe organ playing the "Battle Hymn of the Republic." Many wept openly. The aptness of the prayer and music could not have been lost on the mourners who were well aware that Hopkins' career had been the embodiment of public service, courage, and personal sacrifice. Pallbearers included James Forrestal, Secretary of the Navy; Army General Henry Arnold; British Ambassador, the Earl of Halifax (a pallbearer representing Winston Churchill), and financier Bernard Baruch. Honorary pallbearers who could not attend were President Harry Truman and Prime Minister Winston Churchill. It was very appropriate that the music played and the psalms recited at this funeral service were the same used at the service held for his boss, President Franklin Roosevelt, who had died nine months and seventeen days earlier.[2]

Later in the year, on May 22, at a memorial service held for Hopkins in Washington, actor Burgess Meredith read the eulogy written by John Steinbeck. He emphasized Harry Hopkins' determination during the dark days of the Great Depression when his New Deal programs provided jobs for desperate unemployed Americans. Steinbeck wrote that the physical monuments to Hopkins that emanated from the Civil Works Administration (CWA) and the Works Progress Administration (WPA) – the forests, the highways, the buildings, the art works – will endure but even more important are the millions of people whose security he ensured. Steinbeck applauded Hopkins' dictum that Americans have the right to live in security and government has the responsibility to provide for that security. No longer will the government deny this responsibility, he claimed. The memorial to Hopkins lies in the concept that he embedded in the nation: "Human welfare is the first and final task of government; it has no other. His grave cannot be closed; the man is not dead." [3]

For all of his adult life, Hopkins worked as a public servant for the good of others. Social justice—that is, ensuring that all would be able to share equally in the blessings of liberty promised by the U. S. Constitution— became Hopkins' priority. He was especially concerned for the welfare of so many Americans suffering deprivation during the severe economic depression of the 1930s. From 1940 through 1945, Hopkins became an internationalist and his concern centered on people all over the world being terrorized by expansionist and militaristic dictators. The threat of fascism gave new impetus to this concern for social justice. Robert Sherwood, FDR's speechwriter, biographer, and White House insider, wrote that for Hopkins, "the New Deal provided training in combat conditions for his life was a series of ferocious battles against widespread misery." [4] This battle began in 1933 and ended only when he died in early 1946.

The testimonials at his funeral from leaders, both foreign and domestic, emphasized both his humanitarianism, which defined his work during the Depression as well as during the Second World War. Former Prime Winston Churchill was unable to attend Hopkins' funeral but described how Hopkins' wide-ranging vision and piercing eye countless times kept the often-contentious leaders on track when all seemed baffled. "These were the times when Hopkins would rap out the deadly question: 'surely, Mr.

President, here is the point we have got to settle. Are we going to face it or not?' ... Faced it always was and, being faced, was conquered. He was a true leader of men and alike in ardor and in wisdom, in time of crisis, he has rarely been excelled."[5]

General Dwight D. Eisenhower expressed a similar, if less eloquent, sentiment:

I always found him completely devoted to duty and determined to carry his tasks to a successful conclusion regardless of the effect upon his own health and convenience and comfort. His intense Americanism was equaled only by his determination to preserve the Allied unity.

But Eisenhower added, "I am certain that the public will never fully understand the extent of his contribution to the victory, but I know also that in the hearts and minds of those who were so fortunate as to associate with him at critical times there will never be any doubt on this score."[6] Generalissimo and Mme. Chiang Kai-shek wrote that Hopkins built the foundation for world peace and the British foreign secretary, Ernest Bevin, wrote that Hopkins' "fame would grow with the years."[7]

Yet Hopkins' fame did not grow over the years as Bevin had predicted. Controversy followed Harry Hopkins during his entire public life and persisted after his untimely death at age 55. Ike was right. Despite some recent monographs on his wartime career, there are many today who do not even recognize his name.[8] The ideas that Hopkins left behind, the ones that Steinbeck had praised, may have, in fact, even faded from our collective memories. Thus, it is useful to take a deeper and more personal look at a man whose pragmatism was tempered with idealism and whose belief in *realpolitik* was tempered by a social conscience. These were the qualities that he drew on during the challenging years of the Great Depression and the Second World War. These were the qualities that enabled him to play a role on both the national and international stage that no other person has been able to emulate.

Chapter 1—Beginnings

Harry Hopkins, newly graduated from Grinnell College in Iowa, deep in America's heartland, seemed to be an ordinary young man in search of a life outside of his rural hometown. It was 1912, the century was young and held so much promise; no one anticipated war—progress was the watchword of the era. This particular young college graduate felt only optimism for the future. His destination was New York City's Lower East Side where his older sister, Adah Hopkins, had worked some years earlier at a social settlement house. It held a magical attraction for him; it was where he would make his way in the world. Traveling east across the country, with his college friend Louis Hartson, he insisted that they stop off in Chicago. He wanted to experience the excitement of national politics that was taking place at the Republican Presidential Convention. Hopkins was determined to get a front row seat to experience the political buzz that he was sure was going on. Much to Hartson's consternation, Hopkins actually faked his way into the Coliseum by posing as Elihu Root's secretary[9]. He got there just in time to see ex-President Theodore Roosevelt bolt the convention in fury when he lost the nomination to his successor, William Howard Taft. The result was a third party— the Bull Moose, or Progressive party.

The young men then spent a few days in Washington, D.C., marveling at the sights in the nation's capital before going to Baltimore where the Democrats were holding their convention in the Fifth Regiment Armory. Hopkins had been the president of the Woodrow Wilson Club at his college and was thrilled to witness the success of his hero, soon to be president of the United States. The sights and sounds of party politics thrilled the young Hopkins and left him with a growing desire to get into the game.

Making his way north, he arrived in Lower Manhattan in the late summer of 1912 and, following in his sister's footsteps, immediately went to work at Christodora House, a social settlement. This particular settlement house, located in the Lower East Side of Manhattan, like others provided a wide variety of social and educational services to the largely immigrant residents who lived in neglected urban neighborhoods. After a stint in the Settlement's summer camp for boys in Bound Brook, New Jersey, Hopkins' moved into Christodora House, and began his career as a social worker. Head Worker Christina MacColl, a remarkable woman who became his lifelong friend, assigned him to work as what was then called, "a friendly visitor." His assignment was to climb the dark stairs of the tenements in order to talk with the residents in order to find out what the families needed in the way of services. He would then write reports, and submit them to Miss McColl. This was the beginning of the new profession of social work. The use of case studies, which he was compiling, soon became an integral part of social work. The area he covered, the densely populated Sixth Assembly District of New York, had the greatest proportion of foreign-born persons in the US, mostly living in crowded tenement houses. The area was rife with social problems — poverty, disease, crime, prostitution; but the same area also pulsed with the many cultural contributions that came from such diversity—music, literature, food, art—all provided by the District's largely immigrant population. Hopkins had been at first shocked at the sight of grinding urban poverty. He was familiar with the somewhat genteel poverty of rural Iowa where there was often help from relatives and neighbors for those who had fallen on hard times; but this urban poverty was at first alien to him. He saw people who had no help, no hope, and who were victims of the progress he was so optimistic about. However, he soon began to look for solutions to the problems he found there. To do this, he drew from his education at Grinnell College, an institution that fostered the humanitarian ideals of the Social Gospel Movement. In the midst of the slums of downtown New York City, he began his 25-year career as a social worker.

Hopkins, tall, loose limbed, and affable, was the only man working at Christodora House. It is no wonder that he was highly sought after by the young women working there. Miss MacColl would recruit these women—white, middle-class, Protestant, and educated—who were mostly just taking time off after college and before marriage to engage in some good works.[10] But there was one in particular worker that Hopkins was especially attracted to. Ethel Gross was older by four years and had been living in the area for most of her life. Her family—a widowed mother, an older sister, and two brothers—had left Hungary in 1891, when she was just five years old. They settled in the Jewish Ghetto in the Lower East Side of Manhattan, occupying a small grimy tenement near Christodora House, a place where the child, wanting somehow to adjust to her surroundings, found some comfort. She had left school when she was 12, never feeling like she belonged. Christina MacColl gently mentored the young girl for years. By the time she was in her early twenties, Ethel had become a social worker, a political activist, and a suffragist. Yet she was still an outsider. Unlike the other young women who worked and lived at Christodora, Ethel was Jewish and poor; she did not live at Christodora House but in a tenement with her mother, sister and two brothers a few blocks away. Clearly, Ethel and Harry, attracted to each other, came from two distinct worlds and their coming together at Christodora represented the dual migration that was going on during the early 20th century: immigrants were coming from eastern and southern Europe to urban America and others were leaving rural America, moving east to the cities.

The two met at Christodora House in January 1913 and immediately fell in love; he was fascinated by her beauty, her exoticism; she was taken in by his wholesome Americanism. Harry wrote tender love letters to Ethel every day for the ten months of their courtship; she answered in equally ardent terms. They were married the following October at the Ethical Culture Society by John Lovejoy Elliot. They had their first child, David, a year later. Settlement work did not pay a lot and Hopkins needed a job where he could earn a wage sufficient to support a family. He left Christodora House and the family moved to Staten Island. In 1913, Hopkins landed a position with the Association for the Improvement of the Condition of the Poor, the AICP, a large and long-established charitable organization originally set up to help the deserving poor while at the same time working to improve their moral character. In essence, the poor were blamed for their poverty. However, by the early 20th century, social workers had sluffed off much of the shaming and blaming, and had become champions for social justice, using modern scientific methods to deal with the environmental causes of poverty that seemed so prevalent in urban centers.

In his new job, Hopkins directed his energies to the relief of poverty caused by unemployment. His experiences during this time created a solid platform upon which he built his social work conscience, a concept that would drive him for the rest of his life. With a severe economic downturn in New York City early in the 20th century, Hopkins had plenty to work with. Serving the needs of the poor in New York City, Hopkins came to realize that widows with young children were an especially vulnerable population. In 1915, he enthusiastically accepted a position as executive secretary of the Bureau of Child Welfare (BCW), a state agency that provided "pensions" for needy mothers. These so-called Widows' Pension or Mothers' Pension programs[11] that sprang up in cities during the early years of the 20th century provided widows with young children a government stipend to enable them to stay at home to care for their children. This would prevent needy mothers from farming them out to state-supported or city-supported orphanages. Hopkins honed his administrative skills working for the BCW, learning how to work quickly and efficiently within a state bureaucracy. It was a talent that came in very handy in the years to come.

By this time, Ethel, who had been an energetic suffragist and social worker, found that staying at home minding a child and a household did not make good use of the skills that she had developed at Christodora House or as a suffragist. The domestic sphere did not give her the satisfaction that she needed. Although she was wholly committed to raising their son, she began to resent that her husband's career so often kept him away from home. She also resented his refusal to include her in his projects. After all, she was four years older than her husband and he was already on his way to a successful career. In her mind, she was the one who had introduced him to the city when he was just a hayseed from Iowa. She had been meeting with suffragists and progressive reformers like Max and Crystal Eastman and Inez Milholland while he was still in school. His career was on the upswing, and she felt left behind. Their marriage was beginning to fray.

When the Great War broke out in Europe, Hopkins, like most Americans, was at first opposed to U.S. involvement. However, when Congress declared war in 1917 at President Woodrow Wilson's behest, he changed his attitude. He wrote to his friends at Grinnell, "Much as I was opposed to the war in the beginning, it is my firm belief that everyone should aid in prosecuting it as successfully and vigorously as possible." He later spoke with an old friend about the war and insisted that it was crucial to beat the Germans. "Germany symbolizes militarism and while it exists elsewhere, it is not with the same arrogance and domination."[12] This sentiment, of course, stayed with him for the duration of the Second World War.

Hopkins was exempted from the draft because he had vision problems and was married with a son. Therefore, like many social workers eager to do their part for the war effort, he joined the American Red Cross (ARC). The ARC sent him to New Orleans to be Assistant Director of Civilian Relief serving the Gulf Division. This division of the ARC provided all kinds of support to families of the servicemen who were away at the front, and this was an especially deserving and needy population. Hopkins threw himself into this work wholeheartedly. Drawing on some colleagues from Grinnell, he established a firm basis for a network of professional social workers based in New Orleans at Tulane University.

Clearly, Hopkins built up his career during the time he spent in New Orleans with the ARC. But his personal life exhibited some strain. The couple had a baby girl who died after four months from whooping cough. This devastated the couple. And then Hopkins came down with what was likely the so-called Spanish flu that killed hundreds of thousands of Americans. Ethel nursed him back to health and he survived. Oddly enough, after he recovered, he was healthier than at any other part of his life.

When the war ended, the ARC transferred Hopkins to Atlanta, Georgia, where he headed the Southern Division. Their second son, Robert, was born there in 1921. But although Hopkins gained national prominence because of his work there, the family was not content in Atlanta. Hopkins missed the exciting urban work scene that he had experienced in New York City and the war was over. He left the ARC and began to look for new opportunities in New York City. He now had a reputation as an up-and-coming social worker, and he seemed confident that this would afford him professional choices. After a brief stint with the AICP, in 1922, Hopkins landed a position as Director of the New York Tuberculosis Association. He went to work immediately and grew this agency into a much larger entity, eventually including the Heart Association and covering all of Manhattan, the Bronx, and Staten Island, serving three million people. He worked at a feverish pace and he spent a lot of other people's money creating a large and effective social service agency.

Ethel and Harry now had three boys; Stephen was born in New York in 1925. Ethel felt deeply what she considered her husband's neglect. And, even more debilitating, she felt that her life was withering away by being confined to domestic duties. On top of that she could not come to terms with the realization that while her husband had great empathy for the masses suffering from unemployment, ill health, or deprivation, he could not muster the same feelings for those closest to him. The couple's relationship did not improve with the move to New York City. In 1926, Hopkins met and fell in love with a young woman, Barbara Duncan, who worked at the NY Tuberculosis Association office. He fought against the attachment and even consulted a psychoanalyst, but he was unable to resist his love for Barbara. Harry and Ethel Hopkins separated in 1929 and divorced in 1931. That same year Harry and Barbara married. Their daughter, Diana, was born in 1933.

By this time the Great Depression had caused economic mayhem for the nation and New York City was especially hard hit by the distress caused by massive unemployment. It soon became clear that private charities could not handle the extent of the crisis; they had simply run out of money. When Franklin Delano Roosevelt (FDR) was elected governor of New York in 1928 and re-elected in 1931, he began to look for solutions to mass unemployment and poverty caused by the Depression. Roosevelt convinced the state legislature to allocate $20 million to the Temporary Emergency Relief Administration (TERA), which would use state funds to provide cash relief for unemployed New Yorkers. And he called Hopkins to Albany to run the relief program. With almost 20 years of experience in providing assistance to those in need, he had developed a method of dealing with bureaucracy that proved to be invaluable in the years to come. He would evaluate the problem, look for solutions, and then seek alternatives to those solutions; he held frequent informal meetings, looking for ways to include differing opinions. Hopkins was thrilled to finally have a job where he could create a program from the ground up, one that could become a model for other states and especially one that fit into economic and cultural norms. He cut through bureaucracy, which he regarded as ineffective, ignored organization charts, and placed a great deal of value on consensus. His administrative style emanated from his Social Gospel education, his progressive outlook, and his compassion for those in need.[13]

Hopkins knew that while people needed quick cash just to survive, they also desperately wanted the dignity of earning a wage; so, he added a work relief component to the TERA. This policy dovetailed with Roosevelt's belief that, while an infusion of cash was necessary at first, a job was the solution to the wide spread poverty caused by the Depression.

The TERA allowed Hopkins to showcase his administrative skills as well as to forge alliances. And the governor took notice. Although Roosevelt did not know Hopkins well at this point, the New York experience planted the seeds of what would become a long personal and political relationship between the two men. In addition, Hopkins worked closely with Frances Perkins, Roosevelt's industrial commissioner, and while they often disagreed on tactics, they found common ground on strategies to deal with the problem of unemployment. When Roosevelt was elected president in 1932, he took Frances Perkins with him as secretary of labor; Hopkins saw an opportunity. Shortly after the inauguration, in March 1933, Hopkins went to D.C. and, with Perkin's help, presented the president with a plan that would replicate the TERA on a federal scale. The president liked what he saw. Hopkins moved from Albany into the upper echelons of the Washington political scene with his new wife and daughter. Ethel Gross Hopkins, newly divorced, remained in New York with three boys to raise. While Hopkins would see his sons whenever he could, he and his ex-wife never spoke to each other again.

Hopkins immediately became an exuberant and very effective New Dealer. During his First Hundred Days Roosevelt created the Federal Emergency Relief Administration (FERA) and appointed Hopkins as its director. Roosevelt also gave Hopkins a cabinet-level position as Federal Relief Administrator. The FERA, under Hopkins' direction, provided both direct and work relief for millions of unemployed Americans. Firmly believing that jobs were the antidote to poverty, Hopkins ran massive New Deal jobs programs during the Great Depression: first the FERA, and then the Civil Works Administration (CWA) and beginning in 1935 the Works Progress Administration (WPA). And he spent billions of government dollars doing this. He established a reputation as a no-nonsense, often gruff, and usually cynical social worker turned bureaucrat. He took the president's advice to heart when, in 1933, the President told him to get relief out quickly to those in need and to pay no attention to politics or politicians.

He did such a terrific job as a top-notch administrator who knew how to cut through bureaucratic red tape, that he made a lot of enemies – some called him the Archangel of Spending; in 1936 *The Chicago Tribune* called him "a bullheaded man whose high place in the New Deal was won by his ability to waste more money in quicker time on more absurd undertakings than any other mischievous wit in Washington could think of." But for Hopkins, it was absurd that millions of Americans were suffering from the effects of the economic depression – through no fault of their own. He firmly believed that, in the United States with its abundance of wealth and its commitment to equality and liberty, people should not have to suffer the indignity of joblessness and the resultant miseries of poverty. The federal government, Hopkins insisted, would see to the welfare of all of its citizens. Even in the midst of a devastating economic depression, he was optimistic that this could be done.[14]

The President recognized Hopkins' difficult position as the favored target of a constant stream of negative press. In 1938 Roosevelt appointed him to the post of secretary of commerce, partially in an attempt to distance his friend from the politically dangerous arena of social policy and partially because he was thinking of Hopkins as a possible candidate for the presidency in 1940. This thought did not last longer than a moment because of the political baggage Hopkins carried and because he began to suffer from ill health beginning in the mid-1930s. ·

By the later Thirties, Roosevelt had found that Hopkins' energy and assertiveness in administering the New

Deal jobs programs was very useful. The President was relying more and more on Hopkins for advice and support; they became friends. This established the foundation of the relationship that the two maintained during the dangerous years of World War II.

The basic assumptions that drove Hopkins' career as a social worker and as federal relief administrator during the Great Depression continued to influence him after 1940. The continuity of his social and political mindset can help us understand Hopkins' public career during the war years. As a social worker on the local and state level he had relied on the humanitarian instincts instilled in him at Grinnell College and at Christodora Settlement House. As a New Dealer, he added administrative skills to his instinct to do good when and where he could. According to Dwight Tuttle, Hopkins believed that there would be a new world order created through the efforts of the President with the New Deal as a platform. The welfare of the American people that had concerned both of them during the Depression would be connected to their attention to ensuring the welfare of the world.[15]

Hopkins began his public career with a deeply embedded belief that the government on all levels, but especially those who work for the federal government have not just a moral imperative but the constitutional responsibility to be of service all citizens. In 1933, he was not a politician, but he was a quick study and soon acquired political savvy and diplomatic skills. Understanding this conceptual beginning can help one understand the impulse behind his actions during the war years, sitting at the right hand of President Roosevelt as his personal envoy to the

Allied leaders, most notably, British Prime Minister Winston Churchill.[16]

Chapter 2—The Principles

A complete narrative of World War II must include the diplomatic currents from 1939 to 1945, currents that emanated from the leaders who headed the major nations involved in the conflict. Their interactions had grave and immediate consequences and, therefore, are key to fully understand what happened. Scholars have written about the relationship between U.S. President Franklin Roosevelt and British Prime Minister Winston Churchill, about the fraught relationship between Churchill and Soviet Marshal Joseph Stalin, about Roosevelt and Stalin, and about Roosevelt and his aide Harry Hopkins. However, there has yet to be a full investigation into the significant influence of Hopkins on the wartime relationship between Roosevelt, Churchill, and Stalin (The Big Three).

Since Robert E. Sherwood's masterful *Roosevelt and Hopkins: An Intimate History* was published in 1948, scholars have written about the rapport between the president and his right-hand man, and the role Hopkins played during the thirteen years of his administration. The most complete of these is George T. McJimsey's *Harry Hopkins: Ally of the Poor and Defender of Democracy* (1987), which examines Hopkins' entire public career during the Depression and the Second World War. Dwight Tuttle's *Harry L. Hopkins and Anglo-American-Soviet Relations, 1941- 1945* (1983), and Matthew B. Wills' *Wartime Missions of Harry L. Hopkins* (2004) both treat Hopkins' wartime career adequately. David Reynolds investigates the important conferences in his 2007 book, *Summits: Six Meetings that Shaped the Twentieth Century* and includes an examination of Hopkins' participation in developing wartime policies. Robert Dallek's *Franklin D. Roosevelt and American Foreign Policy, 1932-1945* (1979), shows how the Roosevelt administration, with Hopkins in the inner circle, juggled isolationism and interventionism during these crucial years. Frank Costigliola's compelling book, *Roosevelt's Lost Alliances* (2012), gives the reader helpful insight into how personalities affected wartime politics and foreign policy. Recently there has been an upsurge in scholarly interest in Hopkins' role as Roosevelt's personal wartime envoy. Michael Fulilove's *Rendezvous with Destiny: How Franklin D. Roosevelt and Five Extraordinary Men Took America into the War and into the World* (2013) devotes three chapters to Hopkins in Britain and then in Moscow. Christopher D. O'Sullivan, *Harry Hopkins: FDR's Envoy to Churchill and Stalin* (2014), and. David Roll, *The Hopkins Touch: Harry Hopkins and the Forging of the Alliance to Defeat Hitler* (2012) are excellent investigations into Alliance politics. David Bercuson and Holger Herwig, *One Christmas in Washington: The Secret Meeting Between Roosevelt and Churchill That Changed the World* (Overlook, 2005) covers this important First Washington Conference but does not sufficiently explain Hopkins' role in the creation of the Grand Alliance. None of these excellent books adequately cover Hopkins' relationship with Winston Churchill. Hopkins had planned to write his memoirs after his retirement from government in July 1945 but he never did get around to this—probably because he was too ill. He died six months later. Therefore, his personal interpretations of the war years are somewhat sketchy.

In 1941, the addition of the Soviet Dictator to the wartime Alliance against fascism in June 1940 put Hopkins in the midst of foreign policy complications that affected the politics and the military strategy of the Grand Alliance and thus the outcome of the war. Therefore, a closer look at Harry Hopkins' interactions with the Big Three—Roosevelt, Churchill, and Stalin— is important to the full understanding of World War II history.

While the economic crisis at home occupied the Roosevelt administration from 1933 through 1938, rumblings in Europe and Asia worried him and, toward the end of the decade, the President began to turn his attention to international affairs. Adolf Hitler's Nazi party had come to power in Germany in 1933 about the same time that FDR was inaugurated as president. In direct violation of the Treaty of Versailles, and hoping to bring Germany out of a crippling economic depression, Hitler built up Germany's military and created a huge army and air force. In Italy, Benito Mussolini, head of the fascist government, also launched a military buildup. In 1935 his armies invaded Ethiopia. Despite the threats that emanated from Europe, Americans remained fiercely isolationist. In 1935, public opinion polls suggested that Americans overwhelmingly opposed involvement in foreign affairs. The memories of the Great War—regarded by many in the 1930s as a war to enrich bankers and munitions makers— encouraged passage of the Neutrality Acts of 1935, 36, and 37. The United States could not provide any aid to any nation engaged in conflict. Great Britain also remained neutral. Hitler seized on the neutrality of these two powerful nations as an opportunity for a land grab. In March 1936, Nazi troops seized the Rhineland. Several months later, Hitler and Mussolini extended aid to fellow fascist Francisco Franco in his attempt to overthrow Spain's republican government.

By the end of the Thirties, President Roosevelt and his New Dealers shifted their attention away from domestic economic policy to the disturbing events in Europe and Far East. The American President and his federal relief administrator, Harry Hopkins, became less concerned with economic issues at home than with the rumblings of war in Europe with the rise of fascism and the Pacific with Japanese expansionism in its quest for oil. By 1938, Hopkins' concern switched from providing jobs for the army of unemployed Americans to the storm brewing in the wider world as dictators amassed power and arms. However, he did not lose the optimism that he had acquired during his twenty-five years as a social worker, that social justice could ultimately be achieved. He did, however, redirect his goals to the international stage. His modus operandi remained mostly the same; the work that he did during the war was entirely congenial to his particular social worker's temperament.[17] In his investigation of Harry Hopkins' career, Christopher O'Sullivan draws a distinct link between Hopkins as a social worker and Hopkins as the president's war envoy. It was his background in the Social Gospel ethos that animated his desire to defeat fascism, that convinced him that economic justice and equal opportunity were impossible to exist without peace. Frances Perkins, FDR's labor secretary, who knew Hopkins very well, saw a clear connection between his relief work as a New Dealer and his work during the war as the president's special envoy. She recognized that Hopkins linked economic justice and equal opportunity with peace. He believed that this was only possible in nations where the people were free from oppression.[18]

Historian Warren Kimball sees this connection as well and writes that foreign policy and domestic affairs interact with each other. "What unites foreign and domestic affairs is nationalism—Americanism, if you will—the intellectual and emotional force that is a fundamental link between social and political history."[19] There is no doubt that Hopkins relied on his social work ethos during the war years. In a memo he wrote in 1941, he asserts "the new order of Hitler can be conclusively defeated by the new order of democracy, which is the New Deal universally applied."[20] For Hopkins, the war might be inevitable but his belief in social justice writ large should be not just <u>how</u> the United States responds to Germany and Japan, but <u>why</u> it should respond. His humanitarianism, his concern for the underdog, which was deeply embedded within his core beliefs, set him apart from the rest of those who were in FDR's inner circle. The decisions that he influenced and the actions he took reflected his commitment to furthering the cause of social justice.

This attitude persisted during the rest of the war years. Just months before his death, Hopkins gave a speech on September 6, 1945, that clearly indicates that he never lost his dedication to social justice, whether at home or abroad. This was a time when the nation had to revert to a peacetime economy after the Allied victory over the Axis powers. Hopkins sounds like a New Dealer: "I believe most Americans interpret a good life [in terms of] an opportunity to earn a living" and to be assured of basic rights afforded citizens by a democratic government. In the memo he reiterates his dedication to the New Deal jobs programs when he warns against an unreasoned fear of a "bureaucratic government" taking over or that one's incentive to work would be diminished under such a system. He was a persistent optimist. "I believe that full employment must and can be attained within the framework of our traditional democratic processes," he proclaims. He called upon the nation to look to the domestic economy and for the government to take steps to "assure every man able and willing to work a right to an opportunity to secure the reasonable necessities of life."[21] Clearly, Hopkins' entire Washington career had an important consistency of spirit deeply embedded in it. This might be a clue to his success.

If his social temperament remained intact throughout the war years, the onset of the war and his involvement in international affairs forced him to change his manner of interacting with people, the media, and with Congress. During the New Deal years, he took a lot of criticism from Roosevelt's political enemies. He spent a lot of other people's money. This, along with his inability to tolerate fools or, especially, delays caused by bureaucratic red tape, garnered him enemies. Robert Sherwood notes that in dealing with critics, Hopkins was "addicted to the naked insult." General Hugh Johnson wrote that Hopkins had "a mind like a razor, a tongue like a skinning-knife ... and a sufficient vocabulary of parlour profanity."[22] As President Roosevelt's personal wartime envoy, Hopkins abandoned most of this rhetoric and never resorted to insults in order to get a point across. This was despite the fact that the media constantly attacked him as wielding way too much power.

But history tells us that Hopkins used his influence well. Despite the fears of conservative journalists and most Republicans, this power did not corrupt him. Robert Sherwood notes that "when, with no more authority that Roosevelt's personal confidence in him, [Hopkins] achieved tremendous power in the shaping of historic events [and] he became and remained one of the most incorruptible of men."[23] Of the billions of government money that he spent on his several jobs programs, not a dime stuck to his fingers.

It is important to understand that Hopkins' health was an issue in his public and private life. He had been ill since July 1935 when he was diagnosed with a duodenal ulcer. This resulted in extreme weight loss and debilitation. In December 1937, he underwent surgery for cancer of the stomach. The doctors removed a malignant tumor and, along with it, much of his stomach. This was soon after his second wife, Barbara, died from breast cancer. His father had earlier died from cancer as well. Hopkins had lived with the fear that this would be his fate as well. Although, miraculously, the cancer never returned, from this point on, Hopkins was never fully healthy. He had constant stomach and digestive problems. His intestines were not absorbing nutrition and his weight at one point dropped down to about 100 pounds on his six-foot frame. Although it was not diagnosed at the time, he probably suffered from what is now known as Celiac Disease caused by an allergy to gluten. The treatment at the time for his condition included frequent blood transfusions, injection of nutrients, and just plain eating. The many blood transfusions caused cirrhosis of the liver, which is listed as a cause of death on his death certificate. This explains why some historians conclude that he loved his alcohol. Tuttle incorrectly describes Hopkins as a "high living profligate."[24] In fact, his medical condition precluded any excess drinking. Hopkins certainly enjoyed the racetrack and liked being in the company of interesting and important people, many of whom were also rich. But this was part of his job as presidential envoy. Furthermore, his health problems along with his rigorous work and travel schedule kept him from the high lifestyle described in the media. For example, when he was in England in 1941, he refused an invitation from Lady Astor to join him at Clivedon, responding that he was too busy. Although she was insistent, Hopkins never did see her; Britain was in real trouble and he had more important things to do. Surely, if Hopkins had been interested in hanging out with the rich and famous, he would have made time to see her.[25]

He spent many months at the Mayo clinic in Minnesota undergoing several experimental and painful procedures. Hopkins was quite ill during the years that he was doing extensive and very uncomfortable long-distance travel, meeting with heads of state and military leaders, attending and participating in the wartime conferences, and carrying out his duties as administrator of Lend Lease. However, he almost never let his physical condition deter him from his work.[26] It is a reflection of Hopkins' dedication that he managed to accomplish as much as he did despite his illness.[27]

Roosevelt was a paraplegic as a result of polio, which he contracted in 1921 when he was just 39 years old; he and Hopkins likely developed mutual admiration based partially on the physical struggle each had to contend with. Wendell Willkie, the Republican candidate whom FDR defeated in

1940, and who wholly disliked Hopkins, asked the President why he kept Hopkins around. He called him an unpopular invalid, a "half man." Surely the President knew, Willkie argued, that people distrusted Hopkins because of the influence he wielded at the White House. FDR diplomatically responded that he could understand Willkie's concern but, he said, "'someday you may well be sitting here where I am now as President of the United States. And when you are, you'll be looking at that door over there, knowing that practically everybody who walks through it wants something out of you. You'll learn what a lonely job this is, and you'll discover the need for someone like Harry Hopkins who asks for nothing except to serve you.'"[28] Clearly, Hopkins filled a void in the president's life and they often enjoyed late night card games and lively banter. Their shared disabilities provided common ground for their relationship to grow. Roosevelt's trust in Hopkins was absolute.

If Roosevelt recognized a kindred spirit in Hopkins, he was also aware of his usefulness. Frances Perkins remembered that Hopkins was aware of Roosevelt's position in the world and how important it was for him to filter out the irrelevant and unimportant so that he could do "the right and best thing."[29] But even more than this, FDR knew that he could rely Hopkins' advice. Hopkins did not aspire to political office (except once in a momentary aberration in 1938); while he was always short of money, and he did not strive to acquire wealth. If he had any ambition at all, it was for the power to do what he did so well—serve his boss—and to do it with no interference.[30] The President also relied upon Hopkins to voice his opinions openly, to vigorously debate any issues, and then to follow through with whatever decision the President finally made. He made room for Hopkins in his inner circle and because of this, Hopkins had the President's ear and he had access to power. During the war years, he would use this power to make sure that the Alliance with Great Britain, and then with the Soviet Union, was sturdy enough to defeat the Axis Powers. It was a difficult job and became more difficult as the situation worsened.

In 1937, when the United States was still grappling with economic problems, Japan launched an attack against China and captured Peking, Shanghai, Nanking, and Shantung. FDR began to consult with Britain about a possible war in Asia. Germany, Italy, and Japan had formed an alliance against the Soviet Union in 1936, which was formalized as the Axis pact. And these nations withdrew from the League of Nations. International conflicts began to turn the Roosevelt administration's attention to world affairs. In 1938, Hitler annexed Austria to the Third Reich and then announced that he would take over the Sudetenland, a part of Czechoslovakia inhabited by people of German descent. France and Britain desperately wanted to avoid a confrontation with Germany; they were not prepared for war. Therefore, in September of 1938, the Prime Ministers of the two nations, Neville Chamberlain and Edouard Daladier, met with Hitler in Munich. The British and French agreed to concede to Hitler's occupation of the Sudetenland in return for his promise to refrain from any more territorial expansion. Hitler agreed to this exchange. Chamberlain returned to London and proudly assured the British people that he was able to assure them of "peace in our time." Most seemed relieved that war had been averted, but "appeasement" soon became a pejorative word.

During the early days of the Second World War, amid increased Nazi aggression, an incongruous trio formed an alliance that changed the international balance of power for decades to come. From 1939 to 1945 the conflict demanded cooperation among the leaders who had to put their differences aside to work toward a common goal: the defeat of Nazism. The western allies led by U.S. President Franklin Roosevelt and British Prime Minister Winston Churchill had little reason to work together. They sat on opposite poles of the political spectrum: FDR was a liberal and saw the world from the point of view of a progressive, looking to the future; Churchill was conservative and looked to the past for inspiration. Yet, they formed what scholars have dubbed the "Special Relationship." Consequently, the war years saw a dramatic interaction of strong personalities, working together but often clashing. During the crisis years, from 1940 to 1945, the two received help from what many saw as an unlikely source, former social worker Harry Hopkins. A review of documents shows that as the president's personal envoy to Churchill, Hopkins deftly managed to keep these two formidable men from dangerously colliding. Without Hopkins as liaison between Roosevelt and Churchill, it is likely that the wartime coalition might have been substantially weakened, possibly to the point of collapse.

Historian Mark Stoler stresses the effectiveness of the Anglo-American alliance as it fought against fascism. Despite the occasional ruptures, the Americans and the British managed to keep in communication with each other. Eventually, the relationship between Churchill and Roosevelt became personal rather than managerial. These two men maintained a friendship set the tone for those who served below them. According to British historian, Hew Strachan, "It was a war too important to be left to the generals."[31]

Despite the fact that they liked one another, there is no doubt that the relationship between Churchill and Roosevelt was transactional in nature; it fluctuated relative to circumstance and national need. Nevertheless, what has been called the Special Relationship between the two Western Allies, the United States and Great Britain, rested partly on a common moral foundation and western political traditions embodied by both leaders. This is what lent it at least some stability and allowed a modicum of mutual trust during the five tumultuous years, from 1940 to 1945. The constantly changing war situation as well as the delicate political climate in the United States presented challenges to the American President and to the British Prime Minister as well. They did not see eye to eye on many important issues, but their shared goal of Allied victory would always work to diminish their differences. After December 1941, of course, the Allies were fighting a coalition war and there were many pitfalls to this situation; it was critical that they present a united front to the world in order to wage a successful fight against fascism. Yet there was always the suspicion of treachery. There was always the niggling fear that one of the allies might negotiate a separate peace with the Germans. This cast a shadow on the Alliance. Because the coalition was based largely on expediency, it was fragile.[32]

By 1940, Roosevelt and Hopkins had built a relationship that was both personal and political. They had similar assumptions and similar aspirations although

Hopkins did not aspire to a political position. Both were devoted to American democracy, to capitalism, and to liberal politics. These core beliefs did not change even though they adjusted their actions relative to domestic politics and wartime needs. If their differences were apparent on the surface, in the way they spoke and in how they dressed, they shared a worldview and were certainly on the same page politically. Both believed that the government had the responsibility to use its powers to ensure to the welfare of its citizens. Both were pragmatists and did not adhere to any particular ideology unless it was liberalism. By 1940, not only did Hopkins enter Roosevelt's inner circle, but he occupied a place at its center. And it was this that later allowed Hopkins to gain Churchill's trust. Without full access to the President of the United States, Hopkins would have been of little use to the Prime Minister. Churchill learned quickly that Hopkins was extremely useful when Britain was appealing to the President for military help before Pearl Harbor. But the Prime Minister also liked the frank and often-caustic Hopkins. Upon the two platforms supplied by the two world leaders, while the world was in turmoil, Hopkins built his reputation as a reliable and confidential line of communication between the Prime Minister and the President. He was the "indispensable third."[33]

During the early years of the 1940s, Hopkins became the embodiment of some rather unpopular presidential policies, such as the decision to help the British fight against the Germans and the institution of the first peacetime military draft. Before the Japanese attack at Pearl Harbor, isolationists attacked any hint of assistance to the Allied nations fighting against Nazi aggression. The fear, of course, was that this would drag the United States into what they regarded as another futile European war. Hopkins believed that it was his job to deflect criticism away from his boss and, if need be, he was glad to act as the media's whipping boy. And the media cooperated. He had no official, position to protect; he was entirely reliant on the President for his position and he never feared losing the President's friendship and trust. He acted as "the confidential contact man," allowing Roosevelt to support a particular policy without actually going public.[34] This reputation made him Roosevelt's right-hand man. It also stirred the envy of other powerful men.

However, when asked what he would do if the President asked him to act on a policy that he did not agree with, Hopkins responded that while he might try to influence the decision, once a policy was set by the President, "I'm in there fighting for it fifteen minutes later."[35] And he could act effectively as the president's man because he had the ability to plow through red tape without hesitation and this was extremely valuable to Roosevelt. He could simplify complicated arguments and get to the real argument. Shrewd and at the same time happily informal, he got along well with subordinates. For all his easy manner, however, he never called the president by his first name.

President Roosevelt had implicit faith in Hopkins' loyalty as well his inability to dissemble. This is interesting because Roosevelt knew that he himself did not have that quality of complete honesty, which he so valued in Hopkins. In 1942, he told his friend, neighbor, and treasury secretary, Henry Morgenthau, "You know I am a juggler, and I never let my right hand know what my left hand does. ... I may be entirely inconsistent, and furthermore I am perfectly willing to mislead ... if it will help win the war." Historian Jon Meacham describes both the President and the Prime Minister with insight: "What could make Roosevelt a trying husband and a frustrating friend" and "what could make Churchill a tiring guest and an exasperating friend" were "political virtues" and the very qualities that made them great leaders.[36] FDR's somewhat jovial self-awareness might be commendable, but he did not tolerate anyone who misled him. He knew that Hopkins would never be anything but truthful. This, along with the President's characteristic and unusual reliance on personal, often face-to-face, diplomacy explains much about Hopkins' position of influence in Washington during the war years and why he was such a great asset to the President. Throughout his wartime career, Hopkins made it a point to get behind the outer shell, the public persona, of the people he worked with, from the President on down. He fully understood how important this was to Roosevelt; it was his way to really get to know people through Hopkins. It was Hopkins' job to work closely with all sorts of personalities, military or diplomatic, and explain them to the President. This was a delicate task for the former social worker, especially when it came to interpreting Churchill to FDR and vice versa.

The differences between Roosevelt and Hopkins paled in comparison to the differences between the British Prime Minister and the American President. These two leaders came from similar privileged backgrounds and the United States and Great Britain shared a common history and a common language. However, both were complicated men with different political ideologies who were playing global chess during the war years when the stakes were immense.

They had little in common. Roosevelt was a political liberal. Churchill was a conservative and a champion of the British Empire. Roosevelt abhorred imperialism. He differed with the Prime Minister on the subject of the British Empire and the trading system that went along with it. They had radically different ideas on war strategy and each viewed the Soviet Union through a different lens. Churchill never stopped moving; FDR was a paraplegic. Churchill stayed up late into the wee hours of the morning; FDR liked to retire early. They viewed each other with a wary eye. Hopkins recognized that these important differences in two such temperamental men could jeopardize any rapport the leaders might develop. Later, when he was in London, he described the Prime Minister and the President as alike in some ways but remarked. "If the two were put together in a ship, for instance, they would have terrific rows."[37] The Special Relationship between Great Britain and the United States, forged in the crucible of the Second World War, was merely a product of need and sinuous political bargaining. It was not inevitable. Neither was victory.

Hopkins had his own political views; some of which he did not openly express to Churchill. He believed that the war would likely result in the end of the British Empire. He kept his dislike of colonialism to himself and he never confronted Churchill on the issue—he did not think it important or even politic to pressure allies on issues that were not of prime military importance. What Hopkins did, was to try to mediate. Churchill correctly sensed that Hopkins was more flexible than FDR.[38]

No matter how the Prime Minister enjoyed emphasizing the closeness of the Western Allies to the rest of the world, it becomes clear in hindsight that the Special Relationship might have been continuously on shaky ground. Historian John Charmley emphasizes that it was not America's admiration for the British but the Japanese attack on Pearl Harbor that brought America into the war. Charmley presents a "less romanticized and more realistic account of the so-called special relationship" by dispelling the "Churchillian myth" that there was equality between Britain and the United States. The Grand Alliance certainly suffered from divisiveness. However, to contemporary eyes, America's Lend Lease support and its entry into the war did encourage the public's belief in the necessity of the good will that existed between the United States and Britain whether or not it was actually on shaky ground.[39]

It was Germany that declared war on the United States; FDR would have found it very difficult to persuade Congress to declare war on Germany despite the beating that Britain was enduring. The Prime Minister was on tenterhooks. There was no way for him to discern what the President was going to do because "Roosevelt made and unmade sense from day to day; he was a politician who erected ambiguity and ellipsis into an art form." When it came to making the decision as to entering into the war on the side of the British or not, Charmley argues, Roosevelt "kept his options open and British hopes as high as he dared."[40] Charmley might have overstated this. There was indeed a great deal of personal rapport between the President and the Prime Minister. However, this Special Relationship would not have encouraged Roosevelt to ask Congress to declare war on Germany merely at the request of Churchill. Still, one might conclude that Roosevelt would not have let Great Britain—or Churchill for that matter—founder.

Clearly, the differences between the Prime Minister and the President presented complications in the matter of their alliance before and during the war; here Hopkins played an important role of intermediary and even peacemaker. Trusted implicitly by both leaders, Hopkins was able to ensure that communication between them remained active, correct, and when necessary, secret. He acted as the balancing element, the third leg of a tripod. Clearly, Churchill early on discovered that Hopkins was the best channel of communication between himself and the President and at the same time he was "the main prop and animator of Roosevelt himself." This made Hopkins extremely valuable to Churchill and the interactions between the two men were, according to historian Fraser Harbutt, "sufficiently important and comprehensive" to be called a system.[41] This system endured throughout the war and only increased in intensity as the years wore on and debates among the Allies intensified.

With the entrance of the Soviet Union and Joseph Stalin into the war against Germany in late June of 1941, the influence of Hopkins became even more important. There is no doubt that participation of the Red Army after June 1941 proved to be a decisive moment in the war against Germany. And here, again, Hopkins played a critical role. The participation of the Red Army in the war effort proved decisive for final victory. The fact that Stalin trusted Hopkins' word that the United States would support the Soviets in the war was a great asset to the Grand Alliance. Neither Churchill nor Roosevelt was able to cultivate such a relationship with the Man of Steel.

Had the times not been so desperate, had the British not been so fearful of imminent invasion by the Germans, had their cooperation not been so vital to the victory over Hitler, the President and the Prime Minister might not have been able to fully agree on anything. Even so, during the war years the egos of the two strong personalities could have gotten in the way of any military or political cooperation. In many instances, Hopkins oiled the wheels of the Anglo-American Alliance. He was able to do this because he demonstrated to both of them that the only thing on his agenda was the success of their unified fight against fascism. If Hopkins did not construct the foundation upon which a Special Relationship was built, he steadied it whenever it threatened to falter.

Chapter 3—War

> "History allows us to see patterns and make judgments. ... To understand one moment is to see the possibility of being the co-creator of another. ... History gives us the company of those who have done and suffered more than we have."[42]

Adolf Hitler and his Nazi party came to power in Germany in early 1933 just as FDR was inaugurated as president. The leader of the Nazi party had created a huge army and air force and at the same time, in clear violation of the Versailles Treaty that ended the Great War. Japanese militarism and expansionism added to the threat against democracy. To Americans this seemed vaguely ominous, but for most of the decade attention was focused on our economic woes.

Isolationist sentiment was high, and most Americans wanted nothing to do with the goings on in Europe, much less Japan and China. Both Roosevelt and Hopkins wanted to prevent the United States' involvement in the European war. Congress passed three Neutrality Acts between 1935 and 1937. So, we were legally neutral. Great Britain, having bitter memories of World War I, the Great War, also remained neutral. Adolf Hitler seized on the neutrality of these two powerful nations for a land grab. In March 1936, Nazi troops seized the Rhineland, an area previously demilitarized, which lay east of Germany's border with France. Several months later, Hitler and Italy's fascist dictator, Benito Mussolini, extended aid to fellow fascist Francisco Franco in his attempt to overthrow Spain's republican government. When Spain's republicans appealed to anti-fascist nations for help, only the Soviet Union responded.

The Spanish Civil War, a prelude to the world war that was to follow, precipitated a major debate in America over foreign policy. Conservatives saw Franco as a strong anti-communist whose fascist state would support a stable social order. Political leftists and intellectuals championed the cause of republican Spain. Britain, France, and the United States stayed out of the fight, afraid that it might escalate into a world war. Unofficially some Americans joined the Abraham Lincoln Brigade and fought with the Soviets alongside the republicans. Picasso's famous painting, "Guernica," reflects the horrors of bombing by the Germans and the Italians on the Basque town where 1600 civilians were killed.

International tension escalated. When in 1937, Japan launched an attack against China and captured Peking, Shanghai, Nanking, and Shantung, President Roosevelt became alarmed and he began to consult with Britain about a possible war in Asia. Germany, Italy, and Japan formed an alliance, formalized as the Axis Pact, and they withdrew from the League of Nations. There seemed to be little stability in this modern world. In 1938, Hitler annexed Austria to the Third Reich without resistance — the Anschluss – and then announced that he would take over the Sudetenland, a part of Czechoslovakia inhabited by people of German descent. This area had been taken from Germany and incorporated into Czechoslovakia after WWI. That same year, an uneasy Roosevelt supported a program to increase our navy.

In 1938, Americans were experiencing life very differently from that of the Europeans. Isolationist America seemed as emotionally separated from Great Britain as it was politically and geographically remote. A two-page spread in *The New York Times* Sunday edition of April 24, 1938, graphically depicts this difference in the Rotogravure Picture Section. One side of the page shows a jubilant President throwing out the first baseball of the season. On the same page we see children – well dressed and happily excited – awaiting the annual Easter egg roll on the White House lawn. There is a picture of Henry Ford and Orville Wright dedicating a memorial to the achievements of the Wright Brothers. In Virginia, the Monticello National Guard, resplendent in colonial uniforms, fire a round in celebration of Thomas Jefferson, author of the Declaration of Independence. The collection of photos exudes optimism and national pride. On the reverse side of this page, another vision of 1938 emerges. We see photos of European cities where the swastika lurks in the background. In Vienna, Hitler rides in an open car triumphant over the "peaceful" acquisition of Austria; Italians march into Germany on orders of Mussolini; they are going to work on the farms and they wave swastika flags. Queen Elizabeth[43] of Great Britain inspects tanks and observes defensive maneuvers in Aldershot, indicating uneasiness in England over Nazi moves.[44] Europe seemed more than merely tense.

France and Britain desperately wanted to avoid a confrontation with Germany – neither nation was prepared for a fight. In September of 1938 leaders of the two nations –

French Prime Minister Edouard Daladier and British Prime Minister Neville Chamberlain – met with Hitler in Munich. They affirmed Hitler's seizure of the Sudetenland in return for his promise not to take any more territory. Everyone seemed relieved, not yet aware of the true nature of Adolph Hitler. Consequently, Chamberlain returned triumphant to London and announced to the British people that he had appeased Hitler and the Germans. He assured the British people that the Munich Agreement had secured "peace in our time." Still, the British were uneasy, and "appeasement" soon became a pejorative term.

Seven months later, on November 9, 1938, in Munich, citizens experienced the brutality against German Jews during the Night of the Broken Glass – Kristallnacht. This was the organized destruction of Jewish businesses and the rape and murder of dozens of the city's Jews. This assault was likely the result of Hitler's Nuremberg Speech on September 6, 1938 when he called for racial purity and national self-assertion. Power, he said, is important as a prerequisite for everything, associating pacifism with weakness.

Despite the Munich Agreement, despite his promise to make no more incursions into Europe, Adolph Hitler made plans to invade Poland in 1939, the first step of his goal to take over Europe. However, he was afraid that the Soviets to the east with the powerful Red Army might interfere with his plan. So, he sent German Foreign Minister Joachim Ribbentrop to confer with Soviet Foreign Minister Vyacheslav Molotov and the result was the agreement that the Soviets would not interfere with the German invasion of Poland. As a prize, the Soviets would share in the spoils and get the eastern part of the defeated nation The Molotov-

Ribbentrop Non-Aggression Pact of 1939 gave Germany the opportunity to invade and occupy Poland with no resistances from the Soviets. The Pact also defined spheres of influence and boundaries, giving Latvia, Estonia, and Finland to the Soviets and partitioning Poland so that the eastern part would go to Russia. Both Stalin and Hitler felt good about this pact because it protected their nations from the aggression of the other.

In the midst of the turmoil in Europe, in 1939, Hopkins traveled to his alma mater, Grinnell College, in his Iowa hometown. He spoke to the students there as secretary of commerce. In 1938, Roosevelt had named him to the post, hoping that media criticism aimed at the federal relief administrator would taper off. Hopkins held that cabinet office until 1940. His carefully selected words in the speech reflected his ideas about the proper role of government in the United States. He spoke to the students of the power that comes from banding together for a common cause; it worked during the Depression. This remark could very well have presaged his commitment to facilitating the Anglo-American Alliance. Hopkins wanted to make the students aware of the dangerous world situation. He insisted that the democratic government that Americans so enjoyed had to be protected – "it is the one thing in America that is important." Despite his recognition of possible dark days ahead Hopkins, ever the New Dealer, said to the students, "this country cannot continue to exist as a democracy with 10,000,000 or 20,000,000 unemployed. It just can't be done. ... We have got to find a way of living in America in which every person in it shares in the national income, in such a way, that poverty in America is abolished."[45] Hopkins never abandoned that goal. The nation had to ensure that democracy would be protected at home and abroad.

During this tense international atmosphere Hopkins' illness had worsened. In 1939 he went to the Mayo Clinic for another round of tests, which showed that he was starving; his body was unable to absorb proteins. The prognosis was that he would be dead by Christmas. However, after some drastic and experimental treatments at Mayo, his condition improved enough so that he was able to go home. The diagnosis was "cause unknown." He believed that his public career was over, and he resigned his position as secretary of commerce.[46] Because of the violent conflict gripping Europe, he maintained that the situation demanded a robust public servant who could give full and aggressive attention to his duties. In his August 22nd letter of resignation to the President, Hopkins wrote that the only way to guarantee peace and security of the United States was to "marshal our complete economic strength for the task of defense." He added "the surest guarantee of peace for America" is your leadership in "its gigantic effort to defend itself." In fact, his resignation might have been late in coming. He had become a somewhat of a political liability as secretary of commerce. He was no longer fighting for the underdog; he had lost his patina as a champion of the poor; and the economy was improving. Because of his health, he had not accomplished much during his time on the Cabinet.

Roosevelt reluctantly accepted his friend's resignation but added that the separation would be only from the office and not from the friendship. " ... [It] is possible only for you to break the official ties that exist between us— not the ties of friendship that have endured so happily through the years." [47] However, this was just one of several instances when Hopkins' attempt to leave the President's side failed.[48] In August, he went down to South Carolina to stay with Bernard Baruch at Hobcaw Barony to recuperate. There, in conversations with "Elder Statesman Number One," Hopkins heard Baruch warn that war was coming, and just as Churchill believed, the United States was woefully unprepared. "'I think it took Harry a long time to realize how greatly we were involved in Europe and Asia—but once he did realize it, he was all-out for total effort.'" That same month, Hitler marched through Czechoslovakia, brazenly violating any assurance he had given British Prime Minister Neville Chamberlain at Munich.[49]

In September 1939, Hitler ordered the invasion of Poland with the assurance that his army would be unopposed. This action triggered Poland's allies to act. Consequently, France and Britain, no longer isolationist, declared war on Germany. War had broken out in Europe for the second time in the twentieth century. During the following period, the winter of 1939-40 we have what is called the "Phony War" when nothing much happened – except that people became increasingly nervous. For those in Poland it was a different story. Jews huddled in basements, in attics terrified of getting caught by the Gestapo, terrified of the air raids. Shelters had head counts and Jews were not welcomed. There was a saying among Poles then that exemplifies their stoic cynicism: "Every once in a while, Poland gets quartered into three uneven pieces."[50]

In 1940 Stalin, now in control of eastern Poland, ordered the mass execution of Polish officers who were Russian prisoners of war. This took place during April and

May in the Katyn Forest, near Smolensk in Russia. The Soviet secret police shot 16,000 Polish officers in the head and buried them in mass graves. This cold-blooded act was kept hidden from the public. Three years later, in 1943, well after Barbarossa, the German attack on the Soviet Union when the Soviets became our ally, the Germans discovered the graves and publicly accused the Soviets of the atrocity. Stalin vehemently denied this and countered by accusing the Germans of shooting the Poles. The Russians later exhumed the grave and reburied the bodies, never admitting that they were guilty.

This situation of lies and counter lies about the Katyn Massacre became problematic for the western Allies when they met face to face with Stalin.[51]

On April 9, 1940, what was called the Phony War ended. Hitler's army swept like a knife through Norway, Denmark, Holland, Belgium, and Luxembourg and then the massive German army swept into France on May 10th. Roosevelt's speechwriter, Robert Sherwood, called this lightening war or Blitzkrieg "mechanized barbarism." Just after Germany's Blitzkrieg, the lightening attack against Western Europe, British Prime Minister Neville Chamberlain (stigmatized by appeasement) resigned on May 10th. Winston Churchill gladly stepped up and became Prime Minister of Great Britain, declaring that he had nothing to offer "but blood, toil, tears and sweat." There was no doubt that Britain found itself in a difficult spot, despite the fact that it was able to protect its Royal Air Force from destruction by the German *Luftwaffe* because of it superior air power due to the Spitfire and Hurricane fighters. Still, Britain did not have sufficient resources to defend the island nation much less the vast

British Empire. Churchill was well aware that Britain needed allies and this fact became the "centerpiece of his foreign policy."[52]

The German Blitzkrieg proved to be a ruse to draw Anglo-French troops away from the real German goal of the Belgian-Luxembourg-French border where a strong concentration of German divisions had been waiting. Within three days, the Germans managed to break through the British and French lines and trap Allied troops on the coast of France. When Hitler inexplicable ordered a halt in the German offensive, over 300 Allied troops managed a dramatic escape at Dunkirk. Between May 26 and June 4, the Allied soldiers were rescued by every sailing vessel, large or small, available in England. But the 335,585 rescued men were forced to leave their war machines behind. The Germans captured what were irreplaceable weapons. This severely hurt the British hopes of launching an effective offense against the Germans. According to Sherwood, this was when the United States became "the decisive strategic factor in the war."[53] However, with the Nazis becoming increasingly aggressive, and this being an election year, the American President found that he had to walk a narrow path between internationalism and isolationism.

On June 10, Italy joined the Germans and Paris fell on June 14th. France signed an armistice whereby Germany would occupy Paris, the Atlantic and Channel coasts while the rest of the country would be ruled by a collaborationist government led by Marshall Henri Pétain from the city of Vichy. France had fallen with what Churchill called "astonishing swiftness."[54] It had taken the Germans only two months to conquer a large part of Europe. Britain was left alone to fight the Germans.

Early on, from the very beginning of the rumblings of war in Europe, Hopkins felt the seriousness of the situation as well as an aversion to armed conflict. On August 31, 1939, he wrote a letter to his middle son, Robert. "The European news is too discouraging for words. I am hoping and praying there is to be no war." Clearly, Hopkins was well aware of the dangerous situation caused by Hitler's Germany and by the territorial appeasements made by England and France. His fears came true the next day when Germany invaded Poland.[55].

Hopkins was convinced that it was righteous to fight Nazism using all of our resources — and, ever the optimist, he was sure that social justice and democracy would prevail worldwide. The historical context of this, of course, was imminent disaster. Hitler's army was laying waste to Europe. The Battle of Britain, the relentless Nazi air attack on the island nation that followed the fall of France, had taken a toll on England's defenses; she desperately needed America's help. But in the United States, a national election loomed, and Roosevelt sought re-election to an unprecedented third term. Congress had passed Neutrality Acts in 1935, 1937, and 1939. Pacifist and isolationist oratory abounded throughout the nation. Voters would not look kindly on any possibility of sending American boys to fight in a foreign war. Churchill used every method of persuasion to convince the American President to come to the aid of a besieged Britain, and still the President hedged. Nevertheless, Britain stood alone against the German bombers.

In spite of the national mood of isolationism, Hopkins demonstrated some farsightedness as the situation in Europe heated up. This would sit well with the British Prime Minister. The previous September, the President, whose fears had been stoked by Adolf Hitler's Nuremberg speech, had sent Hopkins on a secret mission[56] to the West Coast to inspect munitions plants with an eye to wartime production. Hopkins agreed with his boss that war was more than likely, and that air power would be a deciding factor in the fight against fascism. However, a good deal of the money for the build-up of the Army and Navy would have to come from federal relief coffers, most probably from Hopkins' WPA. Congress had no intention of allocating money for national defense for a war that might not happen. Eventually, at the urging of George Marshall and with Hopkins' approval, millions of dollars that had been allocated to the WPA were secretly channeled to the task of making machine tools for small arms ammunition. While this was only a minimal effort at rearmament, it did place America well ahead in its preparedness for war.[57]

During the months between the German invasion of Poland and the Blitzkrieg, during the Phony War, Roosevelt feared that the beleaguered British might negotiate a peace settlement with the Nazis; this could endanger the security of the United States. With Britain out of the picture, Germany could well direct its aggression across the Atlantic. The President was walking a narrow path between political expediency and international security. However, "Dr. New Deal" was gradually turning into "Dr. Win the War."

Reflecting the tenor of the times as well as the value he placed on Hopkins' opinions, FDR sent him a poem along with a note bemoaning American isolationism; he was sure that his friend would also resent the fact that Americans would rather shout than fight. Probably this was a reference to the conservative media and the Liberty League:

> Lift up your hands, ye heroes,
> And swear with proud disdain;
> The wretch that would ensnare you
> Shall lay his snares in vain.
> Should Europe empty all her force,
> We'll meet them in array
> And fight and shout, and fight
> For free Amerikay.[58]

Circumstances in Europe began to change American sentiment, subtly at first. May 10, 1940, was a dark day for President Roosevelt. Hitler was laying waste to western Europe; the Polish Army was destroyed, and German panzers were sweeping through France. It looked as if total war was inevitable and might involve the United States. He needed to speak to his friend about the disturbing events in Europe, with Hitler pounding through Europe and a new Prime Minister in Britain. He wanted to assess what impact these events might have on the United States. He invited Hopkins to dinner at the White House. They talked long into the night. At the end of the evening, Hopkins looked so exhausted that Roosevelt asked him to stay the night; he could sleep in the Lincoln Suite. In addition, there were cables that he wanted to review with him. Hopkins accepted the President's kind offer and stayed not just for the night, but he lived there for three-and-a-half-years. He used the suite as his office.[59] Michael Fullilove correctly claims that this was "a new stage" in Hopkins' public life. Occupying the room just down the hall from where Roosevelt slept, he had ready access to the President as his confidante and advisor.[60] Living in such close proximity to his boss worked well for both men. Roosevelt had a difficult job to do; he needed Hopkins close at hand. McJimsey, however, claims that Hopkins didn't much like being a permanent guest in the White House and maybe resented acting as a sounding board or a companion for the President.[61] But Hopkins' position in the White House was much more than this; he took an active part in creating wartime policy and was an integral part of the administration. Hopkins was single with a young daughter; he did not own a house and did not really have a life outside of his job in Washington. His correspondence with his family during this time contained no complaints about his living arrangements. But maybe most of all, the Lincoln Suite had floor to ceiling windows with a direct view to the both the Washington Monument and the Jefferson Memorial. Hopkins likely drew inspiration from this vista as he worked during the war years.

It was clear that Hopkins and Roosevelt were on the same "wavelength." Hopkins could anticipate questions before they were asked, he sensed when to make decisions on his own and when to refer to his boss. During the three-and-a-half years that he lived at the White House he acted as a national security advisor, decades before the position was installed, with a skeleton staff.[62] Hopkins worked from the anteroom with only a card table for a desk; this seemed oddly sufficient for someone who was the second most powerful man in the world. An article in a popular magazine notes that when Hopkins moved in, "he went to war," ahead of the President.[63] Thus began his career as Roosevelt's right-hand man, his political factotum, and his personal wartime negotiator. And, most importantly, Hopkins became the President's connection to the British Prime Minister.

Roosevelt conducted the nation's business relying to a large extent on personal relationships. Frances Perkins, Henry Morgenthau, Averell Harriman, and Wendell Willkie all were close to the President. As Warren Kimball argues, FDR used his friendships to shape policy both domestic and foreign.[64] His penchant was to use nineteenth-century personal diplomacy rather than go through the official channels; Hopkins was very useful here. He did not answer to the state department and because the President did not micromanage, he often made decisions using what he knew the President wanted to have happen. When Churchill visited the White House, which he did on numerous occasions during the war, he had the room directly across the hall.[65] It is not a stretch of the imagination that foreign policy decisions were likely to have been made by men in dressing gowns, one propped up in his bed. Many times, the direct connections among the three men allowed informal conferencing during which military and political aims were discussed.

Hopkins was constantly at the President's side as news from Europe became more and more alarming. The power that Hopkins had by virtue of his friendship with and proximity to the President led some of the administration's enemies to think of him as "an unmitigated menace." He was gatekeeper, the President's best friend, and his sounding board as well as a houseguest. This brought him a lot of vitriol from the media, but Hopkins rarely responded to attacks. He had work to do. It was his job to maintain some sort of equilibrium when there was a dangerous power struggle sparking between (and among) allied leaders. They were unified only by the desire to defeat Hitlerism; each had a different reason for animosity to the Nazis, and their policies and goals rarely coincided. There was little they could agree on. This made for an uneasy and constantly shifting wartime alliance. Beginning in early 1941, with his first meeting with Churchill, Harry Hopkins acted largely behind the scenes delicately pulling strings and settling disputes, ensuring that the relationship between the President and the Prime Minister did not implode. He became, in the eyes of many Washington insiders, "Roosevelt's own personal foreign office."[66] Stalin warily watched from Moscow but had very little on-site interaction with the American President.

In his masterful but often selective memoir, *The Second World War, Vol. III: The Grand* Alliance, Churchill admitted freely that the policy that he formulated with the United States was based on his friendship with Roosevelt.[67] Nevertheless, the documents reveal that the Anglo-American alliance, shaky at best, was held together, to a large degree, by the intervention of Harry Hopkins. He met with Churchill frequently from January 1941 to February 1945, and Churchill dealt with Roosevelt largely through Hopkins. Churchill knew that he could get a message through to the President and that, even more importantly, Hopkins would present it in a way that the Prime Minister could not (or would not). Harbutt explains that Hopkins did sometimes disagree with Churchill, especially over the timing of the Second Front.

Hopkins even threatened to divert much needed material for the cross- channel invasion to the Pacific Theater if Churchill would not ease up on his demand for action in the Mediterranean and a postponement of Overlord. However, the Prime Minister did not vent his anger over this to Hopkins as he did to Marshall, and even Roosevelt.[68]

The month after Hitler marched through Europe, Churchill famously declared, "We shall defend our island. ... We shall fight on the beaches, we shall fight on the landing-grounds, we shall fight in the fields and in the streets, we shall fight in the hills; we shall never surrender." The Prime Minister clearly convinced listeners that Britain would fight on and would never make a separate peace with the Nazis. But Britain desperately needed help from the United States to fulfill that promise. The island nation was running out of munitions and money. Churchill made an emotional appeal to Roosevelt, calling upon to their common history, pleading for the New World to come to the rescue of the Old. It worked, to a degree. FDR made a speech in Charlottesville promising the British "material resources" and he took steps to begin arming the United States for its own defense. According to insider Robert Sherwood, "[t]his was the first pledge of aid to the 'opponents of force'—the first proclamation of the policy" to aid the British with munitions.[69] Nevertheless, this "pledge of aid" was neither wholly altruistic nor humanitarian. FDR still feared that, despite the Prime Minister's high rhetoric, without U.S. aid Britain might make a separate peace with Germany, demonstrating at least some lack of trust in the British to carry on the fight. Still, this was a crucial decision because it laid the groundwork for Lend Lease, which became another plank in Hopkins' platform of power.

After the fall of France in June 1940, the relationship between the neutral United States and the besieged Great Britain took on new dimensions. These were perilous times, politically and militarily. The Germans were bombing British airfields as well as cities; the British people were suffering daily privations and terrors. How long would Britain endure; how long before the nation capitulated to the Germans? American munitions would surely change the game. The President was musing about running for a third term. This was, of course, unprecedented but not unconstitutional. Still, in this political climate of extreme isolationism, Roosevelt could not respond to the British Prime Minister's pleas for military support without taking a serious political hit. Churchill, with his usual hyperbole, declared that if the United States would not help the British, the British would fight alone but would likely be totally destroyed. Nevertheless, he wrote, they would "go down with colours flying and guns blazing."[70] However much the Americans were sympathetic to the plight of the British, they were more fearful of getting involved in another European war. The effects of World War I had left a bitter taste in the mouths of many Americans. Roosevelt seemed to be at an impasse.

One month after he moved into the White House, Hopkins wrote a letter (using White House letterhead) to his eighteen-year-old son, Robert, saying that he regretted very much that he had to miss his Mount Hermon (Massachusetts) high school graduation. The letter is indicative of Hopkins' sentiments when peace seemed to be threatened by the dangerous spread of fascism. Referring to the war in Europe, he tells his son:

> [T]he world is in turmoil. The forces that are now unleashed will cause profound changes not only in our economic life but in your own personal way of living thru the years to come. Already you must have made a deep searching of your heart and mind. What is the true meaning of this terrible and almost unbelievable conflict in Europe? Does it have a significance beyond the age-old struggle for power? Can this country remain aloof from its impact? In what way can it affect our personal lives? You and I, think more thoughts for the first time, of the meaning and importance of these freedoms that make a democracy different from other national political systems. The right to choose your own friends – to speak and think without restraint – to share in whatever religious life gives you deep and abiding satisfaction – to dwell on the surface of the earth as free men, one with the other. I believe that in these things lie all that is important and good in life. I am equally sure they are in danger – grave danger – from forces that represent the antithesis of those things we hold dear. And you and I must decide whether these freedoms are worth fighting for –whether in war or peace – this conflict is upon us. And we shall win not only because of our physical

strength but of our will to be free is strong and indomitable. Signed, Your father, H. L. H.[71]

The sentiments in this rather formal letter to his son, about the probability of war for the United States and about the freedoms that Americans hold dear, can be taken as a clear indication of the assumptions that he held throughout his life. To him it was somewhat of a universal New Deal.[72] Interestingly enough, these ideas preceded Roosevelt's Four Freedoms" speech by about six months; they were also an antecedent of the Declaration of Liberated Europe that FDR submitted at the Yalta Conference in February 1945 in an attempt to ensure democratic freedoms in the post-war world. It demonstrates that the President and his friend had a similar worldview. However, the President was limited in what he could say or even do by our political system, by public opinion, and by his need to get re-elected in November. Hopkins had no such limitations since he did not care a whit about criticism from the media, which flowed abundantly. He wrote this letter to his young son from his heart.

According to Robert Hopkins, he was a frequent visitor to the White House, sleeping in the sitting room adjoining the Lincoln bedroom. His reminiscences reflect the personal relations that the Hopkins family had with the Roosevelts. Eleanor Roosevelt was particularly kind to Robert; he remembers that she taught him to drink coffee for breakfast, which they had together in the blue room downstairs. She did this by adding milk in decreasing amounts during the successive days. Somehow, she felt that she could talk to this young boy and she confided how upset she was over the many divorces her children had, that she had really liked some of the spouses who left especially Elliott's ex-wife, actress Faye Emerson. Robert had heard the rumors that the ghost of Lincoln walked the halls during the night, moaning over the loss of lives during the Civil War. But if this was going to make the young man fearful, it was abated by the fact that the Chief Usher set up a film projector at the end of the corridor so he could watch the latest Hollywood movies. The Roosevelt family itself was intimate and called each other by nicknames. The President called his wife "Babs." Anna Roosevelt's two children were called "Sistie" and "Buzzy." Elliot called his father "Pop." But even though Hopkins and Roosevelt were very close, Robert remembers that he never heard his father address Roosevelt by anything other than "Mr. President."

The President's very human side came out when Robert and his younger brother Stephen visited the White House, he would challenge the boys to a vigorous game of water polo in the pool in the basement. FDR was a very strong swimmer as this was part of his physical therapy; he often beat the young boys at the game. To Robert, the White House seemed as a place of unusual tranquility despite the whirlwind that threatened the world.[73]

As 1940 wore on, candidate Roosevelt, as sitting President of a neutral, isolationist nation, had to steer clear of any war sentiments. He also had to avoid the controversial issue of the third term. Consequently, he remained "Presidential" and made no official statements and directed all questions to his sidekick, Harry Hopkins. Hopkins was nevertheless quietly supportive of a third term for his boss. He was the one who masterminded the President's nomination at the Democratic National Convention in July 1940. The timing for this was providential. France had just surrendered to Germany; there is little doubt that the desperate situation in Europe encouraged Roosevelt to run for the third term. Furthermore, these events just about cinched his re-election.[74]

As the nation entered into an election year and rumors flew that the President was contemplating a third term, the President looked to Hopkins to formulate strategy at the Democratic National Convention in Chicago; he wanted to be drafted. Consequently, Hopkins rallied his strength, took a suite at the Blackstone Hotel, and there set up a private telephone line (in the bathroom of his suite in order to avoid wiretaps) with the White House. He was the only person in the city to have a direct and immediate line of communication with the President. Hopkins heavily edited, and simplified, the first draft of his speech at the Chicago Convention nominating FDR for the third term. In the speech he emphasized that the "great masses of the American people" as well as the delegates wanted Roosevelt re-elected. Hopkins downplayed the "internal economic situation" as a reason for a third term and he only makes one passing reference to the situation in Europe. His emphasis was on the fact that the President would indeed accept the nomination if he were offered it. There was no doubt that FDR would get elected if he accepted the nomination. A *New York Times* article dated August 25, 1940, highlighted Hopkins' activities at the Convention as the "liaison" between Roosevelt and the delegates, directing the campaign to "draft" Roosevelt. This, of course, was an attempt to avoid the possible backlash against the tradition of only two terms.[75] His hard work paid off. Not surprisingly, Roosevelt won the Democratic nomination on the first ballot. However, when Hopkins announced from his suite that the President wanted Henry Wallace as his running mate, mayhem broke out. Democratic party leaders were already itchy because of Hopkins' presumed left leanings and the addition of such a liberal as Wallace to the ballot led to loud objections. At this point, Roosevelt had not yet announced that he would actually run if nominated. It fell to Hopkins, smack in the middle of an ugly controversy, to calm the waters; he did this effectively, behind the scenes, and without written presidential approval. He called upon his old college friend Secretary of Agriculture Paul Appleby to get the delegates to agree to FDR's choice; he persuaded South Carolina Senator James Byrnes to "pass the word." Thus, in the midst of what Sherwood calls "a dreadful display of democracy at its tawdriest," Wallace was nominated on the first ballot and became Roosevelt's vice president. As a footnote, Hopkins convinced Wallace not to give an acceptance speech to the raucous convention. His work here demonstrated that he had become, in fact, a savvy politician.[76]

Chapter 4—Winston Churchill

"I am most grateful to you for sending so remarkable an envoy who enjoys so high a measure of your intimacy and confidence." -Prime Minister Winston Churchill to President Franklin Roosevelt, January 1941.[77]

"The people here are amazing from Churchill down, and if courage alone can win—the result will be inevitable. But they need our help desperately, and I am sure you will permit nothing to stand in the way." -Harry Hopkins to President Franklin Roosevelt, January 1941.[78]

After FDR won his third Presidential election in November 1940, he was able to relax and to speak more candidly about the world situation: it was not good. During the Battle of Britain, the Luftwaffe was taking a terrible toll on the nation, first bombing the RAF airfields and then cities, especially London, during the Blitz. In June 1940, just after Churchill told his countrymen that he could only offer them "blood, toil, sweat, and tears," France fell to the Nazis and Britain stood alone against the Germans. It looked as if the Brits could not hold out much longer, at least this was the message that Churchill continued to send to FDR. Give us the tools, he pled, and we will fight on until the end. For Churchill it was merely a matter of survival. The President's action, however, was limited both by legislation and public opinion. Any loans to Britain were forbidden by the Johnson Debt Default Act of 1934, which went into effect when many countries were defaulting on World War debts. Roosevelt suggested that Britain should sell assets to raise funds to buy munitions from the United States. However, when Secretary of the Treasury Henry Morgenthau reported that this would not raise enough money, FDR relented but still wanted to help Britain.[79]

Churchill's correspondence during this time consistently pled for help from the United States. Before the fall of France, the Prime Minister wrote to the President, dated June 11, 1940, that it was crucial for a strong army to be fighting in France, that the life of Great Britain depended on getting airplanes and destroyers from the U. S. Even more important, the "Italian outrage makes it necessary for us to cope with a much larger number of submarines which may come out into the Atlantic and perhaps be based on Spanish ports. ... Not a day should be lost." Three days later, in another letter to the president, Churchill warned that "with the imminent collapse of French resistance ... the successful defense of this island will be the only hope of averting the collapse of civilization as we define it." That same day he wrote the President that he doubted that it would be possible to keep the French fleet out of German hands. Letters such as these led Roosevelt to conjure up the "destroyers for bases deal" and by mid-August he could write Churchill that the U.S. would send 50 destroyers, some motor torpedo boats, and some airplanes in exchange for "the use of Newfoundland, Bermuda, the Bahamas, Jamacia, St. Lucia, Trinidad and British Guiana as naval and air bases."

Churchill assured the president that the British people regarded "the conquest of the British Islands and its naval bases as any other than an impossible contingency. The spirit of our people is splendid." [80] Letters of this sort continued throughout the year and Roosevelt had become fully aware of the plight and fortitude of the British people. But he had to wait until the election was over to act.

With the election won, Roosevelt needed a break. He, Hopkins, Colonel Edwin "Pa" Watson and Dr. Ross McIntire took a cruise on the President's private yacht, the USS *Tuscaloosa*. Hopkins suspected that while his boss was playing cards and watching Hollywood films that he was actually "refueling." He was right. On board the *Tuscaloosa*, FDR came up with a "masterpiece" of inventive thinking, the idea that the United States would lend Great Britain what it needed to continue to defend itself against the Germans.[81] This was largely response to the increasingly desperate requests that the Prime Minister had already made to the President during 1940. FDR knew that the United States had to somehow pay for waging war against Germany. The immediate inspiration was a long missive from Churchill delivered to the presidential yacht by a navy seaplane, again pleading for help from the Americans. In this 4,000-word letter, which Churchill described as "one of the most important I ever wrote," he presented in detail the situation in Britain as desperate.[82] The nation needed help, needed especially more warships, merchant ships, supply ships, aircraft; but even though Britain did not have any money, the Prime Minister was confident that the United States would find a way to come to the aid of the island nation. According to Sherwood, this letter from Churchill, coming from a plane, "had a profound effect on Roosevelt." It is possible that because he no longer had isolationist rhetoric to muddy the waters, because Morgenthau had given him a disappointing picture of Britain's assets, because he was away from the pressures of Washington, Roosevelt was at last able to seriously consider helping Britain. The United States could help Great Britain hold off the Nazis without having to commit any American troops.

At the same time, Churchill's plea for help had a different effect on Hopkins. It filled him with a desire to get to know Churchill and "to find out ... how much of him was hard fact."[83] He had always favored helping the British in their fight against Germany. Hopkins suggested just giving munitions to the British as a gift, but the President had a different idea. He developed a rough outline of how the United States could provide help for a nation that could not afford to buy munitions. This was the germ of what was going to be the policy of Lend Lease; Britain would get American munitions now and pay for them or later just return them. The Neutrality Acts had been amended to allow for "cash and carry," that is, any nation could buy munitions from the United States if they could pay and ship themselves. But Britain was out of money.

When they returned to Washington, Hopkins encouraged the President to give the idea a positive spin and helped him draft his speech to Congress. This important speech had to encourage the British and the Americans as well. At a press conference, on December 17, 1940, the President – speaking especially to isolationists – drove home the point that the best defense for the United States was a strong Britain standing bravely and well equipped— and alone— against the Germans. Then he used the allegory of a neighbor's house being on fire. One lent one's hose so the neighbor could put out the fire. Once the neighborhood was safe, the neighbor would return the hose, or pay for it if it were damaged. A fortnight later, through the medium of the radio, in one of his most famous Fireside Chats, he entered the living rooms of Americans and reiterated this concept. He spoke frankly about the situation in Europe. He stated that any idea of appeasement or a negotiated peace with the Axis on the part of Britain was not a consideration. We would not enter into a foreign war, but we would do anything short of war to defeat Hitlerism. This included helping the British in any way we could. If we failed to do this, he said, 'We would be living at the point of a Nazi gun loaded with explosive bullets, economic as well as military."[84] This "short of war" policy was what many Americans wanted to hear.

Hopkins often assisted Sam Rosenman and Robert Sherwood in writing FDR's speeches. In this instance, he encouraged the President to include something the public could applaud and suggested the phrase, "We will become the great Arsenal of Democracy." This became the much-repeated phrase that was used to describe as well as justify America's support for Great Britain before the Pearl Harbor attack drew the United States into the war. For most Americans this ideal of being the Arsenal of Democracy was an attractive conflation of the military and the political. In this December 29th speech, Roosevelt established the foundation of his wartime policies. With American assistance, Britain would surely defeat the Axis powers. This would ensure that the United States would never have to send its young men to fight in a foreign war. Aiding the British was the best way to avoid war. However, the President had nothing to base this on except his own exuberant confidence. The treasury department drafted the legislation, the Lend Lease bill, which gave the president a good deal of latitude as to who to aid and what aid to give. Congress did pass the aptly named HR 1776 in March 1941. The Lend Lease Act gave the President extraordinary power based on an 1892 statute authorizing the secretary of war "to lease Army property 'when in his discretion it will be for the public good.'" It would allow the United States' growing Arsenal of Democracy to supply a bankrupt Britain with food and munitions while deferring payment. Germany responded to this optimistic moment for Britain with the worst bombings that the Londoners had yet experienced, timed specifically as an act of terrorism. [85]

While Congress was hotly debating the Lend Lease Bill, there was still a great deal of opposition from diehard isolationists; their fear was that the munitions we would send to the British would surely fall into German hands when the British capitulated, as many feared would happen. Many were uneasy. Hopkins, anxious to get solid information that could ensure passage of the bill, suggested that if he were to go to Britain, he could ascertain the resolve of Churchill and the British people themselves and report back. He was sure that he was the only man who could accomplish this and it was important to let the American people and Congress know the full situation in Great Britain.

The plans for Hopkins' visit to London arose during the Tuscaloosa outing just after the election. FDR really wanted a sit-down with Churchill and when he voiced this, Hopkins asked, "How about me going over." He wanted to arrange a meeting with the two. The president turned him down and sent a series of jibes toward Hopkins about this. It is clear in hindsight that FDR, playing the juggler, had made up his mind to send Hopkins to London; he just was not letting him know just yet. On January 6th, at a press conference, the President told the reporters that Hopkins would act as his personal representative to establish "personal contact" with the British government. FDR's press secretary, Steve Early, brought the news to Hopkins, who was sitting in the Lincoln Suite in his bathrobe. Stunned, Hopkins replied, "Think of it! My father was a harness maker and my mother a schoolteacher. And I am going over to talk to Winston Churchill and the men who run the British government. If that isn't democracy, I don't know what is.[86] Hopkins clearly had a sense of how important his mission was and what it meant to him and to the country.

Contemporary journalist Marquis Childs wrote in the *Saturday Evening Post* issue on April 19, 1941, "The President's Best Friend," that FDR's press secretary, Steve Early, announced to Hopkins that the president had decided to send him to Britain to meet with Churchill. However, the plan to send Hopkins over to take the measure of the Prime Minister and of the British people and to arrange a meeting between the two leaders was actually was Hopkins' idea. He just had to convince the President. Christopher O'Sullivan does not include the Tuscaloosa trip in his book but this event is crucial to understanding the origins of Lend Lease. He also writes that Hopkins' trip to Great Britain was FDR's idea. McJimsey and Tuttle also note that it was the President's idea to send Hopkins to London.[87] In fact it was actually Hopkins, on board the *Tuscaloosa*, who initiated this diplomatic mission and this speaks to how influential he was in 1940-41; he thought of himself as advisor to the president. Childs goes on to write that it was part of Hopkins' job on this trip to "interpret Roosevelt to Churchill and Churchill to Roosevelt. It is one of the gifts that have endeared him to the President— his capacity to get inside another man's mind. His ability to sense another's feelings, convictions, intentions, is almost feminine in its shrewdness." Notwithstanding his sexist flub, Childs did understand Hopkins' role in the Roosevelt administration.[88]

Roosevelt clearly had misgivings about the British Prime Minister and about Britain's ability to hold out against the Germans; U.S. support would be contingent on how any assistance would promote American security. The president needed assurance about Churchill's ability to live up to his pronouncements of British trustworthiness; Churchill resented Roosevelt's hesitancy to send aid. FDR trusted that Hopkins would tell him the full story. He was to ascertain British resolve and find out what the British needed to stay afloat. And he was to arrange a meeting for the two to get to know each other on a personal basis, an integral part of the President's play book. The Prime Minister was fully on board with this. Both leaders believed that "the attitudes, feelings, demeanor, and body language displayed by statesmen in face-to-face meetings could reveal inner thoughts and ultimate intentions leading to significant political and military decisions."[89] Hopkins agreed wholeheartedly. In order to get the support needed to help Britain materially, the President had to first convince Americans that the island nation would not waste America's scarce munitions and would not capitulate to the Germans. If that happened, our munitions would fall into Nazi hands. Simultaneously FDR had to convince Churchill that Americans were indeed supportive of what Churchill described as Britain's valiant efforts to resist the Germans.[90] For better or worse, at this point, diplomatic channels were awkward. Both nations were between Ambassadors. Joseph Kennedy, FDR's Ambassador to the Court of St. James, always pessimistic as to Britain's ability to hold off the Germans, had resigned. And Lord Lothian (Philip Kerr), FDR's much-admired Ambassador from Britain, had died.

According to George McJimsey, when FDR selected Hopkins to be his representative to Churchill, this proved to be the "turning point" in his administration. He had been a loyal New Dealer and a brilliant administrator of relief programs but, more importantly, Hopkins had the ability to bring people to consensus, to resolve differences and win the confidence of people of various political persuasions. FDR knew that he could trust him to represent the White House, to be a valuable instrument of the FDR style of governance.[91] Furthermore, the President trusted Hopkins to the extent that he would share confidential matters with him.[92]

Nevertheless, Roosevelt was reluctant to send Hopkins on a mission, however vital, that would take him out of the country, away from the White House. He had become a welcome and useful fixture. The President, who was in the midst of writing his "Four Freedoms" speech, had an inaugural speech to prepare, budget issues to settle, and the State of the Union speech to write. He was used to bouncing ideas off a man whose opinion he could trust. And on a purely personal level, FDR liked having him around; by then Hopkins had been living in the White House for almost a year. Furthermore, he was not sure that Hopkins would get along with the Prime Minister. In the end, probably due to Churchill's constant and very eloquent pleas for help, Roosevelt relented. The President sent Hopkins to England with orders to set in motion "personal relations" with the British Government. Hopkins would fly to England, take the measure of the Prime Minister and of the country itself, and report back to the President.[93]

Hopkins was the perfect man for this important and very secret mission; or at least he himself thought so. His ultimate goal did gibe with the Prime Minister's. An internationalist by nature if not by ideology, he felt very strongly that unless the United States entered the war, Hitler could not be defeated. Of course, this was the Prime Minister's most desperate hope. The President might have been of the same mind on this subject, but he had to consider political exigencies; as President, he had Congress and public opinion to consider. Hopkins did not. FDR was reluctant to commit anything more than munitions and supplies to the British, which he presented to the American public as a way to prevent our involvement in the war rather than as a step toward sending troops to battle. Because the two leaders suffered from vaguely based mutual distrust – over the monarchy, over the empire, over politics in general – and had only communicated distantly, they needed an intermediary. Costigliola and Tuttle both agree here. Hopkins realized that the two world leaders would not ordinarily be friends and he saw his job as ensuring that they would at least maintain amicable relations during a world crisis. Michael Fullilove calls Hopkins "history's foremost marriage broker."[94] The first meeting between Roosevelt and Churchill, which

Hopkins was charged with arranging, was the beginning of this process.[95]

As a personal envoy, Hopkins' official mission was twofold: to organize a meeting between the President and the Prime Minister and then to assess British needs in the way of munitions. He was also supposed to discover something less tangible: Did the British have it in them to fight to the finish? This was probably the most important part of his mission. Hopkins spent six weeks in Britain figuring this out. His visit laid the groundwork for what later would be called "The Special Relationship," that is, the unique tie between the United States and Great Britain during, and beyond, World War II. Recently, some scholars (notably historian Fraser Harbutt) have emphasized the tenuousness of this relationship and argue that the Anglo-Soviet alliance that began in June of 1941 was more relevant to the outcome of the war than the Anglo-American relationship. It is true that the British were much more invested in the situation in Europe than were the Americans but Hopkins' meetings with the Prime Minister opened up channels between the Western Allies before the Soviets joined in the fight against fascism. The correspondence between Winston Churchill and Harry Hopkins during 1941, when the British were standing alone against German aggression, highlights the fact that Hopkins jump-started the Anglo-American connection, even before Roosevelt and Churchill met for the first time.[96] Furthermore, he kept the relationship stable throughout the war years.

At this point, however, Hopkins lacked diplomatic polish; he didn't need it in D.C., and no one expected it from him. Before he left for London, he met with Jean Monnet, a French banker working with the British as a member of the

Allied Economic Coordinating Committee when France fell
and then with the British Purchasing Commission. Monnet
advised Hopkins not to waste any time with ministers but to
concentrate his energies on Churchill alone. Maintaining his
trademark cynicism, Hopkins replied: "I suppose Churchill
is convinced that he's the greatest man on earth." A friend
who was present advised Hopkins to quit acting like "a
small- time chauvinist" and to get the "chip off his shoulder."
Otherwise, he should just cancel the trip. Clearly, Hopkins
did not expect to like the Prime Minister even though he was
on a mission for his boss to set up communications. [97]
Monnet, who had seen his country, France, go down in bitter
defeat to the Germans, told Hopkins that full military
production should be the primary goal and that "ten
thousand tanks too many are far preferable to one tank to
few."[98] This gave Hopkins food for thought.

Hopkins left New York aboard a Pan Am Yankee
Clipper on January 6th, 1941, arriving in Poole, Dorset on the
evening of the 9th. It was a long flight. Because of American
neutrality laws, the airline was not allowed to fly into
belligerent nations, so Hopkins had to change to British
Overseas Airways Clipper (BOAC) in Lisbon for the last leg
to England. Churchill had sent his secretary, Brendan
Bracken, to meet the plane and welcome the President's
representative. Hopkins was so exhausted after the long
flight that he could not even get out of his seat. Bracken had
to go on board to help him unbuckle his seat belt, get off the
plane, and onto the train that would take them to London. On
the ride to London Hopkins slowly recovered, gazing out the
window at the devastation German bombs had wreaked on
the countryside. If he had originally approached his meeting

with Churchill with a chip on his shoulder, he very quickly brushed it off as the train made its way through the English countryside. He witnessed first-hand the effects of the Blitz, the devastation that the German bombings had wreaked on the British. Even more immediate, he heard the German bombs falling on the track of the Pullman car he occupied just minutes after his train passed.[99] His pro-British sentiments increased with each mile traveled as he became aware of the effects of German aggression. Although Hopkins did not know what to expect from the Prime Minister, a man with whom he had so little in common, politically or socially, he was fully convinced that they had one common goal—to beat Hitler—and this should establish a sufficient foundation for constructive conversation.

At first Churchill had no idea who Hopkins was. All he really knew was that the President of the United States was sending a social worker to confer with him. When Bracken had informed the Prime Minister that an American named Harry Hopkins was coming to meet with him, Churchill asked, "Who?" Bracken, fully aware of Hopkins' importance in the Roosevelt administration, carefully explained this to the Prime Minister. Then, when Churchill had read the letter of introduction that FDR had written for Hopkins, he made sure that the presidential envoy got the red-carpet treatment.

Hopkins knew that his mission could prove difficult. The two leaders did want to meet but Hopkins was afraid that Roosevelt and Churchill might not get along very well – their personalities and ideologies were very different. Just after he arrived at Claridge's, the hotel where he stayed when he was in London, Hopkins met with renowned CBS broadcaster, Edward R. Murrow. Murrow's broadcasts to

Americans during the Blitz had made him famous. Hopkins wanted to talk to him to get more first-hand information about the situation and especially information about the personalities in Britain. He questioned him relentlessly about the people he would be meeting with in Britain, about how the people were standing up to the Blitz, and especially about the Prime Minister. Hopkins turned the tables on Murrow and became the interviewer rather than the interviewee. When Murrow finally got a chance to get a word in edgewise, he asked Hopkins what he was doing in England. Hopkins sat back in his typically relaxed posture and answered, "I suppose you could say that I've come here to find a way to be a catalytic agent between two prima donnas."[100] It was a task that required subtlety and patience, as well as physical endurance.

The first meeting between Hopkins and Churchill took place in London at Number 10, Downing Street. While Hopkins' friendship with the President had evolved over several years in Washington, this was not the case with Churchill. Hopkins' Midwest brusqueness, his utter practicality struck an immediate chord with the Prime Minister. They took to each other right away. The Prime Minister wrote about the first time he met Hopkins:

> On January 10 a gentleman arrived to see me at Downing Street with the highest credentials. ... He was the closest confidant ... of the President. ... Thus I met Harry Hopkins, that extraordinary man, who played, and was to play, a sometimes-decisive part in the whole movement of the war. He was a soul that flamed out of a frail and

failing body. ... He had also a gift of sardonic humour. I always enjoyed his company, especially when things went ill. He could also be very disagreeable and say hard and sour things. My experiences were teaching me to be able to do this if need be. ... With gleaming eye and quiet, constrained passion he said, 'The President is determined that we shall win the war together. Make no mistake about it.' ... And from this hour began a friendship between us which sailed serenely. ... He was the most faithful and perfect channel of communication between the President and me. ...

Together these two men, the one a subordinate without public office, the other commanding a mighty Republic, were capable of making decisions of the highest consequence over the whole area of the English-speaking world. ... There he sat, slim, frail, ill, but absolutely glowing with refined comprehension of The Cause. It was to be the defeat, ruin and slaughter of Hitler, to the exclusion of all other purposes, loyalties or aims. In the history of the United States few brighter flames have burned. ... Harry Hopkins always went to the root of the matter. ... At several great conferences ... when the discussion flagged and all seemed baffled ... he would rap out the question, 'Surely, Mr. President, here is the point we have got to settle. Are we going to face it or not?' Faced it always was, and being faced, was conquered. He was a true leader of men, and alike in ardour and in wisdom in times of crisis, he has rarely been excelled. [101]

Churchill clearly wanted it to be made known that Hopkins was going to be useful. This was indeed a reflection of just how much he thought he needed Hopkins.

As the Prime Minister spent time with Hopkins, he quickly came to realize that this was not just some talented New Dealer. Hopkins represented a direct channel to the President, one that he could fully trust. He rightfully concluded that whatever he communicated to Hopkins would be reported in full to the President and this would be of extreme importance to the British. Their first meeting at No. 10 (the building was described by Hopkins as "a bit down in the heels") was a lunch that lasted for over three hours. When Hopkins suggested that Churchill should make plans to meet the President face to face, Churchill responded, "The sooner the better." Hopkins assured the Prime Minister that the feeling was mutual. The President was anxious for a meeting but wanted to wait until the Lend Lease Bill passed through Congress.

Each time the Prime Minister and Hopkins met their relationship deepened. For the Prime Minister this was important because he needed someone who could get to the American President. Britain needed the help of the United States and Churchill felt that Hopkins would facilitate here. Churchill's daughter, Sarah, recalled in an interview, "the chemistry was right between them." The British people also responded to Hopkins' apparent empathetic reaction to their predicament and his belief in and commitment to ultimate victory over the Nazis. One of Churchill's aides remarked that it was "extraordinary how Hopkins has endeared himself to everyone here he has met." There is no doubt that this was the beginning of the Anglo-American wartime alliance.[102]

Churchill received some much-needed encouragement when he heard Hopkins declare with great emphasis that the President would do anything in his power to defeat the Germans, and would, indeed, stand shoulder to shoulder with the British to defeat the Germans.[103] That remark was pregnant with meaning. The United States was not in a state of war with the Germans. No President of the United States had the constitutional authority to utter these words to a British Prime Minister. Hopkins likely had no right to make such a promise, he probably overstepped his authority, informal as it was, in making such a forthright declaration. But it was clearly meant to let Churchill know that Hopkins, himself, would do everything he could to make sure that the British got the war material it needed to continue to hold off the Germans; by implication, so would FDR. The vital task for both Churchill and Hopkins at this early point was to convince the Americans and the British of two things: 1) that Britain would continue the fight at all costs and 2) that it could not hold out against the Germans without U.S. material support. Both men believed, deep down, that although this was an important first step, there was little chance of final victory unless the United States entered the war.

The Prime Minister quickly took the measure of the man he called a "crumbling lighthouse," recognizing that he would become an integral part of the wartime alliance. But

Churchill was discerning enough to notice something that that Hopkins not just excelled in a time of crisis; in fact, he thrived on it. Churchill recognized that Hopkins' "love for the weak and poor was matched by his passion against tyranny, especially when tyranny was, for the time, triumphant."[104] In other words, Hopkins' concern for the victims of economic devastation in the United Stated during the Great Depression now broadened to include a determination to protect people in Europe from the evils of Hitlerism.

If Hopkins had learned the ABCs of foreign policy at FDR's side, he began his education in wartime diplomacy at Churchill's side during the time he spent in Britain. In true Hopkins style, he sent reports to Roosevelt, not through regular diplomatic channels but by personal courier, thus ensuring that his optimistic missives to the President were not filtered through the State Department. He described to the President Churchill's determination that the British would fight to the finish but would need American munitions to do this. These missives were detailed and personal, and wholly admiring of the Prime Minister and of the British people. They expressed his awe at the Prime Minister's grasp of the war situation and his determination to fight the Germans to the very end. He described to the President the pride that the British had in their country's fight against Nazism. He wrote, "if courage alone can win—the result will be inevitable. But they need our help desperately. ... *Churchill* is the gov't in every sense of the word." This is the point when international relations changed. Harbutt points out that Churchill preferred to do business with either Averell Harriman or Hopkins and Hopkins advised FDR to deal only with Churchill, and this led to the "atrophy of conventional diplomacy." This is true but the two leaders found this wartime personal diplomacy to be expedient. Although it did work, Harbutt is correct in explaining that it worked to the detriment of the state department and Ambassadors.[105]

Hopkins had a very optimistic view of the British and of Churchill. But this was based purely on observation and intuition, not on actual hard data. He was unschooled in military matters and was only just beginning to hone his diplomatic skills. But over the years he had developed an ability to read people, something he had mastered as a social worker and New Dealer. During this trip, the steadfast British people had certainly impressed him and he did not want the United States to let them down. But it was likely the overwhelming personality of the Prime Minister and his eloquent insistence that the island nation would fight to the death that led Hopkins to report to the President that America had to supply Britain with all of the munitions it needed to fight the Germans.

If Hopkins's goal mirrored that of Churchill, he did not possess the eloquence that was so typical of the Prime Minister. Instead, he used the American vernacular and said outright that we had to get on with the "business of licking that godam sonofabitch Hitler."[106] This is what Churchill so admired about Hopkins – his ability to cut through superfluities and get to the essence of the problem. Because of this, the Prime Minister dubbed Hopkins "Lord Root of the Matter," a title that reflected Churchill's admiration for the way this presidential envoy cut to the chase. Despite the fact that they were men from two different worlds, a lasting friendship emerged beginning with their first meeting; it never waned.

Thus, began the "Winston and Harry show" during which the Prime Minister would bring Hopkins along on his travels around Britain while convincing him that Britain would stand fast against the Germans if the United States would provide the military materiels.[107] Hopkins spent several weekends with Churchill at Chequers, the country residence of British Prime Ministers, which did not have central heating and was therefore very cold. He called it the coldest place he had ever been in—and this from an Iowan. The only place where he could work comfortably, the only room with a heater, was the downstairs bathroom and the envoy from the American President found refuge there. Despite the fact that he picked up a persistent cold at this elegant country house, Hopkins accompanied the Prime Minister on inspection tours of military installations. They made an odd couple—the rotund, imposing Prime Minister with the inevitable cigar stuck in his mouth and the unkempt, chain smoking, and often shivering American, together traveling to see the fleet, to inspect munitions factories, to view bomb damage. Altogether, Hopkins spent twelve evenings with Churchill. Biographer Robert Sherwood suggested that this created an "intimacy" almost as strong as that between Hopkins and Roosevelt.[108] Perhaps it was even stronger than the relationship between Roosevelt and Churchill because at that point in time Churchill needed Hopkins more that Roosevelt did. And the fact was that he knew that he could rely on Hopkins steadfast support. True, he had written that Hopkins could "be disagreeable and say hard and sour things" but this was a reference to Hopkins' forthrightness and inability to mince words; this was the quality that the Prime Minister admired. But few words between the Prime Minister and Hopkins were sour at their first meeting; these would come later. Both quickly came to realize the value of the other.

Hopkins kept up with the grueling schedule the energetic Prime Minister had set. There is no doubt that Hopkins felt deeply the heavy responsibility of his mission. He did not mention his illness in any of his messages to Roosevelt and he managed to hide any discomfort from the media. Still, it was an exciting time for him, and the buzz of impending war gave him the stamina to keep up with Churchill. His innate talent to act decisively in times of crisis served him well during this mission. The drama increased daily with the dangers of falling bombs. In any case, for Hopkins, leaping into a bomb shelter was much preferable to spending time in the freezing rooms of Chequers.

In mid-January, Hopkins accompanied the Prime Minister and Lord Halifax to Scapa Flow, where the new ambassador to the United States was to leave for Washington. The weather was brutal with a blizzard and strong winds lowering the temperature to below freezing. Hopkins joined the others in jumping from a minesweeper to a destroyer to a huge battleship but almost fell into the sea trying it. He had to be dragged up, ignominiously, onto the deck of the destroyer by able-bodied seamen. The trip was an endurance test for Hopkins that helped him understand what many British people had been going through for more than a year.[109]

Well into the visit, when they were in Glasgow on a tour of naval facilities in Scotland, Churchill pressed Hopkins for some hint of what he was going to report to the President.

The Prime Minister knew that the President would listen carefully to what Hopkins recommended and he was most anxious to get an idea of what this report might contain. Hopkins had said nothing that would give a clue as to this during their travels. At a dinner in Glasgow, when they were seeing Halifax off, Hopkins unexpectedly stood to give a toast. He presented to the guests a sort of roundabout reply to the Prime Minister's queries, using a quotation from the Book of Ruth: "Whither thou goest, I will go; and where thou lodgest, I will lodge; thy people shall be my people, and thy God, my God." And then Hopkins, very quietly added, "Even to the end." And he sat down. Some reports mention tears in Churchill's eyes because he knew then that he had a good chance of getting American help soon. Lord Moran interpreted this toast as a rope thrown to a drowning man. In this instance, Hopkins did an end run around "the root of the matter." He wanted to give hope to the British people but knew that this would have to come ultimately from the President. So, he did it the only way he knew how, probably echoing his Methodist mother. At this point, the Lend Lease Bill was working its way through Congress and Churchill believed it would likely pass. He might have interpreted Hopkins' toast as a promise of America's participation in the war.[110] Hopkins most likely had thought hard about this toast of his before the dinner; he would not have adlibbed such an important statement.

Towards the end of his stay, Hopkins attended yet another dinner in his honor. This one had been organized by Canadian newspaper mogul, William Maxwell Aiken, later Lord Beaverbrook, who had invited the press. Although there is no record of what was said, one reporter wrote that the

British people had been much encouraged by Hopkins' presence in their country, and he quoted Shakespeare's phrase in Henry V, "a little touch of Harry in the night" bringing hope to the besieged nation.[111] Hopkins had said what the guests wanted to hear—that America was marching alongside Britain. The actuality would only come gradually, first with the passage of the Lend Lease bill and then with the Japanese attack on Pearl Harbor. Still, Hopkins knew that the British people needed hope now and he wanted to give it to them. He told the President in his private dispatches that the United States should give Great Britain whatever it needed to repel Hitler.

Shortly before he returned to the United States, on January 30, Hopkins had lunch at Buckingham Palace with King George VI and Queen Elizabeth. They discussed military issues and ways to ensure that Britain and the United States maintain a close relationship. He wrote in his diary that both "realize that Britain is fighting for its life" and that if Hitler is to win the war, Britain "will be enslaved for years." When an alarm sounded and they had to go to a shelter, Hopkins realized that Their Majesties slept in an air raid shelter every night because of the Blitz. The king told Hopkins that he hoped that FDR and Churchill would meet very soon. Hopkins assured the king and queen that their nation could rely on the United States to give it the aid it needed to defeat the Germans.[112]

Hopkins' final report to the President included praise for Churchill's Cabinet Ministers and Undersecretaries: "They have given me complete access to all confidential information which is concerned with my mission here. I believe. ... I have got a reasonably clear perception not only of the physical defenses of Britain but of the opinions of the men who are directing this nation." He adds that Churchill is "the directing force behind the strategy and conduct of the war ... No matter how fierce the attack maybe you can be sure that [the British] will resist it, and effectively."[113]

Given his newly established relationship with Churchill, Hopkins became, in effect, "Roosevelt's own personal Foreign Office." Hopkins had no title. The American media, having to create some, referred to him as "a personal fact-finder," a personal observer," a "close confidante," and an "unofficial liaison."[114] When Hopkins took over as the Presidential representative for the production, transportation, and distribution of war materials to the Allies, he knew nothing about these matters but he did have "the amazing ability to find out about things quickly;" he was a quick study. And he knew how to get results. He insisted that every effort be given to war production, that all transportation be used for war materials and not "soft drinks, and that planes should be used to deliver ammunition and not people on holiday.[115] These were the sentiments of Lord Root of the Matter that so impressed Churchill. And this was especially true when the survival of Britain hung in the balance.

During the early part of his stay in Britain, Hopkins had found out about the terrifying possibility of a German land invasion of Britain, code named Operation Sealion, and also of the possibility that the Nazis could use mustard gas. In one of his reports to the President he wrote that he believed that this could happen as early as May 1st. Hopkins had experienced the war first-hand in England and this made his reports to the President genuine. In addition, his insights into Churchill allowed him to advise the President from a personal point of view as well as from a platform of emerging military and political expertise, knowledge that would become crucial to the stability of the Alliance. McJimsey notes that Churchill was probably not trying to use Hopkins to maneuver the United States into the war. Hopkins certainly had a great deal of sympathy and admiration for the British but was savvy enough to know that FDR was not going to ask Congress for a declaration of war. He made sure that Churchill understood this.[116]

This first visit to Great Britain initiated a continuous spate of official and unofficial correspondence, some personal and not for the record, between Roosevelt and Churchill—with Hopkins as a "stalking horse." This was unprecedented and opened up many options for the Prime Minister. Churchill could raise issues with Roosevelt indirectly, through Hopkins, if he felt uneasy about going directly to the President. It facilitated interaction between these two leaders, one engaged in war and the other on the brink, until the informal alliance would be formalized after the Pearl Harbor attack. After America entered into the war, this system continued, with Hopkins acting as an intermediary. But this would not happen for another ten months.

Hopkins discussed with Churchill the President's extension of boundaries that would allow American ships to convoy British ships. Churchill appealed to Hopkins to increase the output; eventually Hopkins was able to inform Churchill that more tanks were on the way. Churchill was able to express worries and disappointments to Hopkins, something he would do to the President.[117] His energy and confident persona endeared him to the British people and he came back somewhat a changed man. After his first meeting with Churchill at Number 10, he learned to hold his sharp tongue and acquired diplomatic polish, but he never abandoned his basic assumptions about the value of a democratic system and the responsibility of government toward the people. His experience with the brave British people ensured this.[118]

Hopkins left London on February 8th, having heard Churchill's famous speech in which he pled, "Give us the tools and we will finish the job."[119] The next day he flew home from Bournemouth to pass on his reports in person to the President. By the time he got home, the Lend Lease had been approved by both houses of Congress. FDR signed it into law and named Hopkins as administrator of the program to bring aid to Great Britain, a position that made Hopkins extremely powerful and much more of a public figure. Congress appropriated $1 billion dollars to the Lend Lease program, much to the delight of the Prime Minister who called it "the most unsordid act in the history of any nation." Churchill knew that his new American friend would ensure that Britain would get the munitions and food it needed to survive and to hold off the Germans, for the time being at least.[120]

This initial trip to Britain laid the groundwork, emotionally and politically, for the Special Relationship between Roosevelt and Churchill and between the United States and Great Britain.

Although there was a certain manipulation necessary on both sides of the relationship between Churchill and Hopkins, mutual trust and an evolving affection underlay this. Just before he left England, Hopkins left a note for Churchill:

> My dear Mr. Prime Minister,
> I shall never forget these days with you—your supreme confidence and will to victory—Britain I have ever liked—I like it the more. As I leave for America tonight, I wish you great and good luck—confusion to your enemies and victory for Britain.[121]

Hopkins' return to the United States was front-page news. The New York *Daily News* circulated two editions on February 17, 1941, each with two-inch headlines and photos clearly portraying Hopkins as a returning hero. The articles warn that the Germans were preparing to invade Britain with poison gas sprayed from planes that were similar to American crop dusters, flying in the dark of night. This, of course, had to be terrifying for anyone who had experienced mustard gas in WWI. The paper reported that the Nazis had shut down the Belgian and French coast in preparation for the attack, to the extent that anyone found owning a pigeon would be shot.[122] This news brought home the extent of the crisis in Europe and sympathy for the British increased considerably.

If Churchill at first had suspected that Roosevelt had sent him a social worker to assess Britain, he was partly correct. An editorial appeared in the *New York Post* on January 6, 1941. This was just as Hopkins was leaving London. The article emphasizes his experience with work relief during the depression years that "reflects the reform mood" of the decade. This gives him better insight into how to make use of the "resources of a democracy." The British people, the article explains, will respond to him in a positive way because this attitude is what has most interested the British about his New Deal programs.[123] Hopkins was horrified by the devastation wrought by German bombs. Just after he returned to the United States, Hopkins wrote: "But the new order of Hitler can be conclusively defeated by the new order of democracy, which is the New Deal universally extended and applied." For Hopkins the welfare of Americans was closely connected to the welfare of people everywhere in the world.[124] The New Deal was not over, it did not end with the beginning of economic recovery; the policies of New Dealers like Hopkins were just re-focused to bring help to those suffering from totalitarianism.

Historian Ronald Lewin argues that it was an "enormous achievement" on the part of Churchill to have brought Hopkins, "this shrewd and sceptical (sic) spy" over to his side and, moreover, the Prime Minister exercised "dextrous diplomacy" to accomplish this. His faith in Hopkins "never budged."[125] Hopkins was certainly shrewd and skeptical, but he was not a spy. The mission was secret, but the United States was supporting Britain as an ally and as a bulwark against the Germans. Lewin explains that an unprecedented but official correspondence between Roosevelt and Churchill began through a third party "in whose discretion and judgment each had complete confidence." This would allow Churchill to discuss issues that he could not directly raise with Roosevelt.[126] Hopkins was acting as a "friend by proxy" because this was the only way, at this point in time that Churchill and Roosevelt could establish a relationship.[127] Hopkins' mission to Great Britain established a new relationship between the President and the Prime Minister. His easy style along with his straightforwardness allowed him to act not only as a friend, but as a connection to the President. Consequently, his value to the president grew immensely because of this.[128] McJimsey suggests that there was more to the relationship between Churchill and Hopkins than the envoy merely being a direct channel to the president. The Prime Minister "realized [Hopkins] was a man worth cultivating in his own right" and this is the reason that he did not try to "manipulate Hopkins for his own ends." Hopkins had "an intuitive gift for personal diplomacy and his unaffected friendship" elicited the same qualities in the Prime Minister and this cemented a powerful relationship between the two men. [129]

Hopkins' first trip to Great Britain was successful in that he presented himself to the British people a sympathetic to their plight while at the same time being firm in just how far the United States would go in their support. He had become expert at negotiations and at diplomacy.[130] Hopkins seemed to be encouraging FDR to take a more militant stance against Germany and Japan, believing that U.S intervention was necessary to defeat Germany.

The world situation was hard for Americans to read; Japan's expansionism in the Pacific coupled with German aggression in Europe made for perplexing complications in the minds of ordinary people but also in the minds of those in FDR's administration. In 1941, FDR thought that the Germans were much more likely to attack Indochina or even Russia rather than the British Isles. While Sherwood and Henry Adams claim that Hopkins was pushing FDR toward more aggressive action toward Germany and Japan, Tuttle disputes this to some extent and quotes Hopkins in a memo to Hull: "'It has long been my opinion that Germany cannot be defeated unless the United States is wholeheartedly in the war and makes a strong military and naval effort wherever strategy dictates ... even if hostilities with Japan must be accepted.'" Tuttle argues that Hopkins had the ability to think strategically and that he doubted the efficacy of the President's Atlantic strategy of focusing on the centrality of the Atlantic rather than the Pacific. The President had shifted a portion of the Pacific fleet to the Atlantic even though there was increasing threat from Japan in the Pacific.[131]

As the President's personal foreign office, Hopkins had to keep a rigorous traveling schedule, one that would have exhausted even a healthy man. His illness debilitated him, but he also had personal matters that drew on his emotional energy. Hopkins first wife, Ethel Gross Hopkins, was raising their three sons.[132] Like most divorced couples, money was always an issue; this is revealed in the letters they exchanged. In March of 1941 (just after he returned from his first trip to Great Britain) Ethel Hopkins wrote a letter to her ex-husband informing him that the check he had sent her had bounced; although she knows how hard he is working, she wrote, she "cannot manage on the $170 per month which you send me." She cites school expenses for the older boys and the fact that she is having trouble finding a job. His reply two days later expresses regret that the check was made "out improperly," but "you should organize your life to live within that and not assume that I am going to do something else to earn a larger income later. ... I simply am not in a position to handle your personal affairs beyond the responsibility I have assumed." This letter reflects a testiness that is never apparent in his exchanges with political or military leaders. He was clearly irritated at her request for more money. Later that year a lawyer responded to a query from Mrs. Hopkins about a situation in which her payments might be lowered; he told her that the only contingency would be her re-marriage and added: "In my opinion Mr. Hopkins is doing such great and magnificent work in connection with our war effort, that I feel that he should not be annoyed or mentally harassed in a matter of this kin[d] and at this time."[133] Ethel Hopkins was a remarkably capable woman who did find inventive ways to supplement the alimony from her ex-husband. However, in the mid-20th century it was quite difficult for a divorced woman with three children to find work that paid enough to support a family. That a lawyer would accuse her of harassing Hopkins, whom she admired, would have been devastating for her. Although Hopkins felt the weight of personal problems, it is clear that he also felt the weight of his enormous wartime responsibilities. Tuttle writes that Hopkins was no saint (true enough) and uses as evidence the fact that when he divorced his first wife, Ethel Gross Hopkins, he failed to support her. This is not true. Hopkins was certainly an absentee father, but he consistently contributed fifty percent of his salary to the support of his wife and children. While, at times, this was not enough, he was by no means what we today call a "deadbeat dad." His personal problems, however, never did impinge on his ability to carry out his duties to the President.

Roosevelt began to rely more and more on Hopkins, who had the ability to listen to his boss and to know what he wanted and furthermore to know how and when to present him with ideas. In this sense Hopkins was "a fixer." He often prevented the President from taking a misstep. After he had signed the Lend Lease Act, Roosevelt wrote a "scathing" and "vindictive" speech castigating the media that had opposed him during the contentious congressional debates over the bill. Speechwriter Robert Sherwood witnessed the President's anger and told Hopkins that it would be a terrible mistake on the part of the President to give such a speech. Hopkins replied that the President had no intention of giving the speech and that he was just venting on paper. He suggested to the President that he instead of sending angry letters, he should give a very positive speech praising the American people for supporting Lend Lease. He also advised the President to include a description of the British Prime Minister as the great leader of a brave people. FDR took Hopkins' advice and gave a brilliant and emotionally charged speech.[134] This was a speed bump avoided.

As administrator of Lend Lease, Hopkins expanded his influence with the British. After his return to Washington, he wrote the Prime Minister, "I have great hopes of our ability to be of very genuine help to you. ... I find my thoughts constantly with you in the desperate struggle which I am sure is going to result, in the last analysis, in your victory."[135] If Lend Lease was Britain's lifeline, Hopkins held the rope, and his sentiments were with the British people. In other circumstances, Churchill would have dealt very carefully with any American official having that kind of power. But it is clear from their interactions that he trusted that Hopkins was determined that Britain would get what it needed to fight Nazism.

Hopkins' relationship with Churchill "was especially valuable, forging as he had a bond with Britain's most dominant figure." McJimsey writes that it wasn't just the friendship that Churchill felt for Hopkins that drew the Prime Minister to him; and there was more to the relationship than just Hopkins as access to the President. Churchill seemed aware that Hopkins felt real sympathy for the British and what they were going through. The feeling, of course, resulted from this first visit to England when he saw the effects of the Blitz and witnessed the steadfastness of the British people, Churchill included. The Prime Minister "realized he was a man worth cultivating in his own right." This is the reason that he did not try to "manipulate Hopkins for his own ends." According to McJimsey, Hopkins' candid responses to Churchill and his direct and "unaffected friendship" worked to elicit the same qualities in the Prime Minister and, therefore, created a powerful and honest relationship.

Nevertheless, there was manipulation necessary on both sides of the nascent alliance. The grand chess game that the Allies were playing ensured this.[136] Churchill called him extraordinary, a true leader of men.[137] Whether or not this was actually true, the Prime Minister needed the United States and therefore Harry Hopkins. And even though American security depended on Britain holding out against the Germans, the British needed the United States more than the United States needed Britain. Still, Harold Ickes, no friend to Hopkins, quipped, "I suspect that if, as his personal representative, the President should send to London a man with the Bubonic plague, Churchill would, nonetheless, see a good deal of him."[138] Even if this were true, Hopkins did much more than was expected from him.

During the war years Hopkins used his influence with Churchill, as he did with Roosevelt, to sometimes redirect anger into more positive directions. In late 1943 five U. S. senators toured British military installations and accused Great Britain of using Lend Lease equipment merely to further its own needs in the Empire. The infuriated Prime Minister drafted a speech to deliver to the House of Commons in which he excoriated the American politicians; he asked Hopkins to show it to Roosevelt. Hopkins did show it to the President, but he also warned Churchill that "the inexorable events of the war are rapidly crowding the statements by the five Senators from the front pages" and suggested that he refrain from even responding. Churchill took Hopkins' advice and when questioned on the issue replied, "There would be no advantage in this government taking part in this wordy warfare" while the Allies are fighting "shoulder to shoulder."[139] Hopkins' ability to guide both leaders away from diplomatic gaffes arose solely from the trust both had in him.

Chapter 5—Stalin

"We have taken the opportunity afforded by the consideration of the report of Mr. Harry Hopkins on his return from Moscow to consult together as to how best our two countries can help your country in the splendid defense that you are putting against the Nazi attack" -August 15, 1941, F. Roosevelt and W. Churchill to J. V. Stalin[140]

The 1939 Molotov-Ribbentrop Non-aggression

Pact that gave Nazi Germany the opportunity to invade and occupy Poland with no interference from the Soviet Union had lulled Stalin into believing that his country was safe from German intrusion. Therefore, when Germany suddenly and unexpectedly carried out an attack on the Soviet Union, Operation Barbarossa, on June 22, 1941, it caught the Red Army unprepared, despite warnings from the Americans and the British. Churchill had warned Stalin of a Germany build up and that this presented a potential threat. Churchill had even warned Stalin in April that German maneuvers indicated that Hitler would very likely attack Russia. Stalin did not listen. At the same time, the Prime Minister feared that the German invasion Russia might just be a prelude to an invasion of Great Britain.[141] Therefore, the Soviet leader was entirely stunned when he discovered that Germany had abandoned its campaign against Britain and turned east to attack Russia. He considered this to be treachery of the highest sort; his former partner, Hitler "had suddenly revealed himself as a rabid dog." The Soviet leader furiously declared that the German invasion was "the act of a madman obeying a swift murderous passion."[142] It is illuminating to interpret this outpouring of Stalin's vitriol against Hitler in light of the brutal Soviet invasion of Finland, of Stalin's murder of millions of Soviet citizens, and of the Katyn Massacre; these brutalities placed Stalin on a par with the Nazi leader. Yet, Stalin was now an ally. Two weeks later he sent to Washington a list what the U.S.S.R. would need in the way of armaments. The President had to carefully review this schedule of requirements, costing some two billion dollars, and then get an estimate of when it could be delivered.[143] Roosevelt's advisors anticipated a quick German victory and feared that valuable American munitions would fall to the Nazis. Hopkins was worried about having enough supplies for America's new but uncongenial ally. Both Churchill and Roosevelt, however, had decided that allying with Communist Russia and having the powerful Red Army fight the Germans would trump any ideological "embarrassment" that might follow.

When Churchill heard of the German invasion of Russia, he remarked that Stalin was "a bungler of the first order" because he failed to take note of the German build-up in advance of the invasion, despite repeated warnings from the West. The Prime Minister believed that Stalin's hatred of democracies prevented him from even protecting his own nation.[144] He went on the air and reminded the British people; "No one has been a more consistent opponent of

Communism that I have for the last twenty-five years. ... But all this fades away before the spectacle which now unfolds." He railed against Hitler, "this bloodthirsty guttersnipe" who slaughtered and pillaged, and menaced "with brutal Nazi force."[145] In a speech written on the day of the invasion, Churchill reiterated his hatred of the Stalinist regime, yet he had nothing but very high praise for the Russian soldiers protecting the homeland in advance of the "hideous onslaught of the Nazi war machine." The Prime Minister declared. "If Hitler invaded Hell, he would at least make a favourable reference to the Devil in the House of Commons."[146] Still the consensus was Germany would have a quick and decisive victory. This attitude of pessimism on the part of Britain and the United States certainly had merit. The Red Army did not do well in the Winter War against Finland; the 1939 pact Stalin had made with Hitler demonstrated that Stalin might not be totally committed to the Western Allies and might turn again to Germany if the Red Army faltered.

When Hopkins heard about the invasion, he immediately surmised that Hitler's turn to the east and away from Great Britain was the happy result of America's promise of pending support for Great Britain. This, Hopkins posited, impelled Hitler to surmise that he would not win that battle, so he turned his army east to attack Russia. Now the pressure was off; Britain and the United States would have time to build up their arsenals. Hopkins' relief was short lived, however, for he soon saw the enormous complications that would arise over whether or not the United States should supply the Soviets with Lend Lease materials. While the German invasion of the Soviet Union brought Britain much needed relief from the German bombing, it also brought difficulties for nations that were opposed equally to fascism and to communism. The increasing fear of the spread of totalitarianism coupled with the need for the Red Army to continue to fight led to serious disagreements between Roosevelt and Churchill. The vast majority of Americans, however, opposed giving Lend Lease aid to the Communist nation, as did most members of Congress. Sherwood relates how the day before Barbarossa the Communists were planning an anti-Roosevelt rally in Harlem, condemning the policy of aiding Britain; within a matter of hours, when they got the news that Hitler had invaded Russia, American Communists suddenly became pro-British, pro Lend Lease, and pro Roosevelt.[147]

Churchill was grateful that Great Britain now had time to rebuild its armed forces; he also had an ally in the fight against the Germans—the huge and powerful Red Army. But the Soviet Union was not an ally the Prime Minister would have chosen. Churchill and Stalin had deeply rooted animosities. The Prime Minister abhorred communism. Stalin hated capitalism. Churchill thought that Stalin was "backward." Stalin resented Britain's passivity and inability to engage the Germans, and its refusal to declare war on German allies – Romania, Hungary, and Finland. Stalin suspected that the British wanted the Soviet Union to become a weakened nation, easily controlled after the war. Churchill could not forget that in 1939 Stalin had signed a non-aggression pact with Hitler, agreeing to support German takeover of Poland in exchange for a part of the spoils. The Prime Minister felt extremely bitter over the fact that Stalin sided with the Germans and stood aside while Britain, the only nation holding off the Nazis, was taking a terrible beating. After Barbarossa, the Soviets were now the only ones actually fighting the Germans and looking to Great Britain and the United States for help. This caused deep resentment on both sides.

Roosevelt again looked to Harry Hopkins for a delicate and potentially career-killing job; he, of course, took it. It nearly took his life. In July Hopkins returned to Britain to confer again with Churchill and to finalize plans for a meeting between the two leaders; the situation was now entirely different. The air raids had slackened off and Britain had an ally. The nation was no longer fighting alone. News of Russia's resistance brough hope to the British people but this was tempered by the realization that if Germany defeated Russia and turned again to attack Britain, American help would not be forthcoming.

The Russian picture was indeed complicated. The Red Army, now on the side of the Allies, was the only force holding off the Germans and thus allowing time for the United States and Great Britain to beef up their arsenals. Despite the size and power of the Red Army, however, the President's military advisors did not think that the Russians could hold out against the German army for more than a few weeks; they recommended restraint in supplying them with war material. The secretary of war wrote to the President that that the War Plans Division believed that "Germany will be thoroughly occupied in beating Russia for a minimum of one month and a possible maximum of three months." This was the time for the United States to increase Allied efforts in the Atlantic theater as a way to encourage Britain and discourage Germany. Most national leaders agreed that the Russians would not be able to hold out for long. And when the Soviets fell, then the Germans would turn their attention again to Britain.[148] The Germans themselves had planned on a quick victory before winter set in.

Hopkins proposed concentrating Allied efforts on the Battle of the Atlantic, where German submarines were sinking U.S. ships carrying Lend Lease munitions and food to Great Britain; he avoided the Russian question altogether. Stalin had to assure the Allies that Russia would not capitulate but that Allied support was necessary for the fight; Lend Lease war material sent by the Americans could not be wasted and would not fall into German hands. Roosevelt took a middle road and offered the Russians just enough to hold off the Germans until winter set in. It was clear to Roosevelt, however, that it would be impossible for a sufficiently large number of armaments to be produced and for shipments to arrive before winter. Until then it would be up to the Red Army to hold off the Germans.

The sinking of ships carrying Lend Lease equipment concerned Roosevelt. The loss was shattering for Allied defenses. American convoys would assure some modicum of safety for these ships. So, the President tore out a page from a National Geographic magazine and marked out new boundaries that would allow the U.S. Navy to assume responsibility for escorting British ships through the Atlantic. The line was drawn along Latitude 26 degrees, through the Azores, to the east of Iceland. Hopkins showed Churchill this rough map, which somewhat raised the Prime Minister's spirits.[149] He still wanted Roosevelt to commit to entering the war.

Hopkins wrote an article that was published in *American Magazine* advocating Lend Lease support for Britain, a nation that would rely on its democratic heritage to use the resources that we give wisely—whereas the USSR was a brutal totalitarian state. He did not agree with FDR's foreign policy re the Soviets— he thought FDR was overextending our resources by promising them Lend Lease aid and, furthermore, he feared that the Soviets might well make a separate peace with Germany. This attitude not only reflected his positive assumptions about democracy but also his distrust of Stalin. But Hopkins' attitude toward the Soviet Union did not turn out to be as firm as he thought it was. While he continued to be wary of Stalin's totalitarianism, he was ready to work with him as an ally because he saw the big picture. He knew we needed the Red Army in order to defeat fascism and protect democracy.[150] Hopkins, like Roosevelt, was not an ideologue, and his flexibility here stood him in good stead with both the Prime Minister and the President.

Hopkins' influence became even more crucial at this point. When he met with the Prime Minister in July, the Soviets had held the Germans off for four weeks; maybe the Red Army could continue its defense until the winter. Britain and Russia had come to an agreement for joint action before Hopkins' arrival, whereby each nation would assist the other against Germany and that neither would negotiate for a separate peace.[151] Both were wary of any political alliance.

Great Britain needed munitions from the United States and Churchill had always dealt very confidently with Hopkins as Roosevelt's right-hand man; he was assured that Britain would get the tools it needed to fight.

This neat triangle almost flew apart with the arrival of the Soviet Union and Stalin on the scene. The relationship between Roosevelt and Churchill was shaky even from the beginning. It is important to remember that Roosevelt, as head of state, outranked Churchill who was head of government and Stalin who was head of the Communist party. The President could make his own foreign policy decisions and could take advice or reject it; Churchill had to report to the War Cabinet.[152] Stalin answered to no one. This disparity in the chain of command in each nation often made it difficult to come to agreements, and this was especially true at the two wartime conferences when the Big Three actually met face to face.[153]

Both Britain and the Soviet Union needed American war materials, which were being shipped to England beginning in March 1941. American production was speeding up considerably but still there were limited arms available to be shared under Lend Lease. The United States not yet up to full wartime productivity; more time was needed for America to become the world's Arsenal of Democracy. When it came to deciding whether or not to supply Stalin with the munitions he wanted, there were important considerations. Was the Red Army strong enough to hold off the Germans, did Stalin have the will to continue the fight, or would the Germans defeat Russia and take control of munitions shipped by the U.S.? Was Stalin to be trusted? If the Soviets had joined forces with the Germans as they had just two years earlier, the results would be cataclysmic.[154] The Arsenal of Democracy might be needed to protect our own nation. The President's military advisors recommended restraint when it came to Lend Lease.[155] If the

United States gave a lion's share of its arsenal to the British and to the Soviets, and if these two nations fell, the United Stated would not be able to defend itself against the Nazis, who would surely attack a weakened nation.

The bottom line was that the Allies needed the Red Army and the Soviets needed American materiel, if there were to be any chance of defeating the Nazis. American journalist Herbert Bayard Swope, a member of the Algonquin Round Table, expressed the opinion of many Americans when he wrote to Hopkins: "We are not for Communism, but we are against all that Hitler stands for ... [and] our greatest strength is in unity; our greatest danger is discord." Although Congress did not believe that we should be sending munitions to the Soviets, Roosevelt was committed to providing the Red Army with what it needed and Hopkins was on board. However, FDR preferred to use Hopkins as the conduit for this, side stepping the state department. Churchill fully understood this. Again, personal diplomacy became the favored policy. However, the PM had much more at stake. For the British people, Barbarossa seemed merely a "prelude" to a German land invasion of England, a terrifying thought because England was surely not ready for a land war. [156]

Given the changed situation with the Russia now an ally, Roosevelt was even more anxious to have that face-to-face meeting with Churchill as soon as possible. He believed that this was the only way to get the true measure of the man and he sent Hopkins back to London to arrange this. Hopkins left for his second trip to London in July 1941 in order to arrange the historic first meeting between the President and the Prime Minister. The Atlantic Conference would take place off the coast of Newfoundland. Both leaders, with just a minimal entourage, and under cover of complete secrecy, would sail to Placentia Bay. It was up to Hopkins to lay the foundations for this first meeting between the two leaders.

Hopkins arrived in London on Monday, July 17th, just a few weeks after Hitler launched the lightening attack against the Soviet Union. In an ironic turn of events, Stalin was now an American supplicant. Churchill knew full well that if the United States were to send war materiel to the Soviet Union, it would cut into Britain's own Lend Lease supplies. Warren Kimball argues that the British believed that sharing supplies with the Soviets would be senseless because there was little chance that they could hold out against the Germans for more than a few months. [157] But Churchill trusted Hopkins to keep his promise to provide Great Britain with the desperately needed American munitions. With Hopkins in London the Prime Minister could make sure that this promise was kept. Dwight Tutttle argues that the President did not support or approve of Hopkins' encouragement to the British. However, it is just as likely that Hopkins was following Roosevelt's orders to promise what the President himself could not promise in an election year. Roosevelt wanted to keep the British fighting and he also wanted to avoid the chance that a weakened and desperate Great Britain would look for a separate peace with Germany.[158]

As a mark of that trust, the Prime Minister invited Hopkins to attend a meeting of the War Cabinet—an invitation conveyed to no other American or, for that matter, the representative of any other nation. The President had asked Hopkins to set up the meeting with Churchill, who had "the keenest desire to meet Mr. Roosevelt." The Prime

Minister was convinced that a summit "would proclaim the ever-closer association of Britain and the United States, would cause our enemies concern, make Japan ponder, and cheer our friends." Churchill clearly had high hopes that such a meeting would lead to the United States entering into the war.[159]

Roosevelt also gave Hopkins an additional task: that of assessing the military requirements and resolve of the Soviet Union. Therefore, Hopkins suggested to the President that he go to Moscow, for a week at most, and meet with Stalin. There has been disagreement over whose idea it was to go to Moscow – Hopkins' or Roosevelt's. It seems clear from the Hopkins Papers that it was Hopkins' own idea, made soon after he arrived in London. Tuttle claims that Hopkins' trip to Moscow although "harrowing" was "absolutely necessary" because the Stalin was leery of any alliance with Great Britain or the United States. Only a personal envoy with Hopkins' credentials and abilities could effectively deal with Stalin. And Hopkins knew he was the only one to do it. The Red Army was incurring huge casualties and Stalin was insisting that the Western Allies open up a second front to draw the German away from the Russian frontier. It was this complex situation that led to Hopkins' decision that he had to get the president's permission to meet with Stalin himself. He sent Roosevelt a message on July 25th:

> I have a feeling that everything possible should
> be done to make certain the Russians maintain
> a permanent front even though they may be
> defeated in this immediate battle. If Stalin

could in any way be influenced at a critical time
I think it would be worth doing by a direct
communication from you through a personal
envoy. I think the stakes are so great that we
mean business on a long-term supply job. ...
The grand resistance of the Russian army in
defense of their soul unites us all.[160]

This letter is important because it affirms that the secret
trip to Moscow was Hopkins' idea; it also indicates that
the Alliance was strong and that the Soviets would
possibly hold out against the Germans for some time.

Fullilove believes that it was Hopkins' idea although
Maisky and Winant might have put the idea into his head.
Although the July 25 cable does not directly ask for
permission to go to Moscow and Hopkins veils it in a
question awaiting the President's advice, it seems that he is
strongly suggesting that Roosevelt approve this trip. At this
point he had little confidence that Russia would prevail but
that it would be well worth trying to influence Stalin at this
critical time.[161] However, while in London Hopkins' decision
to go to Moscow and meet with Stalin demonstrated that he
played a significant role, using personal diplomacy, in
insuring that the Soviets got the Lend Lease equipment they
needed to continue to fight the Germans; he assured the
Western Allies that the Soviet leader would not capitulate to
Hitler.

Barbarossa was indeed a game changer. Just before
Hopkins left for Moscow, Churchill sent a letter to Stalin
introducing him to Roosevelt's envoy:

Mr. Harry Hopkins has been with me these days. Last week he asked the President to let him go to Moscow. I must tell you there is a flame in this man for democracy and to beat Hitler. He is the nearest personal representative of the President. ... You can trust him absolutely. He is your friend and our friend. He will help you to plan for the future victory and for the long-term supply of Russia. You could talk to him also freely about policy strategy and Japan.[162]

Hopkins' motive for going to Moscow was to assess the military situation and the resolve of the dictator who controlled the Red Army. Roosevelt needed to know details about Soviet defenses; he had to have absolutely reliable data on the actual situation in Russia. Hopkins believed that he would be able to get this critical information—but it could only come from Stalin himself. The American mission there only received the very sparse information that the Commissar for Foreign Affairs, Vyacheslav Molotov, allowed to circulate.[163] Hopkins urged the president to send him on this mission to Moscow because he believed that it was vital to the war effort.[164] Roosevelt agreed, and Churchill immediately put in operation the plans to get Hopkins to Moscow, and back. The PM did insist, however, that Hopkins return in time to accompany him to the Atlantic Conference, scheduled for August 9th. Hopkins promised that he would not let the President or the Prime Minister down. Everyone knew that it was a dangerous mission. The flight to Archangel was 2,000 miles over German guns in Norway. Still, Hopkins believed the trip to Moscow was worth the risk.[165]

On the evening before he left London, a besieged city still blacked out, Hopkins gave a speech over the BBC. No doubt, it was meant to bolster the British people who had been undergoing terrifying nightly bombings from the Germans. He said, "I did not come from America alone, I came in a bomber plane, and with me were twenty other bombers made in America." He might have been exaggerating the amount of aid America was sending but this speech gave the British a great deal of hope. Again, Hopkins was giving them the confidence that they could rely on the United States to stand by them for the duration.[166] Could the Russians embrace this hope as well?

When Hopkins said farewell to the Prime Minister, he asked him what he should say if Stalin asked about what Russia could expect in the way of British help. Churchill, who had been a virulent anti-communist, said to tell Stalin that Britain only wants to defeat Hitler. Britain's need for the Red Army enabled him to recognize the hard fact that he had to work with a leader whom he had equated with "a devil."[167]

Because the Red Army desperately needed war materiel from the United States, and since Hopkins' approval was required for Lend Lease purchase orders, he was the man Stalin wanted to see. And the feeling was mutual; Hopkins wanted to get the measure of the Man of Steel. Hopkins took a train from London's Euston station to Invergorden, Scotland, on July 27th, accompanied by Brigadier General Joseph T. McNarney and Lieutenant John R. Alison. They arrived the morning of the 28th and then boarded a PBY-5, Catalina Mark I, captained by Flight Lieutenant McKinley; it was the only plane able to take Hopkins on this long trip and get him back in time for the Atlantic Conference. The 24-hour flight to Archangel began one of the most secret missions of the war. The plane had a maximum speed of 175 mph at seven thousand feet (to avoid enemy radar) but realistically could only manage about 135 mph. The plane was not outfitted for passengers and lacked creature comforts; it was cold and the food was minimal. Captain McKinley had not been told of Hopkins' poor health, but even if he needed assistance, there would have been little the Captain could have done to make him more comfortable. Hopkins kept his good humor during the flight even though even though they were flying over enemy territory and could have been shot down at any time, even though he did not like to fly under any circumstances, even though he was pretty sick, it was he himself who had suggested this trip; he knew was going to be dangerous, long, and rigorous and he was determined to see it through.[168]

During the flight, Hopkins, wearing a fine new Homburg with Churchill's initials on it, having lost his old and very thin hat in England, had to sit on a machine-gunner's stool, looking out for enemy planes. Because the Catalina had to fly at a very low altitude and pretty slowly, and because visibility was good (night did not fall in that latitude), it could have been shot down easily. While Hopkins did try to get some rest on the last third of the leg, the arctic cold made it virtually impossible. Due to an error in navigation, the plane flew off course until they picked up a signal from Archangel radio, which enabled them to fly home on the beam.

Once he landed at Archangel, an exhausted Hopkins had to endure a banquet (punctuated by frequent vodka toasts) that lasted an interminable four hours, when all he wanted was to sleep.[169] This, his first experience of Soviet cordiality led him to record the banquet:

> It was monumental.
>
> It lasted almost four hours. There was an Iowa flavor to it, what with the fresh vegetables, the butter, the cream, greens. For some reason the cucumbers and radishes surprised me. They were grown on the farms that hem in the city. Anyway, the dinner was enormous, course after course. There was the inescapable cold fish, caviar, and vodka. Vodka has authority. It is nothing for the amateur to trifle with. Drink it as an American or an Englishman takes whiskey neat and it will tear you apart. The thing to do is to spread a chunk of bread (and good bread it was) with caviar, and while you are swallowing that bold your vodka. Don't play with the stuff. Eat while you are drinking it—sometimes that will act as a shock absorber for you.[170]

He managed only a couple of hours sleep there before getting on the four-hour flight to Moscow. He arrived on July 30 and went directly to the American Embassy where he met with U.S. Ambassador Laurence Steinhardt who informed Hopkins that 1) the Russians would fight to the finish and 2) no foreigner had been able to get any military information of any kind from Stalin's staff. Steinhardt told Hopkins that he was "pessimistic" as to the chances of the Russians holding out against the Germans. [171] Hopkins was sure he was going to change all that. He made it clear that he had the President's authority to carry out policy and that Roosevelt was committed to getting the Russians the help they needed. He announced that he had made this arduous trip solely to meet with Stalin and only with Stalin. The Soviet dictator was the only one who had all the information that Hopkins needed and the only one who could make decisions. The Ambassador informed Hopkins that no one had been able to get any information from the Kremlin, that the diplomats there had no luck in finding out what the actual situation. Hopkins was determined to "break through this wall of suspicion."[172]

Hopkins also carried a letter from the President to Stalin assuring the Russian leader of America's commitment to aiding the Soviets with immediate shipment of munitions. The President wanted to be sure that Stalin knew that he fully trusted Hopkins and that he had the authority to speak for the President himself.[173] The letter informed Stalin that Hopkins was going to Moscow at the President's request in order to discuss "the vitally important question of how we can most expeditiously and effectively make available the assistance the United States can render to your country in its magnificent resistance to the treacherous aggression by Hitlerite Germany."[174] The letter concluded with: "I ask you to treat Mr. Hopkins with the identical confidence you would feel if you were talking directly to me."[175] This might have been difficult for Stalin to understand, for in the Soviet Union no one but the Marshal himself could speak with an authority or make any promises. Now a personal envoy of the President, not even an official ambassador, had the power to decide the fate of the Soviets. This kind of diplomacy again reflected FDR's need for first-hand information through face-to-face conversation. For the President this was the only way to ascertain the truth and Hopkins was the one to ferret it out.

Hopkins' first meeting with Stalin took place at 6:30 pm at the Kremlin. They were not alone; those also present included Ambassador Steinhardt, USSR Foreign Minister Vyacheslav Molotov, and Maxim Litvinov, a former Soviet Commissioner, who acted as interpreter as Stalin spoke no English. Hopkins began the conversation with the Soviet leader by expressing a shared hatred for Hitler and that the United States would give the USSR all possible aid in order to defeat the Nazis. He told Stalin that the President had great admiration for "the splendid resistance of the Soviet army." Hopkins asked what war materiel the Soviets needed and Stalin, apparently well prepared for this question, replied that the nation needed aid immediately, but also for the long term. Stalin asked for guns, ammunition, gasoline, and aluminum. This would allow the Soviets to hold out for several years against the Germans, a clear indication that the Soviets were in the battle for the long run. Stalin also told Hopkins that he wanted the United States to enter into the war but he assured him that if American troops were ever to be sent to the Russian front, they would be able to fight under their own commanders. Hopkins demurred and said that this was not likely to happen; all he wanted to discuss, and all he was able to make decisions on, were war supplies.[176] Actually, what Hopkins really had to find out for the President was if Stalin could hold off Hitler long enough for the United States and Great Britain to manufacture a sufficient level of effective offensive armaments.[177]

During this initial meeting, Hopkins assured Stalin of the United States' support in fighting the Germans if, in return, Stalin would give Hopkins the necessary information about the Soviet Union's industrial and military situation. The dictator agreed to the exchange. Hopkins earned Stalin's respect at first because he spoke honestly and later because he came to realize that Hopkins kept his promises.

The next evening Hopkins had a second meeting with Stalin and the only other person present was Litvanov who again acted as interpreter. They met for three hours in the dictator's own room, an honor rarely extended to foreign visitors, who are usually received in Molotov's office.[178] During these hours, the two men established the beginning of a relationship based on mutual trust if not exactly admiration. Hopkins was very frank in his estimation of what the United States could promise the Soviets. He said that the Allies would do everything possible to assist the Soviets in their fight against the Germans but that, logistically, supplies could not possibly arrive to the front lines before winter. Furthermore, Hopkins asked Stalin to give a full disclosure of the Soviet Union's industrial capacity as an agreed upon prerequisite for Lend Lease aid. Stalin agreed and, surprisingly, gave a full and complete assessment of the USSR's military and industrial capacity. This initial part of the meeting was successful in that the two shared vital information and laid plans for a future meeting of the three Allied leaders.[179] Historian Matthew B. Wills points out that at this second meeting with Hopkins, Stalin was less than transparent about Russia's military might. The Red Army had been beaten by German Panzers in Poland and the

Russian air force had suffered a devastating attack by the Luftwaffe in late June. Stalin knew that if he were to be completely honest about the situation in Russia, the United States might not supply his army with Lend Lease munitions. He also suggested to Hopkins that Germany could not be beaten unless the United States entered into the war. Hopkins told him that he was there only to discuss issues of supply and that the United States would do everything possible to get the necessary munitions to the Soviets as quickly as possible. Wills suggests that while it is not clear that Hopkins actually saw through Stalin's embellishments, it is likely that he did. Hopkins certainly would have known about the defeats that the Red Army had suffered. However, his priority was ensuring that the Soviets continue the fight. He did believe that the Red Army would fight in order to defend their homeland and that Stalin was a ruthless enough leader to ensure that this happened.[180] Cowardice or desertion among the troops was met with instant death.

During the second part of the meeting, after military matters had been concluded, Stalin asked Hopkins personally to convey a message to the President. According to Hopkins' notes, Stalin wanted FDR to know that "Hitler's greatest weakness was found in the vast numbers of oppressed people who hated Hitler and the immoral ways of his Government." Furthermore, Stalin believed that the United States was the source of all "moral strength" and had enormous influence in the outcome of the war. Therefore, if America entered into the war, this could be the tipping point in the fight against Hitler.[181] Stalin made it very clear to Hopkins that he did not want American troops at this time but desperately needed tanks, planes, ammunition, high-octane gasoline, and barbed wire. Stalin assured Hopkins that Russia would win the war, would defeat the Germans because Russia was fighting for the Motherland. The meeting ended with no fanfare, just a handshake. Later Stalin remarked that Hopkins was the only American he had spoken *po duche*, "from the heart." However, this may just have been a result the particular circumstances; the dictator was not used to acting as a supplicant. The sentiments expressed by Stalin must, of course, be interpreted in light of his actions in the Soviet Union over the previous years. Stalin's feelings toward the Germans bordered on pathological hatred. Hopkins saw that when Stalin began to speak of Hitler, "his body grew tense" and his voice became cold. Stalin felt double-crossed and his anger toward Hitler was personal; Hopkins suggests that if Hitler had been in the room at that moment, "Germany would have needed a new Chancellor."[182] At this point Hopkins became the keystone of Anglo-Soviet-American relations. His reports to the President and the Prime Minister assured them that the Soviets would not give up the fight. This was probably the most important result of the wartime missions. Hopkins again expressed amazement at the position of power that he had attained saying that it was "ridiculous yet stupendous" that he, a "rube" from Iowa had risen to such a position.[183]

Hopkins succeeded in his mission to ascertain the specifics of what the Soviets needed from the United States in the way of munitions as well as details of the nation's industrial capacity; arming the Russians would be to America's ultimate advantage but Roosevelt certainly did not want to give them what they did not need. There were many military and political leaders who were wary of the Red

Army's ability to persevere as well as to Stalin's commitment to continue to fight on the side of the Allies. After meeting with Stalin, Hopkins began to believe that there was a very good chance that Russia could actually defeat the Germans. The German press complained that Hopkins, a friend of plutocrats, was merely defending imperialism and communism; some Americans agreed with this assessment. The *Chicago Daily Times* castigated him for supporting Stalin and communist Russia and a Congressman accused him of allying with murderers. However, this media attention from the Nazis only increased Hopkins warm welcome in the Soviet capital.[184]

According to Tuttle, "a triangular relationship between America, Britain, and the Soviet Union had emerged from Hopkins' summer travels" in 1941. His role as go-between had expanded to include all three Allies. His solid relationship with Churchill and now the mutual trust he had developed with Stalin made him the perfect emissary for President Roosevelt. However, such complicated lines of personal communications could sometimes become tangled. During Hopkins' London trips in January and July of 1941, Churchill had interpreted Hopkins' inference as to the United States joining the war, of standing side by side with Great Britain in her hour of need, as a real commitment. This was a serious mistake that would lead to a misunderstanding on the part of the PM during the upcoming conference off the coast of Newfoundland. Again, it is likely that Roosevelt wanted Churchill to be encouraged by the thought that the United States *would* join the war, something the PM desperately wanted. However, just before Pearl Harbor, Hopkins did ask the President why he did not just ask Congress to declare war on Germany. The President responded, presciently, "We need an incident."[185]

Hopkins was in a good position to reassure the Soviet leader of America's intention to support Russia's efforts to drive back the Germans. New York City newspapers such as the *Journal American* and *The Sun* headlined Hopkins' trip on the front page and included articles that described how the Red Army was pushing back the German army that was attacking Leningrad, Moscow, and Kiev. Still, the news was not all good. While Hopkins was there, Nazi troops had come within 130 miles of Moscow; Hopkins experienced two air raids on the city.[186] There can be no doubt that this experience increased his resolve to make sure that the Red Army got the equipment necessary to fight the Germans just as his experience in London during the Blitz led him to insist that the United States send munitions to help the British when they were standing alone against the German attack. But after his meetings with Stalin, Hopkins became one of the few who had faith that the Red Army could successfully hold off the Germans. Possibly the extent of Stalin's fury led him to this belief. But Stalin, himself, knew that defending against the German army would not be possible over the long term without strong allies with military support; America was not yet in the war and Britain was barely holding on. In Stalin's mind, something had to be done to draw the German forces away from Russia. Thus arose the dangerous and contentious issue of when and how the Western Allies would open a second front and force Hitler to redirect his army. Could this be done by invading France from England in a cross-channel attack, or by an invasion through Italy, or by an attack on North Africa?

Churchill had stated very clearly that a cross-channel attack would not be possible in 1942 or even in 1943. The Germans had more men, more tanks, more everything. It would be a bloody disaster. Moreover, there was a narrow path to tread. The United States and Great Britain did not want to run the risk of a German victory and the possibility of Stalin negotiating a separate peace with Hitler. Then Germany could take over all of Europe. Not yet ready for a successful invasion of Europe, Churchill and Roosevelt had to keep Stalin anticipating a successful Second Front. On the other hand, any indication that the Russians were winning without western help, would present the danger of a powerful communist nation at the end of the war.[187]

An editorial in the *Daily Worker*, August 1, 1941, entitled "The Defense of Our country and Mr. Hopkins' Mission," quoted Hopkins as he was interviewed at a press conference at the American Embassy in Moscow. It is an echo of FDR's "short of war" policy:

> We discussed at some length the situation here in relation to the war with Germany. I told [Stalin] on behalf of the President that our country considers Hitler an enemy and that whoever fights Hitler anywhere is on the right side of this conflict. We intend to help them, particularly the Soviet Union, both immediately in terms of supplies, which will arrive here in the near future and also over a long term, no matter how long.

The article goes on to say that aggression against the Soviet Union threatens the United States and, furthermore, support for the Soviets will ensure the peace and security of America.

Thus, the editor calls for the US to come in as an equal partner with the British and the Soviets. Isolationism must end, the article implies, and the American people must support the nation's foreign policy.[188] The communist newspaper reflected a dramatic change in the political balance of FDR's base.

In a report Hopkins wrote after he returned to Washington, he describes Stalin as aptly deserving the name, "man of steel." To a certain extent, Hopkins seems to have admired Stalin—for the way the Soviet leader efficiently carried out the meetings, for his lack of small talk, for the eye contact he maintained with Hopkins during the meeting. According to New York columnist Leonard Lyons, Hopkins asked Stalin why he thought Germany had attacked the Soviet Union. Did Hitler think that Russia was weak enough to defeat quickly? Stalin replied, "'On the contrary. It was because he knew we were strong. Hitler knew that as long as such a powerful war machine was at his back, he could not turn to the front to try and destroy England." Stalin then told Hopkins to give Roosevelt this message: "'Joe pulls through.'"[189]

Although Hopkins respected Stalin's strength, he was not taken in by his outward friendliness. For several days he had had a close-up view of a totalitarian state. He later wrote, "The differences between democracy and dictatorship were clearer to me than the words of any historian, philosopher or journalist could make it."[190]

An exhausted Hopkins flew from Moscow to Archangel in order to catch his flight back to Britain. If the trip over from Invergorden was arduous, the return trip was close to deadly. In the confusion of his departure from

Moscow, he left behind his pack of vital medications. He refused to return to Moscow to retrieve them. There was no time; he was determined to get back to Britain in time to meet Churchill and to sail with him to Newfoundland for the meeting with Roosevelt at the Atlantic Conference.[191] He had made the Prime Minister a promise and he wasn't about to break it. Before taking off, when the Flight Lieutenant asked him if he would like to rest, Hopkins replied, "Whatever the next twenty-four hours may bring it cannot be as trying as the last three days." The PBY Catalina took off in terrible weather and during the twenty-four -hour flight back to Britain on the plane picked us rough weather and enemy fire along the way. This return trip nearly killed Hopkins. Furthermore, when the plane approached Scapa Flow the weather and the heavy seas made it very difficult for the PBY to land in order for the launch to come alongside and pick up Hopkins. After several frightening approaches, the PBY finally landed on top of heavy waves and a much-debilitated Hopkins had to leap over open seas from the pontoons of the plane onto the launch that had managed to maneuver somewhat close to the plane. He landed on the launch, flat on his face, and had to be helped to his feet by the sailors. The PBY crew then hurled his suitcase containing important papers after him. The doctors who attended him did not believe that he would make it through the night; but again, he rallied. After eighteen hours of sleep and some medical attention and he was ready to board the *HMS Prince of Wales* for the trip to Newfoundland where his two friends would meet for the first time. The mission to Moscow nearly did him in; but it was a success and that is all that mattered to Hopkins.

Churchill sent a letter to Roosevelt that reflected his acute sense of history as well as a veiled hope that American intervention would result from the coming meeting: "Harry returning dead beat from Russia but is lively again. We shall get him in fine trim for the voyage. We are just off. It is 27 years ago today that the Huns began their last war. We all must make a good job of it this time. Twice ought to be enough. Look forward so much to our meeting. Kindest Regards."[192]

Meantime, the President of the United States prepared for the meeting with the Prime Minister of Great Britain. In August 1941, as usual, Washington was sweltering in a brutal heat wave. Roosevelt announced that he was going fishing on the presidential yacht, the *USS Potomac*. To some it may have seemed an odd time for the President to take time off. Hitler's armies by now held most of Western Europe and were now attacking the Soviet Union; Congress was squabbling over intervention versus isolation; Britain and the Commonwealth seemed to be losing everywhere.[193] Roosevelt was not going fishing and he did love intrigue. His voyage to Newfoundland had to be top secret. Consequently, on August 4th, Roosevelt left his yacht and boarded the cruiser *USS Augusta*, which continued north. The Presidential yacht, *USS Potomac,* sailed up the coast of New England with a Roosevelt look-alike on board, a jaunty cigarette clamped in his mouth. Only Roosevelt's inner circle knew that the President had left for a conference with the British Prime Minister.

Likewise, Churchill in London secretly boarded a train for Scapa Flow on his way to the meeting. He used a fake newspaper article to convince the British people that he had remained home. The Prime Minister, accompanied by Hopkins, left from Scotland aboard *HMS Prince of Wales*. The destination was Placentia Bay, a large inlet near Argentia, Newfoundland. There, Roosevelt would meet Churchill for the first time under cover of secrecy. Neither the British people nor the Americans knew that their leaders had left the country. It was dangerous voyage, sailing through the U-boat infested Atlantic Ocean. On board ship, Hopkins told Churchill, in detail, about his meeting with Stalin. Churchill listened and realized "all the better why Hopkins was of such value to the President, for he had never before heard harshly objective and salty reporting quite like this."[194] Churchill clearly hoped that this meeting with Roosevelt would convince the President to ask Congress for a declaration of war against Germany. He wrote a letter to the prime ministers of the dominions announcing that he and the President would discuss "the whole field of future action" and that "the President would not have wished for this meeting unless he contemplated some further forward step."[195] It was wishful thinking.

Hopkins' round trip to Moscow from Britain had taken a toll on his health. He wrote to his brother, Lewis, who was a physician, while on the way to the conference, saying that his "mission is nearly complete." He assured his brother that he would tell him all about it as soon as he gets back home. There is an undercurrent of excitement in the letter and Hopkins writes, "I have stood the trip astoundingly well, but I have no doubt I am pretty tired and will feel it as soon as I get back to Washington." The trips had left him exhausted and even somewhat debilitated but the exhilaration he experienced of mission accomplished allowed him to push through any weakness or discomfort.[196] His efforts were not ignored. He received letters of congratulations from Lyndon B. Johnson that begins, "At my age one learns most from watching other men in action" and ends with, "one is very grateful and one has learned much from a friend."[197]

The war news was grim. Germans were bombing Greece, Yugoslavia, and Crete and morale in Britain was plummeting. Americans questioned the chances that Britain could actually continue the fight against Germany. Still, Hopkins maintained his usual optimism although he did not enjoy the boat ride. The five-day crossing from England was rough, with high seas. The ship had to maintain a zigzag course in order to elude dangerous U-boats. Despite the pitching and rolling of the ship and the noisy, cramped accommodations, Hopkins regained much of his strength during the crossing. He even managed to attend a few evenings when he viewed films with Churchill, his staff and the crew. Hopkins had brought two gifts from Moscow, which he presented to the Prime Minister on one of the five movie nights: a tin of caviar and a film clip of his arrival in the bleak Soviet capital. A delighted Churchill played the clip for the party and shouted "bravo" when Hopkins stepped off the plane; "for one evening at least, Hopkins was Mr. Churchill's favourite film star."[198]

During the voyage to Placentia Bay, Hopkins had prepared a report of his talks with Stalin for President Roosevelt. He wanted the information he would give to his boss to be data-driven, full of the cold hard facts he had received from Stalin; this was meant to assure Roosevelt— and Churchill—that the Soviets would hold out until the winter and possibly beyond. Hopkins was convinced that the

Allies should bet on the Red Army and that the United States should send the Soviets the Lend Lease materials that they desperately needed. This position likely resulted from Hopkins witnessing Stalin's fury over the German invasion and Hitler's betrayal of the 1939 Non-Aggression Pact. Hopkins' first words to the President when he later met him aboard the *Augusta* were, "The Russians are confident." Fullilove correctly argues that Hopkins' most important job at this summit was to let the two leaders know what he found out in Moscow from Stalin. The goal was to ensure that the Soviets got what they needed in the way of arms to keep the Germans at bay. As matchmaker, however, Hopkins was also much preoccupied with ensuring that the President and the Prime Minister got along together, and even liked each other. This may have been his primary goal.[199]

Unlike the seasick Hopkins, Churchill, ever the Naval Person, was in his element. He had begun his correspondence with Roosevelt when he was First Lord of the Admiralty and had signed his letters "Naval Person." After becoming Prime Minister, he signed them "Former Naval Person." The fact that both of the leaders had served in the navy departments of their respective governments provided common ground. The Prime Minister was thrilled to be at sea, especially since this was such a dramatic secret mission. If he feared the U-boats it was not for his own safety, nor for the safety of those on board. What he feared was the disruption of the lifeline of arms and munitions churning across the ocean from the United States to Britain.[200] On this journey hung the hope, in the words of a British journalist "of saving the world from measureless degradation."[201] Churchill approached the Atlantic Conference with hopes that he could get FDR to join him in the fight against fascism, relying on his not insignificant powers of persuasion. His confidence was largely due to his meetings with Hopkins although such thinking was more a hope than a reality. Nevertheless, while Hopkins was in Britain, he had managed to lift not only the Prime Minister's spirits but that of the British people as well.[202]

The battle-scarred *Prince of Wales* entered Placentia Bay on Saturday, August 9th; the *Augusta* was already at anchor in the harbor. Thus, the Old World met the New in a remote inlet that Churchill later described as "somewhere in the Atlantic." As the war-torn British ship slid past the pristine American ship, the President doffed his hat and stood in salute as the *Prince of Wales*, camouflaged and battered with guns pointing to the sky moved slowly past. Aboard the *Augusta*, the band struck up *God Save the King*. FDR, recognizing a tune Americans sang with other lyrics, quipped, "Why, that's the best rendition of *My Country, 'Tis of Thee* I've ever heard." The Prime Minister stood on the bridge of his ship as the British band played *The Star-Spangled Banner*, gazing at the American cruiser in her peacetime light grey livery. The difference between these two vessels spoke volumes. It was a historic moment, colored by what a British journalist called, "a touch of danger, humor, secrecy" that would "prevent the carving up of the world and the enslavement of Humanity."[203] For those present this was not mere hyperbole. Everyone on board, Hopkins included, had experienced what Hitler had let loose in Europe.

The same day, Hopkins transferred to the *Augusta* to finalize arrangements for the formal meeting between the two leaders.[204] Much to the relief of Harry Hopkins, the

President and the Prime Minister quickly came to actually like each other, despite their differences. The Special Relationship between the United States and Great Britain took root at sea when these two navel men met at this first summit. This was months before the United States entered into the war. Hopkins had been very impressed with Churchill's comprehensive analysis of the war situation; he wanted Roosevelt to hear the details from the Prime Minister himself. Hopkins was hoping that the Prime Minister might actually convince Roosevelt to take further steps, even ask Congress to declare war on Germany. He was wrong. The President had no intention in going any further that supplying Great Britain with the wherewithal to fight. Still, Hopkins kept his finger on the pulse of this new friendship between one nation at war and another on the brink of war. Here and at this first and at the other wartime conferences, Hopkins' insight into Churchill facilitated compromises and both military and political decisions.

The Atlantic Conference marked, if not quite the beginning of the "Grand Alliance," (Stalin was absent), it did mark the beginning of the Anglo-American partnership, unequal though it was as this point. The resultant document that both agreed on, the Atlantic Charter, was merely a communiqué; it was not a signed agreement. No policies were established. But it was an essential statement of the goals of the allied nations. Hopkins had a lot to do with the final draft of the Charter. When Churchill and Roosevelt were discussing the wording of the Charter, the President, reflecting on the failures of the League of Nations and the dangerous aftermath of the Great War, balked at the idea of an international body such as the United Nations. According to Sherwood, it was Hopkins who facilitated a change of heart for his boss. He convinced the President that the disarmament of aggressor nations and then common disarmament after the war, Point 8 of the Atlantic Charter, would mean nothing without an international body like the United Nations. He suggested that the organization could actually promise world peace. Here Hopkins reflected a commitment to collective security and to the maintenance of the wartime coalition of the United States, Great Britain, and the Soviet Union. Hopkins also convinced the President to agree to changes in Point 4 regarding trade preference given to the Dominions, adding the phrase, "with due respect to existing obligations," which allowed the Ottawa Agreement to stand.[205] This satisfied Churchill who wanted to ensure that the British colonies would get preferential trade agreements. The fact that FDR let this stand likely shows that trade issues and colonialism were not, in his mind, the most important bases for coalition foreign policy; rather the cause of national security informed Roosevelt's wartime decision, even at this early stage, months before the United States was drawn into the conflict. The President was willing to concede to the Prime Minister here in order to keep Churchill on board with the Charter. Although it had no real power, the document as a statement of broad postwar goals was important. The President wanted the world to see the two leaders as being in agreement. Nevertheless, it becomes clear—with decision after decision and conference after conference—that the two had quite different visions of what the world should look like after the war ended.[206] Unity of purpose might have been just an illusion, but it was the illusion that the Allies wanted the world to see.

During the entire Atlantic Conference Hopkins staged the performances of the two leaders, ensured that conversations went smoothly, and created a dynamic that had enormous consequences for the war effort. Still playing the part of matchmaker, he made sure that Roosevelt liked Churchill and especially that he understood the Prime Minister's sometimes quirky rhetoric. The President had to be assured that the British would stay in the war, to the end.[207]

The Japanese menace in the Pacific concerned both Roosevelt and Churchill; it was an important issue discussed at the Atlantic Conference. They agreed that Japanese expansion posed serious problems for the United States as well as for the British Empire. Roosevelt's stated policy was that we would take "counter-measures even though these might lead to war between the United States and Japan."[208] It was important to hold the Japanese at bay. Although both Churchill and Roosevelt knew that war with Japan would be "calamitous," it seemed clear that the President was ready to enter into the war if given proper provocation. Churchill agreed but he wanted the President to state unequivocally and publicly that the United States would aid any power threatened by Japan; certainly, the Dominions were in danger. Roosevelt was worried especially about the Japanese occupation of China. He wrote a note to Kichisaburo Nomura, the Japanese ambassador in Washington, warning him that Japan must end its aggression in the Pacific or the United States would take steps to protect the security of the United States. [209] The warning proved ineffective.

The importance of the Atlantic Conference went beyond the production of the Charter. The First Summit had a "cosmic" effect because the two leaders developed a warm and personal relationship. As Sherwood wrote, "the cigarette-holder and the long cigar were at last being lit from the same match." Maybe Hopkins held the match but he was indeed the "marriage broker" and a "catalyst" at this secret and first meeting when the "prima donnas" were just courting. The coalition was taking shape and the world could see them as firm allies.[210] But as time went on, Hopkins became much more than a "catalyst;" he became a key in the shaping of the coalition that was taking shape. It was Hopkins who very often "interpreted" these two men to each other, who calmed the water when Roosevelt would become frustrated over some of Churchill's antics or even rudeness.

If Churchill expected the President to take concrete steps during the Conference to enter into the war raging in Europe, he was disappointed. Maybe Hopkins' remarks in Scotland and in London had raised the Prime Minister's expectations to an untenable height. But this was the only path to victory that Churchill could see. Britain was broke and could not hold out much longer against the Germans even with the Lend Lease war materials acquired from the United States. He asked Hopkins if there was any hope for Britain, any chance that the United States would declare war on Germany, because he didn't think that Hitler would do anything to provoke the United States to cause this. Consequently, Hopkins relayed to the President that Churchill was depressed and that this might give appeasers in Britain added strength.[211] Conditions for the Allies worsened. The German onslaught against Russia continued while German U-boats attacked U. S. destroyers. Still, Roosevelt was convinced that if he asked Congress for a declaration of war against Germany, it would refuse and this would be politically disastrous. All the Americans could do at this point was to give Britain the munitions under the Lend Lease program and hope the nation would hold out.

On Sunday, August 10, Churchill, Roosevelt, advisors, envoys, and crews attended services aboard the *Prince of Wales*. The service consisted of hymns, prayers, and readings that professed themes of unity. It was reportedly a moving spectacle that moved some to tears. At the end of the conference, Hopkins sent gifts to his British friends, mostly food that was impossible to get in Britain: lemons, candy, ham, etc. He sent a special package to Pamela Churchill, the Prime Minister's daughter-in-law. By the time the two ships departed the harbor on August 12, the Special Relationship had been set in cement.[212]

Chapter 6—The Wartime Alliance

"Among all those in the Grand Alliance, warrior or
statesman, who struck deadly blows at the enemy
and brought peace nearer, you will ever hold an
honored place." Winston Churchill to Harry
Hopkins, May 10, 1945[213]

The personal relationship that had been established at
the Atlantic Conference remained a necessary part of the
underpinnings of the wartime coalition. Kimball calls it "the
most important result of the conference." Churchill wrote to
Deputy Prime Minister Clement Atlee that Roosevelt had
become his "great friend." Although he was gratified that the
President had been so supportive, so friendly, he was also
disappointed that Roosevelt had not been more forthcoming
about specific U. S. assistance. He reached out to Hopkins to
express his dissatisfaction and his need for more from
Roosevelt. He wrote to Hopkins on August 28, 1941, about
"depression" permeating the British government over the
war situation:

> If 1942 opens with Russia knocked out and Britain left
> alone, all kinds of dangers may arise. I do not think
> Hitler will help in any way. Tonight he has 30 U-Boats
> in line from the eastern part of Iceland to the northern
> tip of Ireland. ... You will know best whether anything

more can be done. Should be grateful if you could give me any sort of hope.[214]

By this time, Stalin was an equal and vitally important ally; Hopkins fully understood that the western allies had to overcome some real concerns about working with a communist nation. He had an approach to foreign policy in time of war that included realpolitik. Supporting the Soviet was necessary; he didn't particularly like Stalin and disagreed wholeheartedly with his totalitarian rule. However, he believed that the Soviet leader had given him valid and complete information on the state of the military in the USSR. Stalin had demonstrated to Hopkins' satisfaction that the Soviets would not turn tail and negotiate a nonaggression pact with the Germans--again. And anyway, at the moment, Hitler was more dangerous that Stalin. Roosevelt followed Hopkins' advice and "gambled" on the Soviets. As Kimball argues, the President also appreciated the Soviet Union's potential as a postwar ally. In the aftermath of the Atlantic Conference, it became clear that Hopkins had facilitated a "triangular relationship," one that included the United States, Great Britain, and the Soviet Union with himself standing in the center. One observer commented that Roosevelt, Churchill, and Stalin trusted Hopkins more than they trusted each other.[215]

Although his health was declining, Hopkins had taken up the very arduous job as head of production and transportation of Lend Lease war material. Although he knew little about war production but, as always, he was a quick study. Just as he had demonstrated during the Depression years, his ability to learn quickly and to pick up the nuances of any task the President handed him stood him in good stead in this vital position.[216] Hopkins drew on his "New Deal point of view" in administering Lend Lease and surrounded himself with likeminded men who believed in the capacity of American industry and government "to achieve the utterly impossible." He did know how to spend money and had little trouble spending the $60 billion that Congress eventually appropriated for Lend Lease.[217] Averell Harriman, the "expediter of Lend Lease" reported to Hopkins who had to approve each shipment of aid to the Allies. Roosevelt had confidence in Hopkins' ability to do the job, which could be a political land mine. And Churchill trusted in Hopkins' assurance that Britain would get the munitions needed to continue the fight against the Hitlerites.

Hopkins ran a tight ship. Much to the dismay of Secretary of State Cordell Hull, the correspondence between the American President and the British Prime Minister bypassed the state department and British missives went through Hopkins, this one-man foreign office.[218] Churchill made it clear from the very beginning that he did not like to deal with department heads and would only deal with Roosevelt or Hopkins.[219] However, soon after the Atlantic Conference Hopkins became too ill to continue as Lend Lease administrator. He entered the Naval hospital in Washington in late 1941 and remained there until four days before Pearl Harbor.

Despite the Lend Lease aid given by America and despite the Germans concentrating on the Russian front, Churchill continued to campaign for the United States to enter into the war; it seemed the only way to defeat the Germans. He used Hopkins to express his continued and ardent disappointment at American isolationism. The Prime Minister continuously asked for Hopkins' assistance.[220] However, not even Hopkins could persuade the President to ask Congress for a declaration of war against Germany. FDR was sure it would fail. Congress, and the American people, needed an incident.

With the surprise Japanese attack on the American fleet in Pearl Harbor on December 7, 1941, the United States got its incident and declared war on Japan the next day. Hopkins had just been released from the hospital a few days earlier and was relaxing over lunch with the President in the oval study when Roosevelt received a call at 1:40 from secretary of the navy Frank Knox telling him that there had been an air raid attack on Honolulu. Hopkins thought it was a mistake. Roosevelt believed that it was just the sort of thing that the Japanese might do. Admiral Harold Stark then called and confirmed that the Japanese had attacked the American fleet at Pearl Harbor. Hopkins later noted that when Roosevelt called a meeting with Stimson, Hull, Knox, Stark, and Marshall to discuss what steps should be taken next, that the atmosphere was "not too tense." He wrote in his notes that Hitler remained the prime enemy and that "he could never be defeated without a force of arms." The Japanese attack on Pearl Harbor had given the United States the opportunity to enter into the war.[221]

Parliament declared war on Japan the next day. Four days later, Germany declared war on the United States. After all that the British had been through, Churchill now saw victory down the road; the nation was saved and in his mind the war was won. "Our history will not come to an end," the ecstatic Prime Minister proclaimed.[222] Churchill later wrote that Pearl Harbor was the "Fifth Climacteric" of World War II, the first being the fall of France, the second the Battle of Britain, the third the Lend Lease Act, and the fourth Barbarossa.[223]

After the United States entered into the war, Hopkins' role as a trusted go-between for Churchill became even more significant. Churchill could test the waters, to see where the President might stand on a particular topic or policy, before approaching him directly and risk rejection. The Prime Minister knew that Hopkins could read the President's moods and he knew how and when to present the Prime Minister's often-delicate "suggestions." The road was not always smooth. When Great Britain was suffering crushing military defeats Hopkins, ever the true friend, acted as "the chief comforter" for the Prime Minister when the media viciously attacked him and his policies. To bolster Churchill's spirits, Hopkins would express admiration for the British people in their brave stand against Nazi aggression; he would pass along good news about America's increasingly rapid build-up of munitions.[224] Americans wanted to know that the Prime Minister remained wholly positive and committed to defeating the Germans.

The wartime coalition of the Big Three—Roosevelt, Churchill, and Stalin—had a common enemy and this bound them together, albeit uneasily, from June 1941 to April 1945; there was little else to ensure harmony of any sort. Historian Fraser Harbutt critiques what he calls "The Big Three approach," by which historians see the three leaders working together to defeat the Axis Powers. But there is another approach, he suggests, one that sees the three leaders looking out for their own "national interests rather than the collective good and always subject to variations in homage to power, tempered sometimes by ideological impulses, but essentially rooted in history and always the natural element of the foreign policy establishment in each state." This is especially apparent after the Teheran Conference in late 1943; Anglo-Soviet collaboration became expedient for "a mutually satisfactory postwar order."[225] Thus, each nation and each leader had to consider their own unique needs and history in a way that often subsumed their own ability to maintain an "alliance" mentality. Hopkins, while always in the background, was able to remain above the fray and impose a balancing effect on the two leaders.

Jonathan Fenby, in his book *The Inside Story of How Roosevelt, Stalin and Churchill Won One War & Began Another (2006)*, remarks how difficult it was for the leaders of the Allied powers to submerge their differences in order to join forces and overcome the Axis powers. This feat, the preservation of the Alliance, was "a supreme object lesson in international politics at the highest level."[226] Harry Hopkins played a major role in administering this lesson. He seemed to sense that his primary job during the war years was to keep the three very different and temperamentally difficult leaders on an even keel and to keep each ship of state from foundering. As Harbutt and Martin Folly both argue, the Anglo-American wartime alliance constantly teetered on the verge of collapse. With the addition of the Soviet Union, wartime politics became even more precarious.[227]

Robert Sherwood describes the war years by using the words of journalist Herbert Agar, as a time when "good men dared to trust each other."[228] Hopkins managed to attract or earn the trust of two inherently good men — the two western Allied leaders. FDR relied on him; Churchill admired him; they both trusted. Stalin was certainly not one of these "good" men, but Hopkins did earn his respect. Because of this, Hopkins held this Tripartite Alliance together in a way no one political or military leader could have done. Sherwood also asserts (and as an insider he would know) that the Western Allies were "incorrigible optimists," as was Hopkins. He writes, "A point for historians to consider is that had these Allied leaders not been optimists in the blackest hours, the Germans and the Japanese would undoubtedly have won the war; it was the pessimists like Pétain, Darlan, and Weygand, who went down to quick defeat."[229]

The importance of the Hopkins-Churchill connection during these months, just before Pearl Harbor and America's entry into the war, lies in the fact that Hopkins provided a bridge to the President, a way for the two leaders to connect quickly and intimately, and secretly. Early in 1941 Churchill sent FDR a cable stating "I am most grateful to you for sending so remarkable an envoy who enjoys so high a measure of your intimacy and confidence." Churchill felt that through Hopkins he had established "a definite heart-to-heart contact" with FDR. Robert Sherwood spoke to Churchill at the end of August, after the Atlantic Conference, and the Prime Minister praised the work Hopkins was doing. "His eyes welled up with tears" when he spoke about the "great heart in that frail frame." This reflects the respect that Churchill had for Hopkins during a time when the American President's prestige was ebbing because of America's reluctance to take a more aggressive stance on the war.[230]

ARCADIA, THE FIRST WASHINGTON CONFERENCE

Soon after Pearl Harbor and America's entrance into the war, Churchill and his entourage traveled to Washington to meet with the President at what came to be called the Arcadia Conference. The Prime Minister was more than anxious to get a dialogue started with his new ally, now that America was officially in the war.[231] Churchill's room was across the hall from the Lincoln Suite, which Hopkins occupied; the two communicated frequently as the hallway became the unofficial headquarters for the British. FDR usually retired early but Churchill and Hopkins would stay up late to discuss the war situation. Consequently, FDR changed his schedule and stayed up late, not wanting to miss anything. According to Tuttle, the Arcadia Conference allowed Hopkins to exercise a great deal of influence with Roosevelt and Churchill. "Using the confidence which Churchill and Roosevelt reposed in him, Hopkins worked for a closer cooperation between America, Britain, and the Soviet Union." Hopkins was in a prime position to influence both Roosevelt and Churchill due not only to his living on the same floor in the White House but because both had trust in him. He believed that the Russians would defeat Germany and that the Communists would not put pressure on democratic and capitalist nations of Europe. Hopkins' opinion here wavered and by the Yalta Conference he was fully aware of the danger the USSR posed to postwar Europe.[232]

This was the holiday season but the war news put a damper on the mood; the Japanese had just sunk the *Prince of Wales* and the *Repulse* and Hong Kong had fallen to the

Japanese. But now that the United States was well and truly in the fight, Churchill's spirits were high. The Prime Minister remained at the White House for fourteen days and during this time, he and FDR and Hopkins had lunch and dinner together every day but one.[233] Here the two leaders committed themselves to a necessary if sometimes contentious wartime alliance, with Hopkins acting as the glue that held them together in the dangerous days and years ahead.

At the Arcadia Conference, Churchill and Roosevelt made the important decision to create a joint military command, recognizing that an effective and unified Allied strategy was crucial to the war effort. Thus, they created the Combined Chiefs of Staff (CCOS), insuring cooperation between the British and American military command. When the CCOS met on Christmas Day, General George Marshall, reluctant to share power with the British, proposed that just one man should be in command of the entire Pacific Theater. Churchill did not agree with this strategy. At this point Beaverbrook wrote a note to Hopkins asking him to work on Churchill to convince him that this would be the most effective way to victory. Consequently, relying on his faith in the efficacy of face-to-face meetings, Hopkins arranged a meeting between Marshall and Churchill. The general convinced the Prime Minister that unity of command was essential and that shared power could be detrimental to the war effort in the Pacific Theater. Churchill agreed. According to Sherwood,

This was a demonstration of the peculiar role played by Hopkins at all the major

conferences of the next three years. Because
of the utter informality of his position as well
as of his character he could act in an extra-
official capacity, and thus bring about ready
settlement of disputes, which might have
been greatly prolonged or completely stalled
if left to the traditional, antiquated machinery
international negotiation. There were many
more notes passed to Hopkins under the
conference table and many more examples of
his effective, off-the-record action. He was
rarely confined by the customary channels.

This "ready settlement of disputes," such as that between
Churchill and Marshall was another instance of Hopkins'
usefulness when the allied leaders were making momentous
decisions that reflected the terrible responsibility imposed
upon them by the war. [234]

There was potential divisiveness over war
production. The British consistently were asking for more
and more merchant ships to carry munitions; when Roosevelt
told Churchill that the United States was "at the bottom of the
barrel," the Prime Minister snapped, "Then scrape the
barrel." A "canopy of air protection" would be crucial for the
impending joint North African Campaign. Hopkins fully
supported increased spending for the U.S. Army Air Force.
General Henry (Hap) Arnold, of the Army Air Force, met
with Hopkins and told him that George Marshall had
authorized 115 heavy bombers for late 1942 and this
delighted the Prime Minister. But FDR was unsure about the
success of the spending program necessary to fund this;

presidential approval was necessary for this to go forward. When Arnold had repeated his conversation with Hopkins to the President and assured him that his British counterpart was on the same page, Roosevelt relented.[235] Another dispute settled.

At the Arcadia Conference, FDR and Churchill reaffirmed the crucial decision to concentrate Allied forces to the defeat of Germany and to consider the Pacific Campaign as secondary. This was the important "Europe First" policy. A defeated Germany would surely lead to Japanese capitulation but there was no reason to believe that the reverse would be true. FDR made it clear to Churchill that the United States was fully committed to defeating Hitlerism and would use the Arsenal of Democracy to do this while holding off the Japanese in the Pacific with the help of the Chinese. Still, the Prime Minister had some reservations about the Americans' lack of military experience; the nation, after all, had been intensely isolationist right up to December 7, 1941. The British felt that the early defeats that the United States had suffered in the Pacific, in the Philippines, Hong Kong Bali, Timor, Singapore), and lack of coordination re war production reflected badly on the Americans, who seemed naïve militarily. Nevertheless, the British committed to Anglo-American cooperation with the aim to defeat Hitler first. This strategy continued throughout the war years; the Allies considered Germany as the prime enemy and concluded that Japan would fall as soon as the Nazis were defeated. The two western leaders combined individual documents and drew up a wartime alliance pact called the Declaration of the United Nations, which became the forerunner of the United Nations (a term FDR had been using for the nations fighting against the Axis powers).

Hopkins' negotiating skills were tested to the utmost during this summit. He had an important part in the creation of the Declaration of the United Nations. He suggested changes that recognized that the USSR was not at war with Japan; he argued for the inclusion of all nations ("little countries") as signatories; for the elimination of any mention of the Atlantic Charter; for the inclusion of a mention of religious freedom; for the exclusion of the Free French; and, important to him, a statement of "aims for human freedom, justice, security, not only for the people in our own lands, but for all people in the world." Despite objections from the Russians, religious freedom did remain in the document. The Free French were not included. The signatories (Roosevelt, Churchill, Litvanov for the Soviet Union, and Chiang Kai-shek's brother-in-law, T.V. Soong for China) pledged their full resources to the war and promised not to make a separate peace with the enemy. There was a snag, however. Churchill, ever the imperialist, opposed the inclusion of India on the list as an "associated" member of the United Nations. This issue dogged the allies throughout the war. Litvanov, recognizing the influence that Hopkins wielded with Churchill, invited him to lunch at the Soviet Embassy to complain about the Prime Minister, wanting to shake things up between the British and the Americans. Belittling the position that the British would hold in the postwar world, the Russian hoped to use Hopkins to weaken the Anglo-American alliance.[236] He was not successful; Hopkins confidence in Great Britain was not shaken. By New Year's Day, 26 countries had signed the document, and the foundation of the United Nations was laid.[237]   Hopkins' faith in Churchill and Great Britain had again steadied the Anglo-American Alliance.

Churchill presented the President with the plan for the French North Africa campaign. Land forces would be included so that Americans would get the idea that their nation was well and truly in the war. Roosevelt had agreed to the 1941-42 invasion of North Africa, code-named Operation Gymnast (later Torch). But as President, he had to take public opinion into consideration; troops could not be kept standing idly by while a war was going on. Churchill believed that General Maxime Weygand, commander of French forces in North Africa, could be relied upon to put up no resistance when the Allied forces landed in North Africa. Hopkins disagreed. He thought that Weygand could not be trusted; the chances were that he would cooperate with Henri-Philippe Pétain and fight with the Germans against the Allies. Churchill, Hopkins said, was wrong. Roosevelt was at first in full agreement with Churchill's plan. Hopkins' opinion and a review of War Department memoranda, however, gave the President second thoughts and a few days later he changed his mind. By the end of the conference, Roosevelt and Churchill had agreed that any action in North Africa would necessitate a reduction in operations elsewhere, including a thirty percent reduction of shipments to Russia. Hopkins' mind began to tick over and he figured out that this reduction equaled seven ships and these could be acquired by shifting shipping around. The two Western Allies finally agreed and approved Operation Torch, the campaign to drive the Germans out of North Africa. [238]

Hopkins seemed to be in his element in this environment and he continued to troubleshoot. He convinced

Secretary of War Henry Stimson not to resign over FDR's alleged agreement to turn over troops stationed in the Philippines to Churchill to help defend Singapore. He told his boss that he should be more careful about what he tells the Prime Minister.[239]

After his meeting with Stalin in July 1941 and after the Atlantic Conference, Hopkins became more and more convinced that the Red Army would be able to hold off the Germans and eventually beat them. But would this mean a Communist Europe after the war? At the Arcadia Conference, over a meal with Roosevelt and Churchill, he discussed this and even went so far as to opine, based on probably nothing but his supreme optimism, that the Communism would not prevail over a democratic and capitalist Europe.[240]

Hopkins and Churchill had by this time established a solid and an effective working relationship; the introduction of Stalin and the Soviet Union into the equation would no doubt strain the Special Relationship and thus Anglo-American-Soviet Alliance. There would be increased disagreement among the Allies on military strategy, on the Mediterranean campaign, and especially when it came to the timing of opening up the Second Front. After Operation Barbarossa, Stalin constantly demanded that the Western Allies carry out an invasion of France from England in order to draw the Germans from the Russian front. In fact, from 1942 through 1943, at all the Allied conferences and meetings, the issue of the Second Front always stood in the way of true accord, even between the Western Allies.[241] Churchill knew that going on the offensive and staging an Allied invasion of France was inevitable but the British military needed time to get prepared, to acquire the necessary munitions, ships and men needed for this massive operation. He opposed the launching of any cross-channel invasion in 1942 or even in 1943; it would be a slaughter, he said. The Germans would quickly overpower Allied troops on the beaches of France. FDR and Hopkins did not agree with him. Both feared that, if the war went on much longer, with the Red Army suffering such high casualties, the Soviets might succumb and negotiate with the Germans for a separate peace. It was clear to the President and the Prime Minister that at some point the Allies would have to launch a campaign to draw the Germans from the Russian front and take the pressure off of the Red Army, and to appease an increasingly angry Stalin; they only disagreed as to the timing.

In the aftermath of the humiliating fall of France and the tragedy of Dunkirk, in late October, 1940, Churchill had appointed Lord Louis Mountbatten as Chief of Combined Operations and ordered him to plan an amphibious invasion of Europe. Churchill believed that unless Great Britain made every attempt to defeat the Germans on land, the war could never be won. He gave Mountbatten this overwhelmingly complicated task to go on the offensive. The Prime Minister directed:

> You are to prepare for the invasion of Europe, for unless we can go and land and fight Hitler and beat his forces on land, we shall never win this war. You must devise and design the appliances, the landing craft and the technique to enable us to effect a landing against opposition and to maintain ourselves there. The whole of the south

coast of England is a bastion of defense against
the invasion of Hitler: you've got to turn it into
the springboard for attack.[242]

All agreed that a land invasion of northern France
from England could indeed have the desired effect of
relieving the German assault against Russia. However, the
United States was still gearing up its industry and Britain was
just recovering from the relentless German bombing of the
airfields and of its cities during the Blitz. The Battle of the
Atlantic was raging and precious armaments were lost to
German submarines. Neither nation had the equipment
necessary to defeat the German force after a landing in
northern France. In addition, they were fighting a war in the
Pacific. Churchill, remembering Gallipoli, told Charles
Wilson, Lord Moran and Churchill's physician, "I certainly
entered this war with a mentality born in the last war." He
had good reason to oppose any massive European invasion
of France in 1942, or even 1943. He feared tremendous
casualties because the Allies were not yet ready to face the
Germans.[243]

Mountbatten supported the Prime Minister's
decision to delay and countered the American argument to
push up the date, claiming that an invasion of France
mounted from England had always been part of Allied
strategy. It was going to happen. Although by 1942 the Allies
were committed to a Europe First policy as well as the
creation of the Combined Chiefs of Staff (CCOS), Churchill
and FDR could not agree on when to launch the invasion of
France. Stalin wanted, even demanded, a Second Front
immediately. Churchill stalled. Although FDR did not want

American troops to stand idly by in Europe—he thought it was bad for American morale and a terrible waste of manpower— he nevertheless acquiesced to Churchill's call for delay. He also knew that the United States was not yet up to speed for such an ambitious campaign and he knew that sympathy for the Soviets was hard to come by in Britain. The British had been taking a beating from the Germans for two years while the Russians had signed the infamous non-aggression pact with the Germans and stood by while Britain was getting pummeled by the Germans. Americans were likewise suspicious of Communist Russia. Negotiations were testy.

Historian Jon Meacham notes that the story of the planning for and execution of Overlord, the assault of Nazi occupied France by Allied troops in June 1944, is more a story about the "diplomatic skirmishing" that took place in the years previous to the operation than it is about the largest land invasion to date. American military leaders argued for a cross-channel attack in 1942. Churchill said no, not yet; it would end in disaster. Churchill instead wanted to launch an attack through the "soft underbelly" of Europe in a peripheral operation rather than a frontal attack. Thus, Operation Torch, the invasion of North Africa, and the subsequent invasion of Italy, were the first steps of this strategy. On the other hand, Stalin insisted on a Second Front immediately. FDR, reluctantly but wisely, sided with Churchill until the meeting in Teheran in November 1943 when the President declared the American Arsenal of Democracy ready for Overlord.[244] But to the Russians this was a long time for them to wait for help.

In his memoirs, *Molotov Remembers*, first published in Russian in 1991 and then abridged and published in English in 1993, Russian Foreign Minister Vyacheslav Molotov suggests that if the Allies "had opened up a second front in 1942 or 1943 instead of 1944 it would have gone very hard for us, but it would have helped us immensely!" And further: "We didn't believe in a second front, of course, but we had to try for it. We took them in: You can't? But you promised. ... That was the way."[245] This indicates that Stalin might not have been as adamant about the Second Front as the Allies believed but Molotov's musings years later should be carefully assessed in light of the outcome of the war.

During this critical period of "diplomatic skirmishing" Harry Hopkins honed his skills as the President's unofficial envoy. Roosevelt had been schooling Hopkins in foreign policy since mid-1940. He found an apt and willing pupil as well as a friend. Because of his closeness to the president, the social worker from Iowa had acquired a great deal of political power; he had found his way into the inner circle of Washington and gave up much of his personal life in order to serve his President.

Hopkins had three sons, boys growing into young men whom he rarely saw. He missed birthdays, graduations, operations, and most of the events that make up family life. His young daughter, whose mother had died when she was six, lived at the White House with her father who was away most of the time. Eleanor Roosevelt stepped in as a surrogate parent but until her father remarried in 1942, it was a lonely life for a little girl. Hopkins' children did not resent their father's preoccupation with his job but instead, thanks to a large extent to their mother, were proud of his accomplishments. Yet, Hopkins' personal life did intrude at times.

Hopkins' rapport with Churchill led to interesting interactions between the Prime Minister and a member of the Hopkins family. In October 1942, Hopkins' son, Robert, a corporal in the U.S. Signal Corps who had been assigned to a British Army camp (Lichfield Barracks) was in London on a 24-hour pass. He was to await orders there. On October 17th, Robert received a letter from Commander C. R. (Tommy) Thompson, a personal assistant to Churchill, inviting him to Number 10. Apparently, Harry Hopkins had been having some difficulty getting in contact with his son so he wrote to the Prime Minister to see what he could do. Ambassador Gil Winant, whom Robert had visited earlier, informed the Prime Minister that Hopkins' son was in London. It was probably through the Ambassador that Averell Harriman arranged for Robert to have a three-day pass. Consequently, and surprisingly for the young soldier, Churchill invited him to join his entourage on a defense inspection trip to Dover in the company of Prime Minister of South Africa Jan Smuts, Secretary of the Treasury Henry Morgenthau, Randolph Churchill, and others. Robert filmed the Dover tour with his new color movie camera and then the Prime Minister extended Robert an invitation to spend the weekend at Chequers, a place Robert had never even heard of. But the young soldier was clearly impressed with the place. In an unpublished manuscript, Robert Hopkins described Chequers, "a tremendously English estate." It was built in the late 15th century. Around 1920 it was given as a country home to be used by the current Prime Minister. The huge home had not been updated (other than the installation of modern plumbing) for several hundred years. The rooms were huge with 34-foot ceilings and despite many fireplaces, the place was bitterly cold in the winter, a situation Harry Hopkins always found debilitating. Robert met Clementine Churchill ("tall and aristocratic"), Anthony Eden ("boyish-looking despite his moustache") and Lady Eden. Churchill appeared for dinner in his "zipper blitz suit" that Robert thought looked like a "fancy pair of overalls." After a briefing on the war situation, the Prime Minister phoned Harry Hopkins, who was in Washington, and kindly arranged for Robert to speak to his father. The next day Eleanor Roosevelt arrived with Elliott Roosevelt, who was a Lt. Col in the Air Corps, but since the First Lady left soon after dinner, Robert was only able to have a short chat with her.[246] It was likely this meeting with Churchill that led the Prime Minister and the President to invite Robert to attend the Casablanca, Cairo, Teheran, and Yalta Conferences and create a photographic record of the summits.

Neither Hopkins' friendship with Churchill nor his kindnesses to his son placed him fully behind the P.M.'s insistence on delaying the opening of the Second Front. Neither did he agree with Stalin that the invasion had to be undertaken immediately. He saw both sides of the argument and attempted to use any influence he had with these men to prevent dangerous mistakes. Churchill, however, never lost confidence in Hopkins' commitment to Britain. He received a letter from Hopkins in mid-1942:

> These have been some of the bad days. No doubt there will be others. They who run for cover with every reverse, the timid and faint of heart, will have

no part in winning the war. Your strength, tenacity, and everlasting courage will see Britain through and the President, you know, does not quit. I know you are of good heart for your military defeats and ours are certain victories to come and will be shared together. More power to you. Harry Hopkins.[247]

The timing and the planning of a cross-channel invasion from England to northern France was probably the most important decision that the Allies had to make; it caused serious dissention. How and when could the Western Allies carry out such a huge and complex operation? Or would it be more effective to establish a Second Front through an invasion of Italy or North Africa? The Red Army, and only the Red Army, was holding the Germans at bay. On the other hand, a too powerful Russia at the end of the war could mean a communist takeover of Europe. This would be abhorrent to both Roosevelt and Churchill, to Americans and British people alike. The situation was delicate.[248] It was important to keep Stalin anticipating an imminent Second Front and at the same time have some assurance that the Red Army would continue to fight.

During his secret mission to Moscow in late July 1941, the first instance of a face-to-face contact with the Soviet dictator by a representative of the United States, Hopkins gathered real evidence of Russian needs and intentions re the war. He was not just carrying messages from one world leader to another; he was formulating opinions as to military and political strategy that he shared with the President and the Prime Minister. Hopkins believed that support for the Soviets would ensure the peace and security of the United

States. This attitude proved crucial in making decisions re the planning of the Second Front.

General Marshall, unlike the President, believed that the cross-channel invasion of France was the only way to shorten the war. The President had full confidence in his chief of staff. In mid-July 1942, Roosevelt sent Hopkins, General Marshall, and Admiral King to London on another top-level secret mission. As the President's personal representatives, they were to consult with British on the conduct of the war.[249] It was clear that, despite continuing implied threats from Stalin, no agreement was possible on any date for Operation Overlord. But the invasion of North Africa, Operation Torch, remained a viable alternative for 1942. FDR wanted American troops in on the action with the British.[250] Churchill referred to the President's men as "the three musketeers" and reported in a July 28, 1942, letter to FDR that he was "happy with the result and especially the successful "meeting of minds. ... I cannot help feeling that the past week represented a turning point in the whole war and the now we are on our way shoulder to shoulder."[251]

The defeat at Tobruk on June 21st had devastated the British and conservatives in Parliament called for a censure of Churchill, who was blamed for this. On July 2, he addressed Parliament in his usual eloquent style and consequently survived; the vote was 470 to 25. A delighted Hopkins cabled his congratulations on this success, praising the Prime Minister's "everlasting tenacity." He warns that there will be some "bad days" but victories will come. "More power to you."[252]

Hopkins agreed with his boss that it was not good to have American troops standing idle and he strongly urged the President to name a date for the North African invasion. This would draw German forces from the Russian front and ease the pressure on the Red Army. He argued for speed since the situation with the Soviet leader was so tense, suggesting a date in late October for the invasion. FDR agreed. Operation Torch would go ahead as planned. This "was one of the very few major military decisions of the war that Roosevelt made over the protests of his highest-ranking advisers."[253] However, it is clear that Hopkins' advice did encourage FDR to make that important decision. Additionally, the Allies were going to need assurance from the French in North Africa that they would support the Allies and not the Germans in this ambitious campaign.

It would not be possible for the Allies to mount a cross-channel invasion in 1942 as well as an invasion of North Africa. In addition, there were considerable political risks to Churchill if the former failed. FDR's memo to Hopkins, Marshall, and King ordered them to consider carefully the possibility of opening up the Second Front in 1942 because it "is of such grave importance that every reason calls for accomplishment of it." At the same time, the President wrote, it is imperative to hold the Middle East. Matthew Wills writes that FDR sent his three emissaries to London in order to craft an alternative strategy. His memo ended with "I hope for total agreement within one week of your arrival."[254]

Hopkins' personal life rarely intervened with his wartime schedule but at this particular juncture it did. He had planned to get married on July 30, 1942, in Washington, at the White House where he still lived. FDR insisted that his friend not postpone the ceremony but return to D.C. for his wedding. Churchill's July 28 letter noted that the wedding was still scheduled. Hopkins readily agreed. He arrived back in Washington on July 27th, having stopped over in Iceland to inspect the military installations there. Three days later, he was married for the third time. His wife was the former Louise Macy, a beautiful socialite who had been editor of *Harper's Bazaar* magazine in Paris.[255] The simple ceremony took place in the Oval Office, with just members of the immediate families present: Hopkins' three sons and his daughter as well as Louise's family. The President acted as the best man. It was a remarkably happy interlude for the couple and their guests in the midst of war and despite some very negative press. The media reported unfounded rumors of the honeymooning couple "commandeering" a navy vessel, at public expense. In fact, they spent a couple of weeks in Connecticut.[256]

Hopkins' absence from the Washington scene, though short, left a diplomatic lacuna. It was Churchill with Averell Harriman who had the unpleasant duty of meeting with Stalin in Moscow in August 1942 to bring him news that there would be no Second Front that year. The Allies, they told him, could not possible be ready. An infuriated Stalin vented his anger on the Prime Minister, accusing the British of cowardice. The story, of course, was much more complicated but Churchill had trouble making Stalin understand the Western Allies' position. Earlier, in June 1942, the Germans under General Rommel had just about destroyed British forces in tank battle; the vital city of Tobruk fell on 21st. British supplies were now diverted to the Middle East. This created a dangerous situation for the Suez Canal that threatened the oil supply. In addition, the Germans were sinking Lend Lease ships carrying crucial munitions across the Atlantic at an alarming rate.

The Battle of the Atlantic was eating up valuable resources but was central to Allied war strategy. U-boats were sinking more tonnage than was being manufactured and this led to critical shortages. Well before the United States entered into the war, Roosevelt, through executive initiative, had taken steps to establish a base in Iceland in order to allow American ships to convoy along with ships carrying Lend Lease equipment. From then on, American battleships and planes protected the ships carrying essential munitions to Britain through a security zone; the second leg, from Iceland to Scotland, was under the protection of the British fleet. Harry Hopkins had strongly urged the President to make this decision. Roosevelt agreed and he tore out a map of the Atlantic Ocean from a *National Geographic* magazine, drew a pencil line at longitude 26 degrees that was bent to the east of Iceland and gave the page to Hopkins who was to give it to Churchill. This was an historic decision that had a lot to do with the survival of Britain. In addition, the President declared the Red Sea outside of the war zone, which allowed our merchant vessels to supply the British fighting against Rommel in North Africa.[257]

In this context, Churchill informed Stalin of a tactic that would divert Germans from the Russian front but it would not be the invasion of northern France. Instead, the Allies would draw off the Germans by an invasion of North Africa from the Mediterranean, the "soft underbelly" through which Europe could be attacked. Roosevelt was still pushing for an earlier cross-channel invasion but Hopkins had changed his own mind and now believed that this was too dangerous to undertake before the Allies were fully prepared. He used his influence to convince the President that Churchill was indeed making the right decision in delaying the invasion. Stalin was furious; he threatened to make a separate peace with the Germans. To encourage Stalin of their support, the Western Allies promised that, along with the North Africa campaign, the Allied carpet bombings of Germany would escalate; this would not only cripple German military installations but also serve to damage the morale of the German people. While not happy, for the moment, Stalin was at least placated.

Chapter 7—Wartime Conferences

A good deal of the military strategy was hammered out at the various wartime conferences. However, the Big Three—Roosevelt, Churchill, and Stalin—gathered together only twice, at Teheran in November 1943 and Yalta in February 1945. Still the Soviet dictator's presence was felt at all of the conferences. Issues debated included the conduct of the Pacific War and China's role there, the timing and execution of Second Front, the Mediterranean Campaign, the battle in North Africa, the issue of French leadership, Poland's government and borders, the development of the United Nations, wartime reparations, and the postwar occupation of Germany. Harry Hopkins attended all but one of the major conferences of the Allied leaders.

At end of 1942, Hopkins was optimistic; finally, news of the European War as well as the war in the Pacific seemed positive. His personal life was on the upswing with his marriage; his friendship with the President was solid and the British Prime Minister had full faith in him. Still, living in the very busy White House with a wife and daughter proved to be difficult for Hopkins. Understandably, the family wanted their own home. They subsequently moved to Georgetown where they rented a small house on N Street. Hopkins' move out of the White House certainly did not please FDR. Having Hopkins available to him no matter what the hour certainly was a plus for the President whose mobility was limited and Roosevelt regretted the move. Their relationship, however, remained as strong as ever.[258] Churchill also felt a bit put out by Hopkins' departure from the White House and his new-found marital status. His telegram of October 4, 1942, to Hopkins reflects this.

> Let me know when you are coming over. I am becoming deeply concerned about the layout for 1943 stop there are things I can only say to you. If your visit were to be long-delayed I would send Lyttleton over. Good wishes to all.[259]

Despite the Prime Minister's imprecations, Hopkins did not go to England because it seemed to him that there was

> no good reason why I should make the trip. ... There may be reasons in your mind for my coming to England at once with which I am not fully acquainted but there is so much to do here that I do not wish to come unless it is important to you and the President."[260]

Clearly, Hopkins did not want to leave Washington.

Although historian Warren Kimball suggests that Hopkins' move out of the White House ended his relationship with the president, this is not true. Their close relationship endured until their deaths. When Hopkins wrote a letter to FDR in 1940 resigning as secretary of commerce, citing illness, FDR responded that he could resign the office but that their friendship would go on as before. After that, Hopkins orchestrated Roosevelt's run for a third term, a responsibility that reflected FDR's ultimate confidence in his friend.[261]

Tension between FDR and Churchill, however, escalated over the planning of Operation Torch. The presence of the Vichy French in North Africa could pose a serious threat if they sided with the Germans during the Allied invasion. FDR contacted Admiral François Darlan, the nominal head of the Vichy government who had not only collaborated with the Germans during occupation of France; he also was anti-Semitic.[262] Furthermore, he had allowed German U-boats to use the French port at Dakar to attack Allied shipping carrying Lend Lease munitions. But the President decided to ignore these significant flaws because the Allied troops had to have the support of the French in North Africa for the invasion to be successful. Consequently, General Eisenhower, with the President's support, made a deal with Darlan to support Allied troops when they landed in North Africa.[263] In exchange the United States would recognize him as High Commissioner of France for North and West Africa. General Charles de Gaulle, who proclaimed himself the leader of the Free French, was outraged at this, as were many Americans who considered the "Darlan Deal," which linked us to a traitor, the antithesis of our democracy. De Gaulle especially disliked being omitted from action that was supposed to liberate French territory from German control. But FDR detested de Gaulle, thought him to be insufferably arrogant, and regarded him as a threat to the Allied cause. Churchill, on the other hand, felt that de Gaulle was the strong leader whom the French would need at the end of the war. This difference of opinion further increased the tension between the two Western Allies.

By the fall, however, the tide was beginning to turn in favor of the Allies. Still there was suspicion among the

Allies. In late September, Hopkins send a telegram to Churchill urging him not to send any message to Stalin until Roosevelt approved. "It seems clear to me that what is said to Stalin now and what firm commitments we are prepared to make may well be turning point in the war." Churchill replied, "We are not sending message till we hear from President." [264] In early November 1942 the invasion of North Africa, Operation Torch, successfully replaced the cross-channel invasion. This first Anglo-American land offensive, led by General Dwight David Eisenhower, was successful after three days of fighting. Still, both Roosevelt and Churchill remained cautious. Churchill declared, "Now, this is not the end. It is not even the beginning of the end. But it is, perhaps, the end of the beginning." [265] Roosevelt, relying on his firm belief in personal interaction, suggested that the Allied leaders meet. He was still afraid that Stalin would sign a separate peace with the Germans. [266] For both Churchill and FDR, Stalin was still a cipher. A face-to-face meeting with the Soviet leader might clarify needs and temper disagreements.

Hopkins also believed that a meeting among the three allied leaders could be most productive in this climate of victory in North Africa. Churchill agreed. Consequently, Roosevelt and Churchill, after much bickering, agreed to meet without Stalin in order to discuss war strategy. With the success of the North Africa campaign, and since Morocco was now controlled by the Allies, Casablanca seemed to be a perfect site for a conference. Hopkins told Lord Moran that the President loved the "drama of a journey like this" and Moran told Hopkins that the Prime Minister just wanted to get away from London and the red boxes and escape the "unending grind." [267] Stalin, however, stubbornly refused to attend; the Red Army was engaged in a fierce battle against the Germans at Stalingrad and the Soviet leader did not want to leave Moscow. Historian Kimball suggests that Stalin's refusal to attend the Casablanca Conference based on military needs remains "unverified."[268]   It is also quite possible that Stalin did not want to meet with the Western Allies until he could negotiate from an increased position of strength. He was still a supplicant. And this would be the first time that a U. S. president ever flew in a plane and the first time a president "set foot on foreign soil during wartime." [269] Code-named Symbol, the meeting was scheduled for January 14-24, 1943. Roosevelt and Churchill met amid utmost secrecy at the Anfa Hotel, an upscale resort located on the outskirts of Casablanca. Security was extremely tight and under the supervision of General Eisenhower.

On January 18, the Combined Chiefs of Staff: Lt. General H. H. (Hap) Arnold, Admiral Ernest J. King, General Sir Alan F. Brooke, Admiral of the Fleet Sir Dudley Pound, General George C. Marshall, Brigadier E. I. C. Jacob, Lt. General Sir Hastings Ismay, Vice Admiral Lord Louis Mountbattan, Brigadier General John R. Deane, Field Marshal Sir John Dill, and air Chief Marshal Sir Charles Portal, reported on their deliberations to the President and the Prime Minister. These men had mapped out strategy for the rest of the war. On January 27 Churchill and Roosevelt sent a message to Stalin outlining strategies that included keeping the pressure on Japan but concentrating on the European Theater; supplying the Soviet Union with munitions to enable them to continue the battle against the Germans; clearing a way through the Mediterranean to allow for military traffic; bombing German targets with increasing intensity, which would damage both industry and morale. In addition, a thrust in the Mediterranean would draw the Germans from the Russian Front and, as soon as practicable, the Allies will launch an invasion of Europe. The Western Allies assured of an absent and preoccupied Stalin that "[o]ur ruling purpose is to bring to bear on Germany and Italy the maximum forces by land, sea and air which can be physically applied."[270]

The military successes had given Stalin confidence; the Soviet dictator, recognizing his increased leverage, renewed pressure for a Second Front in northern France. To assuage Stalin, the Western Allies promised him that more effort would be used "to seek out and destroy" German submarines. Furthermore, they promised that Allied bombing of German cities would be again accelerated and Allied forces would move against Sicily and through Italy after the North Africa campaign ended. Arguments raged over whether the Allies should concentrate on Mediterranean operations or plan a cross-channel operation. The American military argued for a cross-channel invasion in 1943. The President and the Prime Minister hedged. Lord Halifax reported to the Prime Minister on a meeting between FDR and Hopkins in late October 1943, in which they discussed Churchill's real intentions about Overlord. "Both the President and Harry Hopkins, of course, agreed that the final decision must and could only be made in light of actual facts at the time the decision had to be taken but the feeling of doubt in the background of their thought plainly remained. ... But I was surprised and a bit disturbed to find the feeling so strong." Eventually, Roosevelt and Churchill agreed that an invasion through northern France would only be considered if it looked like Germany was on the verge of collapse. Otherwise, a date for the cross-channel invasion would be postponed, again. The target date for the cross-channel invasion, now code-named Overlord, was set for May 1, 1944.[271] The situation was still precarious.

On the last day of the Casablanca Conference, January 24, 1943, FDR declared, rather unexpectedly, that the Allies would accept nothing less than unconditional surrender from the Axis enemies. The President declared that this would not only eliminate the power of the Axis nations but also ensure peace when the war was won. Whether or not the President informed Churchill about this earlier has been an unanswered question, although Churchill seemed startled at the announcement. Biographer Robert Sherwood wrote to Churchill asking him if he and Roosevelt had discussed this policy. He replied, "I heard for the first time the words 'Unconditional Surrender" for the first time from the President's lips at the Conference. ... I would not myself have used these words but I immediately stood by the President and have frequently defended the decision."[272] Nevertheless, Churchill agreed to this policy the next day and this was one of the more important outcomes of the Casablanca Conference. General Jacob E. Smart attended the conference and wrote about FDR's announcement to the press that the allies would accept nothing but unconditional surrender from the Axis powers: "That was stunning news. I learned later that the President had acted on impulse, and that Mr. Churchill endorsed his statement. I was certain then (as now) that the planners at Casablanca would not have suggested such a move."[273] McJimsey writes that the Joint Chiefs had been informed before the conference that Roosevelt would make this announcement. Hopkins also knew that Roosevelt was going to make this announcement about unconditional surrender at Casablanca and he did agree with it. Roosevelt himself said that the press conference was so sudden that he had little time to think and the demand for unconditional surrender just "popped" into his head. For Hopkins it was only useful as a wartime strategy. He had earlier discussed this with Churchill, who did not want this to apply to Italy, fearing that it would encourage the Italians to fight harder. Roosevelt, and Hopkins, saw the demand for unconditional surrender from the Axis powers as a way to maintain the good will of the Soviets and to convince Stalin that the coalition was strong and united in its wartime goals. However, although Stalin did not object to this demand, he wasn't much interested; his main goal for the Allies was opening up a Second Front.[274]

In the aftermath of the North African campaign, the Allied leaders faced vital political and military issues. The question of the Free French became especially fractious. FDR had approved Eisenhower's extremely controversial Darlan Deal to ensure French support in the North African campaign, and, after the death of Darlan, now sided with his successor, war hero General Henri Giraud. This position infuriated General de Gaulle, who considered himself the only leader of the Free French. The two Frenchmen heartily disliked each other. Both eventually attended the conference and this led to a situation that dangerously increased the tension. Roosevelt and Churchill both saw Giraud as a possible leader of the Free French and someone who had no connection to the Vichy government in France. But it turned out that, like de Gaulle, his only goal was to be recognized as leader of the Free French. This would lead to tension at the conference as related by a guest.

FDR had invited Hopkins' son, Sgt. Robert Hopkins, a member of the Army Signal Corps, to attend the conference in order to take photographs of the event. It was also a way for the young soldier to see his father.[275] FDR's two sons, Elliot and Franklin, Jr., were also there; Churchill's son Randolph rounded out the family affair. Robert Hopkins wrote a memoir in 2002 recounting his impressions of the people and the problems at the Casablanca Conference; this is an important document because, as Hopkins' son, he had a unique and close-up view of the participants and their interactions. As a quiet observer twenty-two-year-old Robert Hopkins provides us with some insights into the relationship and inner thoughts of the Allied leaders during the war. He writes in the introduction to his piece entitled, "Roosevelt, Churchill, and Stalin: Councils of War and Peace, 1943-1945:" "Because I was often with President Roosevelt and Prime Minister Churchill at informal gatherings and meals when they were at ease, I believe I can relate aspects of their personalities which have not yet appeared in histories of this era." He filmed the invasions of North Africa Italy, and Normandy as well as the Conferences at Casablanca, Cairo, Teheran, and Yalta. In addition, he filmed the Three Kings meeting after the Yalta Conference. [276] He was an important witness to the history of the Second World War because he had easy access to the Allied leaders when they were at their leisure.[277]

In his notes, Robert Hopkins recalls that during the Casablanca Conference he had most of his meals with his father, the Prime Minister, and/or the President. On January

19, after dinner, Churchill took Robert aside and said, "I want you to take a picture of your father and me, walking along the beach discussing the fate of nations, with the mighty surf of the Atlantic crashing against the rugged, rocky shore." This did not happen because the beaches were littered with land mines and barbed wire, and there was no surf. [278] This incident demonstrates that Churchill had a vivid sense of the dramatic and saw this event as something that could improve his image as leader of the British people during a dangerous war.

Robert Hopkins also describes the "thorny problem" having to do with the French. Who would be the leader of the Free French? Both de Gaulle and Giraud were invited to the conference in the hope of bringing this to a resolution. The hope was, according to young Hopkins, that there could be a joint command. It would be very impolitic of FDR or Churchill to back one man; no one could predict who would be on top at the end of the war. On the morning of January 20th, the CCOS met and Robert took photographs of the 14 men who would make critical decisions as to the direction the war would take. That evening he had dinner with FDR, his father, Harriman, Elliot Roosevelt, and Robert Murphy. Murphy, whom the President sent to North Africa to negotiate the Allied take over, was especially concerned about negotiations having to do with the role of the French after the North African campaign was over. De Gaulle had initially refused the invitation to attend the conference, not wanting to meet with Giraud; this irritated FDR. At the dinner, the President likened de Gaulle to a groom who was reluctant to meet with his bride. When de Gaulle did finally show up, the President greeted him coolly. Churchill and

Roosevelt finally convinced de Gaulle and Giraud to work together with Giraud in command of the Free French Armed Forces and de Gaulle in charge of uniting the French struggling against Nazi occupation of France. At a photo-op toward the end of the conference, de Gaulle, Giraud, FDR, and Churchill sat for a photograph. According to Sherwood, it was Hopkins who managed to manipulate the two Frenchmen into a position for a photo. Moran' diaries confirm that Hopkins had planned all along to bring the two French leaders together even though he was well aware that they hated each other. Churchill saw it as an historic moment and wanted it to be photographed so the party moved to the back of the president's quarters. De Gaulle, "stiff-necked," offered his hand "without the flicker of a smile" that apparently amused FDR to no end. He threw his head back "in hilarious enjoyment of the moment" while Churchill sat "demurely on the edge of his chair, his face wearing the expression of a child who has the sixpence in his hand and is anxiously waiting for the opposite side to call 'Up, Jenkins.'"[279] The two Frenchmen stood and shook hands, although stiffly, for the camera. In the photograph, the awkward postures of the two men, standing stiffly and not looking at each other, clearly show how reluctant the two were to work together.[280] Hopkins had advised the President and Churchill that the enmity between the two French leaders was a serious problem. He insisted that the sovereignty of France rested with the French people and that the United States had to assure them that they would enjoy self-determination after the war. The issue of colonialism seemed to be a subtext of many of the discussions at Casablanca as well as who would lead the Free French. De

Gaulle felt he was the only one who represented the French people; in his opinion Giraud only represented the hated Vichy government.[281]

Twenty-five years later, a Frenchman, Louis de Villefosse, who had fought against the Vichy government in World War II, wrote an article for *Contretemps* describing his 1972 visit to Robert Hopkins, who was then living with his wife in Georgetown. In the article, de Villefosse states that although Churchill and the British were well aware of the importance of Harry Hopkins, the French were not. Hopkins was not concerned with fame, he wrote: "Yet, if one had to count on the fingers of one hand the men who carried on their shoulders the heaviest responsibilities during the Second World War, certainly Roosevelt and Hopkins would have to be among them. The effort caused the death of each."[282] In December of 1941, according to de Villefosse, he was in Ottawa when he spoke to the U.S. Minister to Canada, a Mr. Moffat. "Mr. Minister, you can tell the President that the Free French will never do anything which can annoy the United States." Several days later, On December 18, 1941, de Gaulle disavowed this by ordering the occupation of Saint Pierre and Miquelon. This was extremely divisive for the Allies who were just beginning the plans for the Second Front. This, the author claims, was the beginning of the de Gaulle-Roosevelt animosity. The American President was clearly angered by this action of the French; it was not in synch with Allied strategy at the time—and he had not been informed of it. After that he did not trust de Gaulle; the French leader seemed to be fighting his own war against the Germans with little thought to the Allies. In FDR's mind, de Gaulle wanted to establish his position after the war ended while the

President just wanted to win the war.[283] According to Tuttle, the United States needed the cooperation of the Vichy French for the planned invasion of North Africa and this incident could upset the balance between the Western Allies. Hopkins, who had little sympathy for the Free French, acted as intermediary between FDR and Churchill, who supported de Gaulle. Hull entered into the picture when he tried to convince the Vichy French to end connection with Germany. Churchill then accused the secretary of state of "going behind his back." Hull blamed Hopkins for the mess and accused him of vindictiveness. Tuttle notes correctly that this feud only outlined the growing power that Hopkins had amassed among the Allies.[284]

At the Casablanca Conference, Hopkins ran interference between the two western leaders and kept tempers down, hoping this would allow issues to be resolved. Churchill had arrived at Casablanca with a large entourage. This irritated Roosevelt because the agreement had been that only minimal staff would accompany the leaders to the conference. Hopkins stepped forward to prevent Roosevelt from an angry exchange with the Prime Minister. When Churchill discovered to his horror that there would be no alcohol served at the dinner in deference to the Sultan of Morocco, Hopkins smoothed his ruffled feathers, assuring him that there would be drinks after dinner.[285] This complaint and Churchill's general discomfort may have had more to do with the Prime Minister's fear of a sensitive discussion over British and French colonialism rather than the lack of spirits.[286] These several incidents, taken together did threaten the ties that bound the western alliance and the coalition that was so necessary for victory over fascism. The decisions made at this conference—to postpone the invasion of France until 1944, to accelerate the war in the Atlantic against German submarines, to select a leader of the Free French, to continue the bomber offensive against Germany, to plan the assault on Italy, and to demand unconditional surrender of the Axis powers—were some of the most significant of the entire war.

It is interesting to note that just a few weeks before the Casablanca Conference, FDR hosted a New Year's Eve party in the White House during which he showed the newly released, very anti-Vichy motion picture, *Casablanca*, starring Ingrid Bergman and Humphrey Bogart. The Oscar winning film, a critique of the President's policy in North Africa and toward the Free French, celebrated democracy over fascism, loyalty over deception and romance over everything. Kimball sees the film as bringing a message to Churchill that "what romance remained was only for the Americans; the British were nowhere to be found." Raskin argues that America's military needs in North Africa led FDR to maintain relations with the Vichy government, a position that the film decries. He also points out that "Casablanca" can be translated as "White House," with Rick standing in as Roosevelt, merely waiting on the sidelines.[287]

After the Allied victory in Tunisia, Roosevelt and Churchill, with their respective advisors, met in Washington, D.C. for what Sherwood calls "the largest gathering of high-ranking officers that had yet taken place in the war." Hopkins' notes on this Washington Conference, code-named Trident, refer to discussions on issues relevant to China and the war in the Pacific; on the intensified bombing of Germany by the Mighty Eighth Air Force, peaking in April 1944, in an attempt to deplete Germany of fighter planes; on the deployment of British and American troops in England in preparation for Operation Overlord, which was set for May 1, 1944; and on plans to get Italy to surrender.[288]

Discussions on the war in the Pacific were limited to plans to eject the Japanese from the Aleutians and to continue Allied operations in the Marshall Islands. Still, the war strategy for the European theater took precedence over the Pacific campaign. The most important part of any strategy concerned the discussion of cross-channel invasion. It was crucial that there would be enough personnel, tanks, landing craft, and munitions for this ambitious and very dangerous operation. The atmosphere was optimistic, however, for this was the first wartime conference when victory over Germany seemed possible, if not assured. Much to the relief of the Western Allies, de Gaulle and Giraud finally agreed to a unified government-in-exile for the French.[289]

Still, there were disagreements. The British wanted an immediate invasion of Italy while the Americans argued that they should wait for the planned invasion of France. Hopkins had made sure that Roosevelt was fully informed about the importance of a Second Front and did not want the Prime Minister to change his mind and opt for another postponement. The Allies were winning the war and now was the time to strike. A cross-channel invasion would also be a sign to the Russians of Allied support. Churchill was not happy with this strategy and claimed to be discouraged over the President's unwillingness to support his Mediterranean strategy. Hopkins took advantage of his friendship with Churchill to confront him and bluntly warn him that he would not be able to change the President's mind about the

Mediterranean and Italy. The Prime Minister relented and later wrote that Hopkins had acted as a "mollifying and also dominating influence on the course of Staff discussions."[290]

When the conference ended, the President and the Prime Minister, accompanied by Hopkins, went to Marrakesh, a trip of about 150 miles. Along the way there was an American soldier every one hundred miles as protection. When the party stopped for lunch, fighter planes provided additional security for the party. They all admired the beauty of the Atlas Mountains at sunset from the rooftop of a nearby house. Churchill was so taken by the sight that he insisted that Roosevelt see it also. Two servants made a chair with their arms and carried FDR to the rooftop, with "his paralyzed legs dangling like the limbs of a ventriloquist's dummy" so he could experience the purple hills in the changing light. In the morning the Prime Minister, wearing his red dragon dressing gown, saw the Americans off at the airfield. Later Churchill painted a picture of the Atlas Mountains, the only picture he painted during the war.[291]

FIRST QUEBEC

Amid tensions over war strategy, Hopkins accompanied the President and the Prime Minister to the First Quebec Conference (Quadrant) scheduled for August 1943. There clearly was a good deal of tension, much of it having to do with Operation Overlord. Hopkins wrote a letter to General Eisenhower's aide, Lt. Commander Harry C. Butcher: "We are off tonight for the Quebec Conference and we are not going to let the British push us around. Give my warmest congratulations to Ike."[292] Did the Americans feel on the defensive? This reference is a clear indication that there was some dissention between the Western Allies. The issues on the table were 1) the tenuous situation in Italy, 2) the part that the Soviet Union would play in the Pacific War, 3) who would be named the commander for Overlord.[293]

By this time, Britain's war production was beginning to flag while the American Arsenal of Democracy was on the upswing. According to Stoler, Roosevelt's staff did a superior job in preparing for the conference compared to the British. This resulted in the United States presenting a united front that was so crucial to the maintenance of the wartime coalition.

At pre-conference meeting at Hyde Park, Hopkins played mediator and pressed FDR to fully support Churchill's policy to delay Operation Overlord until late May 1944 and to name an American to command the operation. Conversely, Hopkins was determined to ensure that Churchill would commit to the date; he wanted the Prime Minister and the President to have a meeting of the minds. Stimson warned Hopkins that the Prime Minister was still wary of a too-early invasion, fearing a devastating defeat. True to Hopkins' fears, at the first meeting of the CCOS at Quebec, the subject Overlord proved to be challenging. Churchill still believed that it was too dangerous and it was still too early. The Prime Minister's inability to commit to Overlord irritated Hopkins and while discussions were often heated, they did not become overtly adversarial. In the end, the American position prevailed and Churchill agreed to launch Overlord on May 1, 1944, with an American in command.[294] Churchill had agreed that command for Overlord would go to an American since U.S. troops would outnumber British troops by a considerable amount. The President and Hopkins supported George Marshall for this important post but others high in the administration and in the military thought that the general was too valuable in Washington to be given the post.

At the First Quebec Conference, Hopkins had access to a document (source unknown) that referred to Russia's position in the world after the war. With Germany defeated, the Soviet Union would be the most powerful force in Europe and the spread of Communism continued to be one of the great fears of the Western Allies. In addition, the United States needed the assistance of the Red Army to defeat Japan after Germany fell. The document that Hopkins read stated: "Since Russia is the decisive factor in the war, she must be given every assistance and every effort must be made to obtain her friendship. ... Finally, the most important factor the United States has to consider in relation to Russia is the prosecution of the war in the Pacific."[295] During the Conference, FDR received a promise from Stalin that the Soviets would join the Pacific War six months after the Germans surrendered.[296] For Roosevelt, this was a most critical issue to be settled, and it would carry over during all the summits, ending up on the agenda at Yalta. One wonders, however, what happened to the strategy behind the Europe First plan established at the Arcadia meeting in Washington. By 1943, neither Roosevelt nor Churchill were convinced that victory over Germany would lead to the capitulation of Japan. Because of this, FDR was adamant that Stalin would give the United States assurances that the Red Army would turn to the Pacific after Germany surrendered.

The absence of Stalin at these conferences proved to be troublesome. Hopkins was fully aware that Stalin and the Soviets would wield a great deal of power after the war ended. With the defeat of Germany, there would be no power strong enough, not even Great Britain, to oppose the forces of the USSR. Therefore, since the Soviets were the "decisive factor in the war," every effort should be made to ensure friendly relations with Stalin and with Russia. Hopkins recognized the validity of Soviet fear of Germany as a corridor for invasion and recommended that diplomatic relations would settle the problems even before victory. Roosevelt felt that he, himself, could establish a personal relationship with Stalin and that through the force of his own personality could solve any future problem of dominance. Hopkins disagreed; it would take more than personality to deal with Stalin. [297] Hopkins here had the advantage over his boss; he had already met with the Man of Steel.

FDR desperately wanted to talk to Stalin; it was important that they meet face to face. He had used this method with Churchill three years earlier when he sent Hopkins to set up a meeting, and this had positive consequences for the United States and Britain. The Atlantic Conference began the Special Relationship. This methodology reflected the President's commitment to personal diplomacy—his confidence in the power of his own personality. It certainly can be called arrogance but it also reflected a reliance on a very effective negotiating tool. Consequently, he suggested a tripartite conference of the "Big Three" to be held in utmost secrecy in about six weeks with Russia, Great Britain, and the United States. Stalin and Churchill both agreed with Roosevelt that a meeting of the three Allied leaders would be extremely helpful as a way to establish personal relationships while planning strategy for the rest of the war, and afterward. Hopkins was very much involved in this decision because he knew from personal experience how important such meetings could be. He also knew from his 1941 meeting with Stalin in Moscow that he was the only one who could make decisions, that he held all the power in the Soviet Union.[298]

FIRST CAIRO

The First Cairo Conference is important largely as a prelude to the planned Teheran Conference (Eureka), where the Big Three met for the first time.[299] Code-named Sextant, it had been planned in haste. Originally, it was to be a meeting between FDR and Stalin. Roosevelt had hoped to meet with the Soviet leader alone. He had planned the meeting without including Churchill. He wanted to lay the groundwork for what he hoped could be a personal relationship and get to know the man who controlled the USSR. When Churchill discovered that Roosevelt had invited only Stalin to the meeting, the Prime Minister was furious and bellowed that he would attend the summit even though he did not think it would be an important meeting. The Prime Minister was afraid that the United States was growing closer to the Soviet Union at the expense of Britain.

The main topic of conversation would be the Pacific Theater but when FDR invited Chinese leader Generalissimo Chiang Kai-shek, Churchill's rancor increased because he thoroughly disliked Chiang and did not regard China as a great power; he spent little time or energy on issues having to do with the Pacific War. Although originally Stalin was going to join the reluctant Churchill and the enthusiastic Roosevelt, he eventually refused the invitation when he heard the Chinese were to attend. The Soviet Union had signed a pact with Japan and Stalin did not want to interfere with the supposed neutrality of the Soviet Union in the Pacific War. On the other hand, the Chinese leader did not want to meet with Stalin; Chiang had been waging war against Mao Tse-tung and the Communists in China. So the conference included only Roosevelt and Churchill with Chiang in attendance. Churchill was pleased because he did want to meet with the President before they both sat down for this important meeting with Stalin in Teheran. When FDR then invited Molotov to the Cairo Conference to represent the Soviets, this did not sit well with Churchill who merely wanted a free and frank discussion by himself with the President. He planned on merely ignoring Chiang. The Prime Minister did not want any Russian interfering in the affairs of the Western Allies. So, as Averell Harriman explained, "the Chinese would go to Cairo without the Russians, and the Russians to Teheran without the Chinese."[300] Hopkins regarded Chiang as a weak leader and head of a corrupt government, this probably added some tension to the meeting.

Harry Hopkins' son, Sgt. Robert Hopkins, also attended the Cairo Conferences. He had again been invited by the President to attend as an official photographer. His diary reveals some of the intricacies of the conference. He made his way to Cairo through Tunis, North Africa, and met up with his father and the President on November 20, at a Kirk Villa aptly called "The White House." The party included General Marshall, General Eisenhower, General Spotts, Sir Charles Portal, Air Marshal Tedder, Admiral King and Admiral Leahy. The next day, Ike took the party on a tour of various sites involved in the North African campaign and then stopped for a picnic lunch. That evening they boarded two planes for the flight to Cairo. On the morning of the 22nd, the plane flew into Cairo over the Sahara, which was, according to young Hopkins, "the most bleak, God-forsaken landscape I have ever seen." This spectacle brought home to him the "terrific ordeal" that the troops must have endured in their march from El Alamein to Tunis. The first plane arrived at 7:10 am but the second one, the one that carried FDR and Hopkins, arrived later. It had come the long way, up the Nile so that the President could see the Valley of the Kings. While the wartime conferences involved tedious and uncomfortable and often dangerous air travel for the President, they also allowed him an opportunity to actually sightsee. The house assigned to the President had a direct view of the Pyramids and the Sphinx.[301]

Churchill and his entourage had arrived on the 21st and the Prime Minister invited the President to join him for a tour of the Pyramids. (Hopkins did not go because of an appointment.) The President later hosted a Thanksgiving party at his quarters on November 25th and served his guests a traditional American menu, turkey, cranberry sauce, pumpkin pie. His guests included Churchill and his daughter Sarah Oliver, Churchill's secretary John Martin, Averell Harriman, Elliot Roosevelt, Chip Bohlen, and others. The Chinese did not attend. During the meal there was some conversation as to who would command the cross-channel invasion planned for the following year. Harry Hopkins did not even know for sure who this would be but the names of Marshall and Eisenhower were high on the list. [302]

The meal was topped off by toasts from the President and the Prime Minister. The President told the guests the story of Thanksgiving in America, how it had spread from New England to the rest of the country; with so many American soldiers in every part of the world, it was now an international holiday. The President then addressed the Prime Minister and told him how gratified he was to share this holiday with him, a friend who had worked side-by-side during "their united struggle." Churchill's toast ("a masterpiece of eloquence and drama") began as usual with no notes, his voice rising and lowering at appropriate moments. According to Robert Hopkins, there came a point when Churchill was formulating a particularly complex sentence and seemed to come to a point where he could not finish it. He remained silent for two full minutes, to the discomfort of many at the table. Then, 'with the flair of a magician, Churchill drew from his extraordinary memory, the only word in the English language to fit so precisely in this sentence. It seemed to have been chiseled from crystal to fit this particular situation. There was an audible sigh of relief from the listeners who had held their breath in concern." At the end of Churchill's speech, Robert heard the President say, "This is the happiest moment of my life." Harry Hopkins had arranged for the army band to play after dinner and discouraged any in the party from talking business. The band took requests. The Prime Minister was partial to martial music while the President preferred songs from the 1890s. Eden requested Noel Coward's "Let's Not Be Beastly to the Germans," but the band understandably didn't know it. It seems that all these leaders, in the midst of war and with so much on their minds, were actually jovial by the time the dinner broke up at 12:30 a.m.[303] Clearly the Western Alliance was secure on this particular Thanksgiving in Cairo.

The primary topic of discussion at Cairo was the Pacific Theater. With America's entrance into the war after the Japanese bombing of Pearl Harbor, China's position in the international chess game rose in importance. The nation now had a strong ally against Japan, which had invaded China in 1937. China, Asia's largest landmass, had 450 million troops that had for seven years kept one million Japanese at bay while the Allies concentrated on the European Theater. However, China's leader, Generalissimo Chiang Kai-shek, had a different wartime agenda than either FDR or Churchill. While the Western Allies focused their attention on the European Front and saw China's role as merely holding off the Japanese until the Allies defeated Germany and not of primary importance, Chiang wanted China to be the main stage. This, of course, was not at all compatible with Anglo-American strategy. To make matters worse there was a real lack of cultural understanding between the Chinese and the Americans. FDR felt that China was backward, that the government was dishonest and that the military was badly managed. He had good reason for these opinions. However, Chiang's Nationalist Kuomintang armies had been fighting both the Japanese and the Communist Mao Tse-tung's rebel army. In January 1942 FDR sent General Joseph Stilwell (Vinegar Joe) to China as his personal representative and his reports back to the President reflected his belief that Chiang was more concerned with fighting the Communists than fighting the Japanese. With Chiang asking for more U.S. aid in the form of Lend Lease munitions, this presented a problem. The fear was the Chiang was stockpiling weapons to be used against Mao after the war. Chiang did not trust Stilwell, Stilwell had no respect for the Chinese, and FDR did not trust Chiang. When Chiang requested that Harry Hopkins replace Stilwell, believing him to be more of a friend of China than Stilwell, FDR, although he recognized the problem, refused; he needed Hopkins in the European Theater. Instead, President Roosevelt sent Lauchlin Currie, one of his economic advisors, to China, along with Wendell Willkie. Currie had a dim view of Chiang's leadership and even his trustworthiness while Willkie thought Chiang to be a strong leader.[304]

'Vinegar' Joe Stilwell was thoroughly familiar with China and was eminently qualified for the appointment, militarily. However, the personalities of Chiang and Stilwell., who remained in China, clashed to a dangerous degree. With disagreement over military strategy, the situation worsened. Britain entered in the fray over the debate on how to re-open the Burma Road[305] (Burma was still a British colony), relighting old animosity and mutual distrust between China and Great Britain. Churchill saw no need to expend Allied energy here, much to the anger of Chiang. In addition, Chiang resented the fact that China had not received its fair share of Lend Lease equipment. This complicated his regard for Hopkins. There was also a good deal of conflict over the use of air power. Chiang wholeheartedly supported Claire Chennault's Flying Tigers, composed of American volunteers, as an important defense while Stilwell felt that air power was useless as long as ground forces were available. Even more divisive, Chiang refused to use the Chinese

Communist forces to fight the Japanese and used his own military to fight against the growth of communism, seen as the greater enemy, troops that could have been used against the Japanese.

Despite his lack of confidence in the Chinese and their leader, FDR succumbed to his penchant for face-to-face deliberation and he was the one who invited Chiang to the Cairo Conference. Chiang wanted to convince FDR to take China seriously; he wanted a seat at the negotiating table but he had never been out of East Asia, did not speak English, and had little knowledge of the workings of western governments. Americans, likewise, had little knowledge of Chiang or the Chinese. Earlier, Willkie, who supported Chiang, had suggested that Mme. Chiang Kai-shek visit the United States on a good will tour to encourage FDR to change his priorities and abandon the Europe First policy, or at least recognize her husband's legitimacy as an ally. The very attractive Soong Mei-ling spoke English fluently and had been educated at Wellesley College. The first lady of China found a friend in Harry Hopkins who recognized that, despite its leadership failings, China was strategically important in the fight against Japan. When Mme. Chiang made plans for her U.S. tour in late 1942, Hopkins helped manage the trip. Both Roosevelt and Churchill approved. Madame Chiang Kai-shek told Hopkins that the Chinese did not really trust the U. S. when it came to the Japanese; she said that the Americans needed to defeat Japan before Germany, and she warned him that morale was low in China, because the people were critical of the Allies in general. Moreover, she admitted, probably unnecessarily, that she didn't like Stilwell.[306] Hopkins understood the situation and remained diplomatically polite.

As for the British, the Prime Minister felt that China was not fighting hard enough against the Japanese and that Chiang was merely a lightweight. Knowing this, Mme. Chiang pled her case to Roosevelt through Hopkins. She insisted that Chiang did have control over the government and the military and that China deserved a place at the negotiating table with the rest of the Allies. Hopkins urged FDR to meet with Mme. Chiang even though he also had suspicions that the Chinese were doing less than their best against Japan. He also knew that Chiang had little interest in any struggle outside of China. Still, a strong China in the postwar era could be a counterbalance against the spread of communism. Therefore, Hopkins emphasized to the President that China could play a crucial part in Allied war strategy. Chinese officials appealed to him when they needed war materials and used him as a liaison with the President. Just as he had understood that the Allies needed Stalin's cooperation to defeat Germany, no matter how reprehensible the dictator was, he knew that China was holding off the Japanese, even if the government was corrupt and the military in disarray. In April 1942, General Marshall sent General Stilwell a message in which he referred to the "incompetence" of the Chinese troops and their "disregard of orders." He further accused them of cowardice in battle. The message made it clear that Stilwell was on his way to Chungking to have a "'show-down' with the high command."[307]

If Chiang did not carry a lot of weight with the American public, Mme. Chiang did. Washington, D.C., she made powerful speech on behalf of Pacific War. If she impressed the public, she did not sway the President who was committed to the Europe First policy. Still, she hoped to change the president's mind and had long talks with Hopkins re shipment of planes and her plans for China after the war. She wanted China to be at the peace table. Recognizing the influence that Hopkins wielded, she was anxious for Hopkins to visit China but he demurred graciously and said that he saw no real reason for him to go.[308]

Hopkins took his son Robert to meet Madame Chiang Kai-shek on the afternoon of November 26th and Robert was charmed by her attentiveness and ease. Robert, of course, had no knowledge of the conversations that had taken place around the conference table or of the often-acrimonious debates that went on over military strategy in the Pacific.[309]

The discussion at the conference centered on issues relative to China-Burma-India (CBI). Churchill did not think that opening the Burma Road was very important while Chiang felt it to be crucial to the war effort. Churchill and even FDR were very suspicious that Chiang was holding back Lend Lease supplies to use against the Chinese Communists after the war ended and not using them to fight the Japanese. General Marshall even questioned how vital the Chinese actually were in winning the war in the Pacific now that our strategy had changed from using China to hold back the Japanese to island hopping. On another level, many of those present at the conference resented the presence of Madame Chiang, who acted as interpreter for her husband. She had no official position and some thought that the presence of an alluring woman at such an important conference was distracting.[310] All of this disturbed Chiang who had to take something substantial back to his nation to demonstrate that China had a place in the coalition. His reputation was at stake. He even threatened to pull his troops out if he did not get a commitment from the Western Allies to the Burma Road campaign. It was an idle threat. The Prime Minister did not think that China should be treated as a big power and regarded any interaction with Chiang as a waste of his time.[311] Roosevelt, however, knew that China would likely emerge as a world power after the war as a stabilizing force in Asia. Churchill disagreed and, therefore, believed that no effort should be made to retake the Burma Road.[312]

During the Conference, Hopkins met Charles (Chip) Bohlen whom Harriman had just brought from the Moscow Embassy. Hopkins wanted to pick his brain as to what he had learned during his time in Moscow. The two struck up a friendship and later Hopkins recommended that Roosevelt appoint Bohlen to a position in Washington as a liaison with the state department.[313] Cordell Hull resigned as secretary of state in November 1944 and Edward Stettinius took his place. Hopkins now had "a twin power base from which to pursue his role as the President's prime alliance agent and was the one senior figure who could rise above departmental divisions."[314]

There has been a lot of scholarly debate as to the significance of this conference. Sherwood argues "the effects of these meetings on the progress of the war on history was negligible." The summit in Teheran, which immediately followed Cairo, had far more import.[315] The Cairo Conference might even be called a failure because it interfered with the planning of Overlord and with the overarching need to commit men and munitions to the upcoming invasion of France. The political confusion that emerged as a result of this conference led to problems that the next President would have to face.

Lord Moran wrote in his diary that he met Hopkins on November 25 and "found him full of sneers and jibes." Hopkins made it clear if Churchill continued to push for the Italian campaign and postpone Overlord, "the Americans will support the Russians." Certainly, Hopkins was influenced by Marshall in this approach and there probably was some "hardening of purpose in the American camp," as Lord Moran suggests in his diary. But Hopkins also was aware of Churchill's dread of the consequences of an unsuccessful invasion of France. To Moran, Hopkins seemed to think that Churchill was backing out of his commitment. Hopkins snarled, "Some of us are beginning to wonder whether the invasion will ever come off." "Sure, you're not going to tell me that Winston has cold feet," he snapped to Moran. The Prime Minister's brooding threatened to damage his friendship with Hopkins and fuel dissention with the President as well. Roosevelt understood Churchill's reservation about Overlord but he also listened to his advisers. He sought a compromise and Hopkins helped to find one. If the Allies did not have sufficient forces to launch Overlord then operations in the Mediterranean would weaken the Germans until the forces are built up. The P.M. agreed. The difficulty Hopkins faced here was that to the Americans, Churchill was "explosive and obstreperous." Roosevelt was wavering. Hopkins knew that there would be battle at the Teheran Conference because of the tension generated at Cairo. It would be his job to keep things from exploding. Hopkins was dealing with the British as

Roosevelt's man; he was speaking for the President when dealing with a difficult Prime Minister. This was probably for the best because, as he said, one can "never be sure what will happen when Winston and the President get together." [316]

About a week after the Cairo Conference ended, President Roosevelt put General Eisenhower in command of Operation Overlord. Churchill agreed with this appointment. "I am all for President announcing Ike as proposed and that His Majesty's Government will nominate the new Allied Supreme Commander in the Mediterranean. ... I should like however to announce at the same time Montgomery to command British Home Forces and Alexander to command the Allied Armies in Italy."[317] Roosevelt gave Hopkins the unhappy job of telling Marshall the news. The General, who had expected this appointment would be his, was sorely disappointed, but like a true soldier, accepted the fact that FDR needed him in D.C.

By late 1943, China had become less important to the Allied effort; the Pacific strategy changed after the First Quebec Conference in August of that year. And when later at the Teheran Conference in December Stalin promised to bring Soviet troops into the Pacific to help defeat the Japanese, China's position became even less important. This strengthened Chiang's resolve not to use the Chinese Communists to fight the Japanese; in his opinion they were not needed. Historian Ronald Heiferman asserts that FDR and Chiang were basically "incompatible" and much of the difficulty between the two leaders emanated from a lack of understanding of the other's culture. However, disagreements over strategy and structure only exacerbated an already serious problem.[318]

The Cairo Conference did not accomplish much and, according to Churchill, was just a waste of time. There was still a deep rift between the western leaders over the timing of Overlord. The British argued that there had to be some flexibility as the situation changed. Churchill wanted to be able to change plans and strike when the circumstances were most favorable and not be tied down to any strict timetable. Furthermore, he did not want to sacrifice troops fighting in the Mediterranean in order to set an early date for Overlord. The Americans, on the other hand, wanted a firm date set in order to be able to assure Stalin of Allied support with a definite date for the cross-channel invasion.[319] This divisiveness continued into the year and it set the stage for the complications that would emerge at Teheran. Robert Sherwood describes the nature of the interaction among the Allied leaders at the first meeting of the Big Three:

> ... here were Titans determining the future course of an entire planet. This was indeed the Big Three. Churchill employed all the debater's arts, the brilliant locutions and circumlocutions, of which he was a master, and Stalin wielded his bludgeon with relentless indifference to all the dodges and feints of his practiced adversary; while Roosevelt sat in the middle, by common consent the moderator, arbitrator, and final authority. His contributions to the conversation were infrequent and sometimes annoyingly irrelevant, but it appears time and again—at Teheran and at Yalta—that it was he who spoke the last word.[320]

During the war years Hopkins used his influence with Churchill to sometimes redirect the Prime Minister's anger. In late 1943, five U.S. senators made a tour of various military bases and accused Great Britain of using equipment to further their own ends in the Empire. The infuriated Prime Minister drafted a speech to the House of Commons in which he excoriated the American politicians and asked Hopkins to show it to the President; he was used to using Hopkins as his own personal ambassador. Hopkins did show it to the President but also warned Churchill that 'It would be unwise to mention five Senators. ... [Their] backstage talk will get less attention during the coming week but you will get much more of the same thing from unfriendly or misinformed people over here. Would it not be better to postpone the statement for a week or more in order not to put yourself in the position of answering these particular Senators." Hopkins added in a telegram 10/15/43, "Anything that has been said by the five Senators is rapidly getting off the front pages by the inexorable events of the war," and suggested that he wait to respond.[321] Churchill, grateful for guidance from his friend was able to "gracefully duck" questions put to him by MPs on the issue by echoing Hopkins' advice: "There would be no advantage in this government taking part in this wordy warfare" during a crucial time in the war when the Allies are fighting "shoulder to shoulder." [322] Hopkins used three steps to prevent Churchill from taking a misstep: first he would calm the PM down, then he would recommend moderation in his reaction to something or other that had upset him, and lastly he would send an "educative note."[323]

TEHERAN CONFERENCE

The Teheran Conference (Eureka) took place just after Cairo, from November 28 to December 1, 1943. At this historic meeting of three Allied leaders, Churchill, Roosevelt, and Stalin made decisions as to military strategy that remained in place for the duration of the war. The Big Three finally committed to the date for Operation Overlord: May 1944. This summit proved to be contentious largely because of the different personalities and wartime goals of the three as well as the jealousy and distrust each had for the other. In addition, the city was fraught with rumors of assassination plots.

Hopkins and his son, Robert, had flown in on November 27, 1943, and both were taken to the Russian compound where FDR was staying as a matter of security; there had been reports of possible attacks by Nazi agents on the Allied leaders and their entourage. The fact that Hopkins and FDR were quartered in the Soviet Embassy piqued the Prime Minister. The British were quartered a good distance away. He was further irritated when the President met alone with Stalin the following afternoon. Although this impromptu meeting was informal and there were no photographs taken, Churchill felt that he had been insulted. He felt that he was becoming the junior member of the triumvirate. For the Big Three the stakes were unimaginably high and feelings were easily hurt. Hopkins had his work cut out for him in keeping tempers on an even keel. He had to call on his years of experience in Washington to deal with, not only two "prima donnas," but with a dictator who saw no need to compromise and who had little in common with

American ideals or with western foreign policy. His only objective for this meeting was to ensure an early date for Overlord from allies who were too cautious and whose goals were murky.

On their way to their rooms, Robert Hopkins asked his father, "Why are we dealing with the Russians? Russia is a dictatorship and we are a democracy. They don't share our concept of freedom and justice." Hopkins replied, "We're helping them because they are holding down 95 Nazi divisions. Without our help to the Russians, the Nazis would be victorious and they would turn those 95 divisions against us. That's why we're dealing with them."[324] Hopkins knew that the expansion of Communism in Europe after the war was a real danger and he did not minimize the ruthlessness of Stalin. He had seen it first hand in Moscow. But he was also fully aware of not only of the power of the Red Army but of the absolute power that the Man of Steel had over his country. The Allies had to negotiate as partners in a war that was yet to be won.

From 1942 through 1943, the Red Army had suffered enormous casualties while holding off the Germans. The Western Allies knew it was crucial for Britain and America to support the Soviets and, especially, to assure Stalin that they stood beside him; the possibility of a separate peace between Russia and Germany always loomed large. Anglo-American assistance and cooperation with the Communists did not sit at all well with Churchill although the Prime Minister did recognize the strategic necessity for such a wartime coalition. Roosevelt, while he was not naïve about the threat posed by the Soviet Union in post war Europe, believed that a personal approach to Stalin would allow him to control the dictator after the Axis Powers were defeated. Hopkins told Lord Moran that Roosevelt could never convert Stalin to democracy but FDR had great faith in his charm and charisma; he had "spent his life managing men, and Stalin could not be so very different from other people, so could come to terms with him."[325] In addition, it was obvious by this time that Britain's power was waning. Roosevelt and Churchill disagreed over the timing of Overlord; over the need for Anvil, the southern France operation; and over the Mediterranean campaign.[326] This could prove dangerous for the Western Allies. Hopkins well understood the problems inherent in coalition warfare. Even though he was not a military strategist was awfully good at keeping peace within the coalition.

Hopkins was the only one that FDR conferred with before the sessions at Teheran. As in most of the conferences, Hopkins stood in the background but Roosevelt always had his ear tilted toward his advisor. The President knew that although Stalin was an extremely powerful and callous dictator, the United States needed to have the Soviet leader on our side, for the time being at least. According to historian Keith Eubank, the fact that the President relied entirely on Hopkins' advice and received no briefing from the State Department, made this conference "unique."[327] Hopkins understood the tension that was building up between the President and the Prime Minister. Churchill felt that Roosevelt and Stalin were "double-teaming" him. Hopkins had to draw on all his skills to ensure that there would be no permanent rift between them; cooperation between the western powers acted as a balance against the military power of the Soviet Union.

Stalin trusted Hopkins as a result of their meeting in July 1941 and because Hopkins made good on his promise to send Russia much needed Lend Lease munitions. Still, the dictator was suspicious of the Western Allies because of the confusing delay over the Second Front. He felt that the U. S. and Britain wanted to delay the invasion and weaken the Soviet Union. The President wanted to allay the fears of his powerful Russian ally. Hopkins was an asset here. When Stalin greeted Hopkins at Teheran, Averell Harriman noted "he displayed more open and warm cordiality than he had been known to show to any foreigner."[328]

An indication of the relationship among the Big Three when they met for the first time at Teheran is an anecdote that Molotov's editor, Felix Chuev, related to the foreign minister:

At the Teheran conference Roosevelt and Churchill got tired of Stalin constantly pressing them about his proposals. They decided to trick him. In the morning before the regular session Churchill said, 'I had a dream that I became ruler of the world!' "And I dreamt," Roosevelt said, 'that I became Master of the Universe! And what did you dream of, Marshal Stalin?' 'I dreamt,' Stalin casually replied, 'that I didn't confirm either of them."[329]

This was a rare exhibition of Stalinist humor but also had a tinge of animosity toward FDR and Churchill.

On the evening of the 29th, a large dinner party took place to celebrate Churchill's sixty-ninth birthday. FDR made a congratulatory toast to the Prime Minister, and then Stalin made a long and congratulatory toast to the United States, a nation capable of turning out 10,000 planes a month, many more than Great Britain or the USSR. An irritated Churchill was unable to contain himself. He stood and interrupted Stalin, rattling off figures of British war production exceeding anything that Russia could produce. Stalin did not react but merely went on to claim that if it had not been for American Lend Lease equipment, Russia would have lost the war long ago. Then Stalin turned on Sir Alan Brooke claiming that he was unfriendly to the Red Army. It seemed to Robert Hopkins, who attended the dinner, that Stalin was deliberately trying to provoke the Prime Minister.[330]

Hopkins played a role "of paramount influence on Roosevelt" at the Teheran Conference, probably more than at any other conference. He knew that it was the President's intention to establish a personal relationship with Stalin; it was FDR's style, one that Hopkins was very familiar with. The President wanted to understand, and be understood by, Stalin. Teheran is where he planned to do this. Hopkins kept the President constantly informed, rarely leaving his side, bringing him as much information as he could garner. Stalin admired Hopkins' candor and forthrightness.[331] Cadogan remarked that Hopkins seemed to be the only member of the American delegation who acted with practicality and effectiveness, "even if his methods are a trifle unorthodox." At the Teheran Conference, Hopkins had to use every bit of his Washington experience to help him deal with a dictator whose approach to foreign policy was very different, who had no desire to compromise, and had no apparent moral compass.[332] Plans for the continuation of the war in Europe took center stage. Hopkins feared that Churchill would again try to delay the Second Front and continue to insist that the Allies focus on the Middle East. Hopkins believed that the Battle of the Atlantic was most important and that the British were expending valuable resources in the Mediterranean, which was a losing battle. The President wholly agreed.[333] When the Foreign Ministers met, Hopkins stood in for Cordell Hull and had to deal with Molotov (whose agenda was clearly the same as Stalin's) and Eden, who argued that Turkey should be encouraged to enter into the war on the side of the Allies. Hopkins insisted that plans for the Second Front had been set for May '44 and should not be changed. Stalin had threatened that if the invasion did not happen in May, the Red Army would not be able to continue. In supporting Stalin, Hopkins knew he was relating the President's policy here at the expense of the Prime Minister. Any planned action in the Mediterranean, which Churchill insisted upon, would merely divert necessary war materials from the cross-channel invasion.[334]

Despite blowback from Churchill, Operation Overlord was scheduled and, even though the Prime Minister feared for the loss of Allied lives, he accepted the decision. Churchill used Hopkins as an intermediary when he wanted to "correct" FDR. In a telegram to Hopkins in early February 1944, the Prime Minister writes, "I would be glad if you would put these points on nomenclature to the President when convenient." He goes on the say that the object of Overlord is the liberation of Europe. The Allies are not invading.

The word 'invasion' must be reserved for the time when we cross the German frontier. There is no need for us to make a present to Hitler of the idea that he is the defender of Europe which we are seeking to invade. He is a tyrant and an ogre from whom we are going to free the captive nations.[335]

Churchill had finally agreed to Operation Overlord for May 1944 but he was adamant that the terms used in the directives should reflect the real nature of the conflict. The President agreed to use the word "invasion" only to refer to the crossing of German borders. European operations would be described as "enter[ing] for the liberation of Europe."[336] Stalin agreed to launch an offensive against Japan once Germany was defeated. Each of the three Allied leaders recognized the contributions that Hopkins made to the war effort. At one of the dinners Churchill asked Roosevelt and Stalin to join him in a toast to Hopkins. FDR quietly said, "Dear Harry, what would we do without you?"[337] demonstrating the warmth of his relationship with the President.

Immediately after the Teheran conference, Hopkins entered the Naval hospital and remained too ill to continue his work. For seven months he left FDR's inner circle. The timing here was crucial. Victory was imminent and the Allies began making plans for the postwar world. According to Stoler, it was clear that America and Roosevelt would be able to dictate the terms of any arrangement. However, Stalin still had chips to play and the Allied victories after the Teheran Conference gave him confidence as to his bargaining position.[338]

Chip Bohlen remarked that at Teheran, Hopkins acted as "a paramount influence on Roosevelt." As Cadogan noted that Hopkins seemed to be "the only practical and more or less effective member of the [American] entourage, even if his methods are a trifle unorthodox ... his language is refreshingly emphatic." Hopkins position, however, was difficult for as Fenby writes, he was "dealing with a dictator who saw no reason to compromise and for whom the moralism and legalism which infused the American approach to foreign policy meant nothing."[339]

SECOND QUEBEC – OCTAGON

By the end of 1943, the entire Hopkins family was involved in the war in one capacity of the other. Just about everyone knew that Harry Hopkins was either at FDR's side counseling him or acting as the President's personal envoy far afield or recovering in a hospital. His first wife, Ethel Gross Hopkins, the mother of his three boys, was working with the American Red Cross. His eldest son, David, had joined the Navy and was assigned as Lieutenant JG to the aircraft carrier *Essex*. His middle son, Robert, was in the Army Signal Corps participating in and taking photos of the European battles. The youngest son, Stephen, joined the Marines just after he graduated from high school in 1943. He trained at Parris Island and was quickly sent to the Pacific Theater. He was killed February 2, 1944 on the island of Kwajalein in the Marshall Islands. He had just turned 18 and it was the first time he had seen action. The family was devastated but took solace in the fact that, according to those who were there, he had died bravely. Hopkins was in the

Naval Hospital when he got the news of Stephen's death. He then went to Miami to recuperate. Churchill understood Hopkins' grief. He recognized that his friend must have felt guilt at not having spent more time with his children and also guilt that decisions made because of his reports might have precipitated his son's death. The Prime Minister sent Hopkins a scroll, written in beautiful calligraphy, with a quote from Shakespeare's *Macbeth*:

Stephen Peter Hopkins
Age 18
To Harry Hopkins From Winston S. Churchill
13 February, 1944

Your son, my Lord, has paid a soldier's debt;
He only liv'd but till he was a man;
The which no sooner had his prowess confirm'd
In the unshrinking station where he fought,
But like a man he died.

Shakespeare[340]

In March Hopkins had had exploratory surgery at the Mayo Clinic and while the doctors found no recurrence of cancer, he had lost a good deal of weight (down to 133 lbs.). Halifax wrote to the Prime Minister that when he visited Hopkins, "he struck me as rather shrunk and frail though just like himself and gay till he got a little tired."[341]

After six months convalescing at Ashford General Hospital at Sulphur Springs, Hopkins returned to Washington. Sherwood wonders if the relationship between Roosevelt and Hopkins had actually weakened. Did FDR lose confidence in his friend because he had been sick so often and not available to him for advice and direction?[342] Certainly FDR had come to rely on Hopkins' constant counsel and utter willingness to undertake any mission the President might assign to him. In the absence of this, it might seem reasonable to presume that the friendship might waver. However, one must wonder if a President of the United States can really have friends in the same way "ordinary" people do. It is probably not possible. Despite their closeness, Hopkins always maintained a formal relationship with his boss; he might have voiced disagreements with him but he always addressed him with respect.

There is no doubt that Hopkins' health was continuing to decline. (He was only 54 years old but looked much older.) However, if Hopkins was not constantly at FDR's side in the physical sense, he remained his friend throughout his illnesses and hospital stays. Their correspondence reflects the President's concern for his friend's welfare and he kept abreast of his progress back to health. This would never happen, of course, but the bond that held these two together was never completely broken. The President still needed Hopkins' advice and support.

Hopkins was away from Washington for six months, and the Prime Minister also kept careful track of his health. Throughout most of April 1944, much of the correspondence concerned Hopkins' health. On July 6, 1944, Hopkins sent a telegram to the Prime Minister: "I am back in Washington feeling ever so much better." Churchill obviously missed his friend, missed the ability to get messages to the President through him. In an answering telegram on July 19, the Prime

Minister wrote he was "delighted" to hear that Hopkins had recovered enough to return to D.C.

> I greatly needed to say some things through you which are of importance. ... Although we look like winning the War a most formidable set of problems is approaching us from every side, and personally I do not feel that anything but duty would make me encounter them. Our affairs are getting into a most tangled condition. We have to deal with the affairs of a dozen States, some of which have several civil wars brewing and anyhow are split from top to bottom, by means of the concerted action of three great powers or four if you still include China, every one of which approaches the topic from a different angle and in a different mood. ... Our affairs are getting into a most tangled condition.[343]

The timing here was crucial, and Churchill's temperament reflected the disquiet that permeated the Alliance. It also reflected his reliance on Hopkins for balance. Hopkins wrote the Prime Minister on July 20, "The war seems to be going extremely well and I think we have Heine Hitler really on the run."[344] Was Hopkins merely buoying up a clearly morose Prime Minister or did he have a very different perspective of the outcome of the war? It does seem that Hopkins' optimism was still intact.

During, 1944, an election year for the United States, the Allies were debating the strategies relative to the attacks on southern France that would support the invasion across the channel from England. The Western Allies planned the

Second Quebec Conference (Octagon) for September 12-16, 1944, to firm up these plans. They had every reason to believe that victory was at hand in the European Theater and there was also good news from the Pacific Theater. Hopkins apparently had not recovered sufficiently to attend this conference, the only major conference he did not attend. It was only at the last minute that Hopkins wired Churchill telling him he would be unable to go to Quebec due to ill health. "I will not run the risk of a setback in health by attempting to fight the battle of Quebec on the Plains of Abraham where better men than I have been killed."[345] This worried the Prime Minister who relied on Hopkins as a stabilizing influence for the Allies. Churchill was extremely disappointed and blamed the failure of the conference on his absence. The system that their relationship began seemed to be faltering due to Hopkins' illness.

In the 1940, air travel was often rigorous and uncomfortable. Hopkins' illness only increased the difficulty he had in traveling, especially by air. An article in a Virginia newspaper in 1942 reflects this:

> Harry Hopkins' record in administering relief during the depression years did not impress the nation, but Harry Hopkins' work during the war will be found of a different and higher level. The plain truth is that Hopkins is an ill man. He knows it. Frequently he has to slip away from the White House for a day or two and get blood transfusions. Then he comes back, and though he scarcely is able to keep on his feet, he is deep in his duties as chief of lease-lend. At that post, believe it or not, he is displaying much sagacity.

Those who most deserve his support are getting it wholeheartedly.

Now Hopkins has gone once more to London—this time by bomber and doubtless on the 'straight-away.' That is a severe ordeal for a man in perfect health and with flesh enough to keep him from feeling the extreme cold of a flight at more than 20,000 feet. Often strong men have to take oxygen as they speed through the cold, thin air four or five miles above the sea. To Hopkins, thin and bloodless as he is, the flight must have been literally so many hours in hell ...

You may not like his former administration and you may not have forgotten the bitterness of his tongue during the days when he was dictator of relief expenditures; but you have to take off your hat to him now for as fine a display of persistent, day-to-day courage as this was has offered in America."[346]

Historian David Roll suggests that Roosevelt did not invite Hopkins to the Second Quebec Conference, because their friendship was beginning to fray. Whether Hopkins did not attend because he was ill or because the President felt he no longer needed his counsel is debatable. Harbutt argues that Hopkins suffered from Presidential disfavor rather than illness. There is no question that Hopkins was very sick; he had been so since 1937. He was in the Naval Hospital from August 26 to September 13, 1943 and again from January 5 to February 11, 1944. He stayed at the Mayo Clinic in Rochester, Minnesota, from March 9 to May 7, 1944. He learned of Overlord from his hospital bed. It is likely true that FDR resented his absence, having been so reliant on him in the past. Whether this indicated that Hopkins had lost the support and confidence of the President is debatable, however. Hopkins returned to Washington in time for the Fourth of July 1944. The relationship, if it actually suffered from a rift, would soon heal, however, for Hopkins played a key role for the President at the Yalta Conference. FDR was, of course, also ill.

Churchill believed that illness was merely a rather lame excuse for Hopkins to miss the conference. A debilitated Hopkins surely would have wanted to avoid air travel. Churchill noted this and wrote of this time, "It was remarkable how definitely my contacts with the President improved and our affairs moved quicker as Hopkins appeared to regain influence. In two days, it seemed to be like old times." Christopher O'Sullivan writes that Hopkins had reclaimed his alliance with the President before Yalta, indicating that there had been a rift. But, although Hopkins' illness did at times limit the times that Hopkins could be at FDR's side, there was never a time when the President did not rely on his advice and counsel. [347]

There was set agenda and the Second Quebec Conference certainly did not go as smoothly as it might have if Hopkins had had a hand in its organization. When the issue of the imminent German surrender came up, Secretary of the Treasury Henry Morgenthau presented his plan to level the entire country, strip it of its industrial centers, and send it back to the feudal era. Here, at this conference that the President, absent the counsel of Hopkins, made the mistake of signing off on the extremely controversial and radical Morgenthau Plan. The President was probably not thinking clearly when he initialed it. Had Hopkins been there, this would have never happened. Churchill looked to a strong and friendly Germany as a bulwark against communism in postwar Europe.[348] FDR soon realized his mistake; he eschewed the Morgenthau Plan and recognized how much he really did need Hopkins who surely would have prevented him from approving the document that Morgenthau presented to him. According to Stoler, both Roosevelt and Churchill concluded that Germany might present a real menace to European peace but would also be necessary for postwar economic health. The United States State and War Departments and the British Foreign Office objected strongly to the decision at Quebec to "pastoralize" Germany and no final decision was made at Octagon or at Yalta.[349] FDR later regretted he had not just insisted that Hopkins attend the conference. He knew that his friend had been ill before but never opted out of a conference just because of his health.[350] According to Fraser Harbutt, Churchill wanted to pastoralize Germany for economic reasons; trade would devolve to Great Britain with Germany's collapse. With Hopkins absent, Morgenthau seems to have been dominant.

For Hopkins the war had always been personal and he was well aware of the lives that had been sacrificed—one of them was his young son— and still more soldiers would be lost. For him victory was the answer. The war was not merely statistics on a report or a subject to be debated around a conference table. The work he and all those involved in strategy decisions had consequences for all families touched by this devastating world war. Hopkins was proud that his boys were doing their duty. Robert volunteered to join the D-Day landings in order to take photos but was distressed when he discovered that he would not be allowed to go in the first wave. Hopkins wrote a letter to Eisenhower: "I hope you will let Robert go on the invasion whenever it comes off. I am fearful—and I am sure Robert is too—that because one of my other boys had some bad luck in the Pacific that Robert's C.O. may be a little hesitant about putting him in. The war is 'for keeps' and I want so much to have all of my boys where the going is rough."[351]

Chapter 8—Yalta

"We have learned the simple truth, as Emerson said, that the only way to have a friend is to be one."
-Franklin Roosevelt's Fourth Inaugural Speech, January 20, 1945.

In the aftermath of the Teheran Conference, Hopkins' health kept him from participating fully in the war effort. He was hospitalized during early 1944 and the doctors at Mayo Clinic considered his physical condition to be precarious. He was clearly unable to function at his normal frenetic level at FDR's side. He underwent another surgery and seven weeks later he retired to White Sulphur Springs, where he convalesced at the Army's Ashford General Hospital. The President missed him and clearly understood how important Hopkins was to his administration's war efforts; he needed him healthy and pled with him to stay until he was well enough to return. Churchill also hoped that Hopkins would be back in good health. The PM wrote a note 2/28/45 to Hopkins: "Please take every care. You are needed so much." [352]

Churchill expressed a need to meet with Stalin in order to discuss post-war policies having to do with southeastern Europe. By this time, although the British had a strong presence in Greece, Russia had occupied Finland and Bulgaria as well as Poland and the Baltic states. This worried

Churchill; he needed to talk with Stalin. But FDR was in the middle of a Presidential campaign—his fourth—and couldn't leave the States. Therefore, Churchill (who didn't think that the Soviet leader would wait until the American elections were over) and Eden went to Moscow to meet with Stalin and Molotov in order to discuss post-war spheres of influence: the Tolstoy Meeting. Hopkins felt that there should be an American there and wanted FDR to make it very clear that any decision made between Churchill and Stalin would not be validated by the US until the three nations conferenced together. When Hopkins found out that FDR had cabled Churchill saying that he would let the Prime Minister speak for the United States, Hopkins was aghast. It was a terrible mistake. He took it upon himself to stop the transmission of that message to Stalin from the Map Room; he immediately told the President what he had done and why. The President quickly realized that Hopkins was right and that he had almost made a serious mistake. FDR and Hopkins then redrafted a message to Stalin stating that he hoped that there would be no bi-lateral meeting with Churchill and that it was vital that the three leaders meet together. The President reiterated that only all three could determine the answers to global problems.[353] "I choose to consider your forthcoming talks with Mr. Churchill merely as preliminary to a conference of the three of us which can take place ... any time after our national election."[354]

Consequently, since Hopkins was sick, FDR sent Averell Harriman to Moscow to attend as a U.S. observer to the Tolstoy Meeting but not as a participant. He would not commit the U. S. government to any policy that might be discussed by the Stalin and Churchill. At this Moscow meeting, Churchill and Stalin came to an agreement on postwar spheres of influence in the immediate aftermath of the war, the infamous "percentages agreement." During this meeting in Moscow (Tolstoy), October 9-17, 1944, Stalin and Churchill seemed to collude to establish spheres of influence and divide up postwar Europe. This became known as the extremely devious Percentages Agreement: Churchill wrote in his memoirs re the October 1944 meeting with Stalin in Moscow:

> Let us settle about our affairs in the Balkans. Your armies are in Rumania and Bulgaria. We have interests, missions, and agents there. Don't let us get at cross purposes in small ways. So far as Britain and Russia are concerned, how would it do for you to have ninety per cent predominance in Rumania, for us to have ninety percent of the say in Greece, and go fifty-fifty about Yugoslavia?' While this was being translated I wrote out on a half-sheet of paper
>
> | | |
> |---|---|
> | Rumania | |
> | Russia | 90% |
> | The others | 10% |
> | Greece | |
> | Great Britain | 90% |
> | (in accord with the United States) | |
> | Russia | 10% |
> | Yugoslavia | 50-50% |
> | Hungary | 50-50% |
> | Bulgaria | |

Russia	75%
The others	25%

I pushed this across to Stalin, who by then had heard the translation. There was a slight pause. Then he took his blue pencil and made a large tick upon it, and passed it back to us. It was all settled in no more time than it takes to set down.[355]

The Soviets would control 90 percent of Rumania, Great Britain and the United States would control 90 percent of Greece; the Soviets would get a 75 percent control of Yugoslavia, Hungary, and Bulgaria. Although Churchill recognized the cynicism and reflected in the "offhand" manner in such decisions had been made, he was indeed anxious to have Greece within Britain's sphere of influence. Roosevelt had adamantly refused to discuss territorial issues until after the war and this agreement wholly violated his policy. The agreement also led to a public uproar in both Britain and the United States. Anglo-American relations fell to a new low as a result.[356]

Churchill's Percentages Agreement with Stalin clearly violated Roosevelt's policy of delaying any issues having to do with territorial settlements until after the war. The President, remarking on Russia's promise of help in the Pacific War after Germany surrendered, assured Stalin of his "complete acceptance of the assurances that we have received from you relative to the war against Japan." Stalin replied that he had mistakenly understood that Churchill would be speaking for the United States as well as for Great Britain and that he was very glad for the clarification from the President. Hopkins had again intervened between Roosevelt and Churchill, avoiding a potentially dangerous political and military impasse. Not for the first time, and not withstanding Hopkins' absence from D. C., FDR recognized his value to the administration and to the war effort and especially his "willingness to act and ask for authority later."[357]

If Hopkins had not interrupted the communication to Stalin that Churchill would speak for the President, Roosevelt would have been implicated in this agreement. Roosevelt considered these talks as merely preliminary to any conversations among the Big Three. Although Harriman was not present at the meeting between Stalin and Churchill, he did report the spheres of influence agreement that emerged. Hopkins and Hull opposed any such arrangement until after the war; FDR told Harriman that he was only interested in making sure that the Balkans were protected against future invasions and that the question of spheres of influence must be left open until after the war was won. Churchill feared the encroaching power of the Soviets and wanted to ensure that Britain would retain influence in Greece and Yugoslavia.[358]

The American and the British press responded angrily when this information was aired and this seriously damaged the Grand Alliance. There was little that Roosevelt could do to remedy the situation. The Western Allies seemed to be drifting apart over more than just military strategy; the politics of postwar territorial arrangements and spheres of influence let to disagreements between Churchill and Roosevelt. And this, of course, was a concern for Hopkins, whose goal was to project a spirit of unity among the Alliance to the rest of the world. Churchill clearly valued Hopkins' counsel. The PM sent him a letter 12/17/44: "I hope you will not hesitate to telegraph me on any points which you think we, or I personally, have been in error, and what you would advise, because I have great trust in your judgment and friendship, even if I may at times look at matters from a different angle."[359]

Even though Hopkins was hospitalized, he again assumed the role of mediator in in the aftermath of Tolstoy when Churchill became embroiled in controversy over British actions in Greece in an attempt to restore the monarchy; the result was deadly violence and a civil war. The Prime Minister almost lost a vote of confidence as a result. Furthermore, Churchill was irritated by a statement issued by the new American secretary of state, Edward Stettinius, that seemed critical of British actions in Greece. The Prime Minister was further angered when an order was issued forbidding the British to use American ships to support their troops in Greece. Admiral King had prevented supplies from reaching the British. Churchill contacted Hopkins and informed him that he was going to send an angry cable to President Roosevelt protesting this action. Hopkins, not wanting the argument to go public, convinced Churchill not send a divisive letter and he then got the naval order rescinded, much to the Prime Minister's relief. Hopkins' willingness to take quick and decisive action in this situation prevented a serious rift in Anglo-American relations[360]

Hopkins now was back on duty and, in spite of his physical debilitation; he still had a lot of work still to do. The October 1944 Moscow meeting between Churchill and Stalin and the resultant "Percentages Agreement" had created divisiveness between the Western Allies but it could have been a lot worse if Stalin had believed that Churchill was speaking for the United States as well for Great Britain while carving up eastern Europe. In January 1945, just before the Yalta Conference, Churchill said that the "informal and temporary arrangement" that he had made with Stalin at the Tolstoy meeting was never meant to "govern or affect the future of these wide regions once Germany was defeated."[361]

National politics again came into play in 1944, when Roosevelt was running for his fourth term and while his nomination was a foregone conclusion, there was debate over his vice-Presidential choice. It was apparent that Roosevelt was ill and that he might not actually serve out his full term of office; it was very likely that the vice-president could succeed him before the term ran out. Therefore, the choice of a running mate was very important. Hopkins had a lot to do with the decision to select Harry Truman to run for Vice-President. (The predictions were correct because nine months later he became President.) Hopkins sent a brief telegram on November 8th to Churchill merely saying, "It's in the bag." Churchill's response reflected joy as well as some relief: "Thank God all is well."[362] Hopkins looked forward to participating fully in political and military decisions that would lead to victory and to being influential in post-war foreign policy.[363]

But now plans for the Second Front were well settled. Operation Overlord, led by General Dwight D. Eisenhower, was the largest amphibious operation ever launched. The assault on the beaches of Normandy (code-named Utah, Omaha, Gold, Juno, and Sword) involved 2 million British, Canadian, and American troops and thousands of ships, as well as 12,000 aircraft. It began on D-Day June 6, 1944. Failure would have been catastrophic. But the Allies had made remarkable progress in their military buildup. The landings were successful and opened up the long-awaited Second Front. This inspired Stalin to cable Churchill that Napoleon failed and Hitler had failed to cross the Channel, but Overlord was "unprecedented in military history as to scale, breadth of conception and masterly execution."[364] The Allied invasion of northern France just about assured victory over Germany but the war was not yet won. Churchill seemed not too happy with Allied progress in August 1944 and in a telegram to Hopkins on August 8, wrote, "I am grieved to find that even splendid victories and widening opportunities do not bring us together on strategy. ... Of course, we are going to win anyway, but" the Prime Minister was not happy about Allied strategy in France when it came to Anvil, later Dragoon.[365] Hopkins was adamant that it was not a good idea to change strategy at this point in the war. He wrote to Churchill, "To change this strategy now would be a great mistake and I believe would delay rather than aid in our sure conquest of France. ... A great victory is in store for us."[366] Hopkins' confident optimism served as an interesting backdrop for the Prime Minister's pessimism in personal correspondence with Hopkins. Still, it would take nine more months for Germany to surrender.

The culmination of the wartime summits took place at Yalta, on the Crimean Peninsula, in February 1945. Here the Big Three, Churchill, Stalin and Roosevelt, met to outline what they envisioned for the postwar world. Hopkins acted as a behind-the-scenes facilitator. He smoothed over sticky relations between FDR and Churchill; greased the wheels on the Polish question and backed compromise when it came to reparations. The outcome of this conference has been debated for over six decades. Most agree that this marked the beginning of the Cold War.

Hopkins was committed to ensuring that the upcoming conference would establish the groundwork for postwar peace. It was crucial that all three Allied leaders be on the same page and on a level playing field. But all was not well with the Grand Alliance. The United States and Great Britain had rather testy relations with the Soviet Union; Britain's power had been on the wane for a year; Stalin remained an enigma to both Roosevelt and Churchill. There were going to be several unsettling issues on the table at the Yalta Conference: Poland, the United Nations, German Occupation, the Pacific War, and the Soviet presence in post war Europe. Churchill's plans for post war Europe proved to be central to policy debates at the Conference. This was going to lead so some difficulty for Hopkins. With the defeat of Germany, Communist Russia would be the most powerful nation in Europe. Hopkins also knew that Britain was going to be bankrupt after the war and that the United States and Soviet Russia would be responsible for keeping the peace in Europe, and in the world. Still, he was very concerned about reports he received that the Soviet leader might be negotiating a separate peace with Germany. Furthermore, the Russian people did not know the full extent of the impact of Lend Lease shipments that the United States was sending to the Soviets—food and munitions. In fact, Britain seemed to have closer relations to the Russians than did the United States. At this crucial point, we had the ineffective William Standley as ambassador to the Soviet Union. Hopkins refused to accept the ambassadorship, instead recommending

Averell Harriman. In any case, Roosevelt preferred to conduct Russian foreign policy through Hopkins.[367]

Well aware on the nature of Stalin's dictatorship and the threat that communism brought, Hopkins also knew the value of the Red Army; the war could not be won without it. The Big Three had to continue to work together. "Since Russia is the decisive factor in the war, she must be given every assistance and every effort must be made to obtain her friendship. ... Finally, the most important factor the United States has to consider in relation to Russia is the prosecution of the war in the Pacific." This sentiment guided the policies Hopkins supported at both Teheran and Yalta when the Western Allies met with Stalin.[368] However, after the successful landing in Normandy and the Allied push through France, the Soviets had less need for U.S. or British support. Stalin was no longer a supplicant. Neither Roosevelt nor Hopkins was naïve as to the very real threat posed by the Communists. In early 1941 Hopkins had written to New York City mayor, Fiorello La Guardia: "It seems to me that we have to find a way of dealing with the communists. From my standpoint they are just as much our enemies as the Germans."[369]

The Yalta Conference had been a long time coming but had been continuously in the minds of the Allies. Churchill had wanted to meet with FDR and Stalin in the autumn of 1944 but failed in his attempt to arrange this. Roosevelt had been thinking about venues for a Big Three conference even before the '44 election. He discussed choices with Hopkins, who suggested the Crimea. He recognized the importance of this summit and also knew that Stalin would not leave Russia because the war was at a crucial stage;

Gromyko confirmed this. The Soviet dictator also hated to fly. Stalin wrote the President suggesting Yalta as a place where the three leaders could meet. Neither Churchill nor some of the President's closest advisors could agree with this plan and soundly criticized Hopkins for his suggestion. According to Churchill, "we could not have found a worse place for a meeting if we had spent ten years of research."[370] Yet, the venue was set. Indeed, getting to Yalta involved complex travel plans for the Prime Minister but even more so for the President; first to Malta and then a flight to Saki and then a five-hour drive to Yalta. The accommodations were somewhat primitive except for the leaders, of course. Still, Churchill was anxious for the meeting and grudgingly agreed to the location.

A rift between the Western Allies emerged when Churchill became enraged over criticism in the American press of the British Empire. He retorted that he had not become Prime Minister to oversee the end of the Empire and relations between the White House and Number 10 became strained. Accusations that the British and the Americans were kowtowing to the Russians further angered Churchill. He seemed to be in a permanent bad mood. His distress, however, rarely included Hopkins. He wrote on December 12, 1944, "I have great trust in. your judgment and friendship even if I may at times look at matters from a different angle." And then in a Christmas greeting on the 23rd, Hopkins wrote the Prime Minister: "I am well aware of the heavy burdens you carry. Since our first meeting I have tried to share them with you. I would share them now ... What a gallant role you play in the greatest drama in the world's history no-one knows better than I." [371]

The Prime Minister's temperament still threatened to undermine the conference scheduled for February at Yalta. Hopkins suggested that he go to London to placate Churchill. FDR thought that this was a good idea. Hopkins flew with Chip Bohlen on the Sacred Cow, an airplane rigged up so FDR could enter in his wheelchair through the undercarriage and not have to be publicly carried up the steps. After his arrival on January 21st, he met with Churchill twice and allowed the Prime Minister to vent his displeasure about the venue and the explosions were "volcanic." Apparently, as Chip Bohlen declared, "The boil was lanced" and Churchill's mood improved.[372]

Hopkins and Bohlen then continued on to Paris in the hope that they could assuage the anger of General de Gaulle over not being invited to participate at Yalta. Roosevelt hoped that a visit by Hopkins could temper the situation and calm the volatile Frenchman. Hopkins felt that de Gaulle would be pleased that the Allies might be able to offer France an occupation zone in Germany after the war. But the General was not pleased at all and Hopkins' welcome was chilly. There was really no way that de Gaulle would be invited to the conference table. Even Churchill did not want de Gaulle to take part in any of the discussions; the Prime Minister found him to be "unbearable" because of his claim to represent all Frenchmen. According to the French general, the President's envoy was supposed to "sugar-coat the pill." De Gaulle asked Hopkins why there was such discord between the United States and France. Hopkins discarded any diplomatic polish he had recently acquired and replied:

> The cause is above all the stupefying
> disappointment we suffered when we saw
> France collapse and surrender in the disaster of
> 1940. ... Add to this the fact that those French
> military or political leaders in whom we
> successively placed our trust. ... did not show
> themselves worthy of our hopes.

De Gaulle then reminded Hopkins that Washington had done nothing to help the French or taken any steps to encourage Paul Reynaud to keep on fighting. But then they both cooled down and Hopkins did acknowledge what he had accomplished; and de Gaulle recognized America's part in the liberation of France, but he could not accept that France would have no say when the future of Europe was being decided at Yalta. Nevertheless, at Yalta, Hopkins did support Churchill's belief that France would be crucial for the containment of communism in the post war era. Hopkins eventually persuaded Roosevelt to agree to a French zone in a divided German and thus France had to have a role in the Control Commission. This would certainly improve Anglo-French relations for the future.[373] Although hesitatingly, de Gaulle did accept Hopkins' invitation to meet with the President when the conference was concluded. He later reneged on that acceptance. De Gaulle actually refused to meet with the President in Algiers after the conference ended; the President wrote an angry and insulting reply. He did not tolerate rudeness. Hopkins stepped in and, again, tempered the President's response and convinced Roosevelt to rewrite the letter in more polite terms.[374]

Hopkins continued from Paris to Rome (where he had a twenty-minute audience with the Pope), to Caserta, to Naples, and then to Malta where the CCOS had been meeting to set out plans for the final assault on Germany. Here Hopkins put on his social-work hat and began work on plans for the relief and rehabilitation of Europe. It seemed to fit him still. He insisted on leaving enough shipping available in order to meet the needs of the civilian population not merely military needs. He realized that there could be no lasting peace, no enduring democratic governments, or no economic recovery, if the people were starving. Marshall and King agreed. From Malta transport planes took off shuttling 700 people, including Roosevelt and Churchill, to Saki airport on the Crimean Peninsula. From there, they would drive to Yalta and meet up with Stalin.[375]

The Yalta Conference—its location, its schedule and its staffing—benefitted from Hopkins' influence, even if Churchill found the place cold and uncomfortable. According to McJimsey, it was one of the best-prepared conferences of the Second World War. It "represented the maturing of the Hopkins Shop in the conduct of American diplomacy."[376]

The conference took place at Livadia Palace, which housed the American delegation while the British stayed at Voronstov Palace and the Russians occupied Yusupov Palace located between and about five miles away from the American and the British headquarters. The first meeting between these FDR and Stalin took place somewhat unexpectedly; certainly it was not planned. Stalin arrived at Livadia Palace unannounced; FDR was unable to alert Churchill. Stalin and FDR sat on a couch in front of a beautiful inlaid table and chatted while Robert Hopkins took photographs. Stalin's interpreter, Pavlov, ensured that they understood each other. Both leaders had martinis and, although the conversation seemed very cordial to the young photographer, Stalin was nettled that he could not have a lemon in his drink. The next day FDR received from Stalin an entire lemon tree with 200 lemons, ordered directly from Georgia.[377]

The relationship among the Big Three during the Yalta Conference has been the subject for historians and political scientists for decades now. FDR and Churchill considered Stalin to be rough and inferior; Stalin felt that the Western Allies were class enemies. These rather extreme differences between East and West certainly made decisions difficult and meetings often contentious. Still, FDR hoped that what he regarded as his personal relationship with Stalin would transcend these differences and lead to the possibility of peace in the post war world. Although there was much personal interaction at this historic meeting, the business at hand was the fate of postwar Europe and especially what to do with a defeated Germany. Each of the Big Three had his specific objectives. Stalin wanted to be sure that a weakened and divided Germany paid reparations and he wanted a sphere of influence in Eastern Europe; FDR wanted to establish the UN as a peacekeeping institution and wanted to ensure that the Allies remained allies in the postwar era. The President was sure that he could act as a conduit for this.[378]

The President was especially concerned with getting assurance from Stalin that the Red Army would help in the defeat of the Japanese when the European war ended. He was also concerned about establishing fair rules for voting in the

UN Security Council. The President refused to discuss post war borders until after the war. Churchill, on the other hand, was more concerned about the division of Germany and the fate of Poland; FDR was concerned about Poland only insofar as getting an assurance from Stalin that the Poles in London would be included in the elected government in Warsaw. Churchill was just as concerned with this issue. Parliament would not tolerate failure to establish a liberal government in Poland—Great Britain had declared war because of the German invasion of Poland. It could not let that nation fall to the communists.[379]

First Plenary Meeting[380] took place on February 4, 1945, just after Stalin had paid that unexpected courtesy call on President Roosevelt; Churchill had not yet arrived. Sergeant Robert Hopkins acted as photographer; there were no civilian photographers at conference. Robert gave his father a 10-ruble banknote on which he wrote his name, the date and "Short-Snorter" and he asked if he could get Churchill, FDR, and Stalin all to sign it. When Stalin balked at signing the note, FDR explained that the Short Snorter Club was started by American bomber pilots; anyone who flew over the Atlantic was welcome to join if sponsored by two members. When Stalin noted that he had not flown over the Atlantic and was therefore not eligible, FDR said that he was taking the initiative and waiving the requirement. Stalin signed the note. The young soldier was thrilled with his souvenir. He also recognized that this was the most important conference of the war and urged his colleagues, the assembled photographers, to record it as accurately and completely as possible.[381]

Hopkins was ill during most of the Yalta conference, actually bed-ridden. He did, however, get out of bed to attend all eight of the meetings where Roosevelt and Churchill and Stalin were present; many of the lower echelon meetings were held in his bedroom.[382] According to McJimsey, Hopkins' major contributions were during the discussions over the UN. Still, he used his influence re the future of the Polish government and the nation's boundaries. He was able to placate Churchill on the issue of French occupation of Germany as well as on the issue of Poland's western boundaries. Churchill wanted a strong Germany as a bulwark against encroaching communism while FDR and Hopkins agreed with Stalin that Germany should be dismembered. Hopkins acted as mediator between Stalin and Churchill by suggesting that the matter be referred to the foreign ministers. Stalin refused and Churchill had to agree to the President's proposal to include dismemberment of Germany in the surrender terms.[383]

Lord Moran writes in his diary, February 5, 1945: "Hopkins is, of course a valuable ally, particularly now when the President's opinions flutter in the wind. He knows the President's moods like a wife watching the domestic climate. He will sit patiently for hours, blinking like a cat, waiting for the right moment to put his point; and if it never comes, he is content to leave it to another time. The battle is not lost yet, but I wish Harry was in better fettle."[384]

By this time, the Red Army was advancing toward Berlin and Stalin was no longer the supplicant pleading for Allied help. This gave him leverage at the conference table. At the second plenary session, the issue of what to do with Germany after the war proved to be a divisive issue, especially when the discussion turned to the role the French would play in any occupation plan. How would the Allies treat a defeated Germany? Would Germany be completely dismembered, be forced to pay huge reparations, and even be forced to turn over its industry to the victors? Just previous to the second plenary session, FDR met with Hopkins to discuss dividing Germany into zones, reparations, and dismemberment. Hopkins urged the President to postpone any decision until the war was over but to be sure that the Ruhr and Saar would be under Allied control.[385]

Stalin was evasive on the fate of Poland, on the voting issue in the UN but he did agree to aid the United States in the Pacific War when the fighting ended in Europe. He, however, insisted on maintaining the borders that had been established by the Molotov-Ribbentrop Pact of 1939. Although there were no formal minutes taken at the meetings of the Big Three, records published in 1955 by Bohlen, Alger Hiss and H. Freeman Matthews indicated that Stalin did have the upper hand. It was his Red Army that had held the Germans at bay for years before the Western Allies stepped; his army suffered enormous casualties in the fight against Nazism; and, consequently, his army occupied a good deal of Eastern Europe.[386] The expansion of communism in Europe was of especial importance to Britain's Prime Minister.

The Polish question was probably the hardest fought and the most controversial issue discussed by the Big Three at Yalta. In February 1945, there were two Polish governments. The Polish government in exile in London had the somewhat mild support of the British while the Soviet-backed Polish government situated in Warsaw (also known as the Lublin government). This latter government accepted the borders established by the Soviets; Stalin insisted that Poland remain with the Soviet sphere of influence and thus wanted to ensure a puppet government in Warsaw. The Western Allies and the London Poles emphatically disagreed. Poland should emerge from the war as a democratic nation with representatives from noncommunist and anti-Nazi political parties that would government provisionally until elections could be held. Hopkins worked tirelessly here to negotiate some kind of consensus. Stettinius agreed with Hopkins' strategy: establish agreement among all three leaders and then let the ambassadors work out the details.[387]

The issue of Poland's boundaries arose as a contentious issue among the Big Three. Roosevelt and Churchill had earlier agreed upon Polish borders when they met at Teheran. The eastern border would be the Curzon Line based on ethnic boundary between Poles and Ukranians just as it was at the end of First World War. After Barbarossa, Stalin accepted Curzon Line but he never lost desire to retrieve land that the Soviets wanted as part of USSR. The Western Allies wanted a plan that would satisfy the Poles and at the same time not antagonize the Soviets.[388]

At Malta, immediately previous to the Yalta conference, the British essentially agreed on the Curzon Line being the eastern border of Poland, giving Lvov to the USSR. The United States did not agree and wanted Lvov to remain as part of Poland. At Yalta, Churchill, used all of his diplomatic wiles to mitigate the situation. He said that he supported US position and admitted that because of "sacrifices" made by USSR it probably deserved claim to Poland but the Soviets (i.e. Stalin) should "make a gesture of magnanimity to a much weaker power" that would be much appreciated by the western powers.[389]   FDR was less concerned about Poland's boundaries than about the establishment of a democratic government for the beleaguered nation. Churchill could not disagree; Great Britain had gone to war over Poland and certainly wanted to ensure that its people had the opportunity to elect a government that represented them. The Prime Minister was not about to recognize the Lublin Poles. Conversely, Stalin saw the London Poles as merely obstacles to international recognition of the borders that had been established under the Molotov-Ribbentrop Pact in 1939. He intended to maintain these borders that benefitted the USSR.

Hopkins again intervened here. He understood that the President did not have the constitutional power to approve any international boundary change. However, he was fully aware that if FDR hesitated here, he would risk antagonizing Stalin. He sent a note to the President warning him about this and suggested that he speak to Stalin in private explaining that he did actually accept the boundary that benefitted Russia but could only do so in very general terms publicly. FDR did this but then had to mollify the Prime Minister. He did this by allowing Churchill to draft the statement establishing the boundaries for Poland, with an emphasis on the western boundaries instead of on the eastern. The three leaders signed.[390]

Stalin was intent on securing a strong and dependent Poland, a nation that would be capable of resisting any future attack on the Soviet Union from the west. Poland had been the route through which invading armies had tried to destroy Mother Russia and Stalin was determined to prevent this from happening again. Poland was a security issue for Stalin while it was a political issue for the Western Allies. Churchill reflected that if Britain recognized the Communist-controlled Lublin government as legitimate, it would be seen as a refutation of its promise to secure free elections in the nation. At the same time, it was crucial for the three Allies to maintain a relationship in which they could negotiate these very delicate matters. They could not let the Polish question destroy the Alliance. All agreed. The Western Allies desperately needed the Red Army, the largest land army at the time despite the millions of casualties it suffered during the war. But it was not yet over. Battles in the Pacific still raged, the Germans still had hundreds of divisions on the front. Roosevelt and Churchill needed Stalin's compliance. Stalin needed the Western Allies to ensure that a defeated Germany would not again threaten the Soviet Union and to negotiate reparations from the Nazis.[391]

After Stalin agreed to support the United States in the Pacific and agreed to membership in the UN General Assembly, the President did not want to risk these gains by forcing Stalin on the very contentious issue of a democratic Poland. The UN concessions apparently made by Stalin were linked to any concessions by the Western Allies on Poland. In essence, both the President and the Prime Minister capitulated to Stalin on this issue. Stalin was not going to compromise.[392]

During the Plenary Sessions, Hopkins sat behind Roosevelt and Stettinius apparently passing notes to the two, giving advice. He saw his job as supporting the President in his efforts to maintain the Alliance rather than to gain any specific objective. He again played the role of an "honest broker." For Hopkins, reaching an agreement on the United

Nations, especially the issue of the veto powers, was critical. He advised the President to allow Stettinius to present the American point of view since FDR would be presiding himself over the plenary session and it might be awkward if he brought up the subject. The American proposal was that permanent members of the Security Council would have veto powers but could not veto discussions of any issue. Churchill agreed but Stalin remained wary.[393]

Hopkins then sprang into action and advised Stettinius before the foreign ministers' meeting. During the afternoon session, the Russians agreed but asked for more seats in the General Assembly. According to McJimsey, Hopkins had informed FDR and Churchill that the United States would take the lead in opposing such a request from the Soviets; it might be awkward for the British because they had requested a seat for India, part of the Empire. During the discussion over these issues having to do with the UN, Hopkins noticed that FDR had begun to stall for time, speaking at length about apparently nothing. He clearly wanted to avoid the issue. Hopkins sent his boss a note: "I think you should try to get this referred to the Foreign Ministers before there is trouble.'" FDR agreed and suggested a UN conference in March, at which point Churchill vigorously rejected this idea. He needed to consult his War Cabinet. At this point, Hopkins sent another note to the President suggesting that he just drop the subject. He needed to sit down with the Prime Minister and come to some agreement with him first. Stalin was amenable to tabling the issue and the meeting ended on a calm note.[394] At the same time, Churchill sided with Stalin over extra votes for the USSR. Hopkins again stepped in. He talked to the President and then told Sir Charles Wilson, Churchill's physician, that FDR had decided to side with the Russians on this issue. Hopkins also encouraged Stettinius to hold the UN conference in some place in the middle of the United States. In the end Roosevelt told Stalin that he would get the extra votes.[395]

A final UN issue to be decided upon was the status of those nations that had not yet recognized the Soviet Union and of those Latin American countries that had not declared war on Germany. Hopkins told the President that the nations that had not declared war on Germany did so because they were not strong enough to wage war. FDR made the suggestion that these countries be invited to join the UN because of the support they had given to the Allies in the form of raw material. They could belatedly declare war on Germany, sign the UN declaration and join. Hopkins insisted that even Turkey should do this, a nation that had essentially jumped from one side to the other. Hopkins' influence on the UN discussions was invaluable.[396]

Roosevelt and Churchill agreed on many issues at the Yalta Conference but differed on how to treat Germany. The occupation of a defeated Germany again led to disagreements among the Big Three especially over the issue of what part France would take. When Churchill and Stalin argued over whether or not France should have a seat on the Allied Control Council, Hopkins again stepped in as mediator and suggested that France be given a zone in occupied Germany and that the foreign ministers decide if France should have a seat on the Council. Calm prevailed. At the Third Plenary Meeting on February 6, Churchill said that it was vital that France be a part of European security. Great

Britain alone would not be able to protect approaches to the English Channel from the west. The Prime Minister, concerned over the stability of Europe in the face of the Communist threat, wanted a strong Germany both as a "counterweight" to the Soviet Union and as a strong economic power. Stalin and FDR wanted to dismember Germany to ensure that it would never again take up arms. Hopkins urged the President to again defer to the foreign ministers to devise surrender terms that would treat this issue. He convinced the President to mollify Stalin by telling him that this crucial matter should be left to the ministers. It worked. Churchill eventually agreed.[397]

The issue of German reparations led to a face-off among the Big Three. The Russians demanded reparations in the amount of $20 billion of which they would get half. Great Britain and the United States objected. The post WWI debacle loomed. Gromyko informed Hopkins that Stalin was not pleased with FDR's apparent defection. Hopkins suggested that the President again speak privately to Stalin. This did not work because Stalin did not accept the President's explanation and angrily declared that his country had lost millions of soldiers, had made sacrifices that neither the British nor the Americans had. The Soviet leader reiterated the concessions he had made so far at the conference—the UN, France, Poland, the war in the Pacific—and nothing could make up for the efforts of the Red Army. Hopkins send a note to Roosevelt:

> 'The Russians have given in so much at this conference that I don't think we should let them down. Let the British disagree if they

want to—and continue their disagreements in Moscow. Simply say it is all referred to the Reparations Commission with the minutes to show the British disagree about any mention of the 10 billion.'

Hopkins' actions during the conference demonstrate why Churchill dubbed him Lord Root of the Matter. He actively participated in discussions, generally acting as mediator. When FDR and Churchill disagreed, as they often did, Hopkins stepped in to provide solutions that both could live with. He also acted as mediator between Churchill and Stalin, having the confidence of both leaders. [398]

Just after the conference ended, Hopkins wrote to his wife Louise: "The days have gone by with eventful swiftness and it seems as tho the fate of the world—at any rate the one that we know and like—are [sic] being determined. Perhaps I exaggerate this because I am so close to it."[399] Clearly the import of the Yalta Conference was not lost on the one person who was closest to the President. The influence that Hopkins exerted during the fateful days of the Yalta Conference is reflected in a recollection by Commander William M. Rigdon, who was one of the few who had access to Roosevelt's map room and who accompanied the President on every trip. He writes of a seemingly minor but very telling incident at Yalta when Hopkins asked Pa Watson and Admiral Wilson Brown (Naval Aide) to let Churchill have their room so the Prime Minister could have a much-needed nap. When at first they angrily refused, Hopkins gently offered to take it up with the President. The two left, if reluctantly. Rigdon reflects that Hopkins had "the power to get things done ... that he was closer to the President than others. The President trusted him completely. Everyone knew that he could, if he chose, speak for the President and would be backed up in what he had done."[400]

The Americans, including Roosevelt and Hopkins left Yalta feeling exuberant, confident that their British colleagues also believed that the conference had been a success. The President received many congratulatory messages on board the *Quincy* on his way home. Hopkins remarked to Robert Sherwood:

> We really believed in our hearts that this was the dawn of the new day we had all been praying for and talking about for so many years. We were absolutely certain that we had won the first great victory of the peace — and, by 'we' I mean *all* of us, the whole civilized human race. The Russians had proved that they could be reasonable and farseeing and there wasn't any doubt in the minds of the President or any of us that we could live with them and get along with them peacefully for as far into the future as any of us could imagine.

He did add the caveat that this rosy picture would be possible only as long as Stalin is alive and in the Kremlin.[401] Churchill wrote, "Our hopeful assumptions were soon to be falsified. Still they were the only ones possible at the time."[402] Hopkins regarded the outcomes of the Yalta Conference as "the first great victory of the peace" for all the world, not just the Allies. He believed that the Russians were "reasonable" and "we could live with them" peacefully in the future.[403] Moran writes that the Americans left Yalta, where the Allies made decisions that would affect the world, with a sense of achievement. Clearly, Hopkins prediction of a utopia reflected the confidence of the Western Allies that the Yalta agreements were the best they could get.

Decisions made at the Yalta Conference on post war borders, spheres of influence, the balance of power, the war in the Pacific, the division of Germany, Poland—were made with the knowledge the Western Allies had at hand. Averell Harriman was appalled by the Soviet refusal to help Poland when Germany was attacking Warsaw; the Katyn massacres hung in the background of most of the wartime conferences.[404] Nonetheless, Hopkins did not want Soviet attitude toward Poland to get in the way of any future negotiations between the United States and the USSR. FDR hoped that what he considered his personal relationship with Stalin—begun with Hopkins' meeting in Moscow and furthered by the Teheran Conference—would ensure the Russian leader's cooperation at Yalta and after the war. The President desperately wanted the Soviets to help defeat Japan after the war in Europe was won. After the successful cross-channel invasion, Stalin was in a much stronger position in the Alliance; no longer was he in the position of a petitioner, begging for the Second Front. The Western Allies, on the other hand, still needed the Red Army to win the final battles of the war. Stalin clearly had some leverage in the negotiations that he could use to fulfill his goal: the occupation of most of Eastern Europe.[405]

Chapter 9—Endgame

En route to Yalta, when he stopped at Malta, Roosevelt made a spur of the moment decision and he issued an invitation to King Ibn Saud of Saudi Arabia, King Farouk of Egypt, and Emperor Haile Selassie of Ethiopia, to meet with each one separately, after the Yalta Conference, aboard the *Quincy*, in Great Bitter Lake. When the conference ended on February 11th Roosevelt merely announced his plan to Churchill, who was somewhat taken aback at this unexpected get-together.   A rather disturbed Churchill sought out Hopkins to find out what the President intended to accomplish at these meetings. Hopkins responded that he didn't know and suggested that it was probably "a lot of horseplay" so that Roosevelt could "enjoy the colorful panoply of sovereigns of this part of the world." Churchill did not participate in what was dubbed The Three Kings Meeting. He was, however, concerned that such a meeting might compromise the British position in the Middle East. This was a legitimate concern because, according to Hopkins, the President did intend to speak with Ibn Saud about Palestine and Jewish refugees. Churchill made plans to meet with the Three Kings on his own in Egypt.[406]

Hopkins' memo, written after he returned to the United States, reflecting on the meeting between FDR and Saud is especially enlightening. Saud, a dignified and educated man, was a powerful king and a born soldier; the President had no pre-knowledge of who he actually was. He was therefore surprised when the monarch answered his request to admit Jews to Palestine with a blunt "no." The Jews, supported and armed by the Americans and British, were clearly a threat to the Arabs. Saud declared he would fight before he would agree to admit more Jews to Palestine.[407]

Hopkins wrote a letter to his wife describing the meeting of the Three Kings with the President, how Saud wore gorgeous robes, spoke in surprisingly blunt language, brought his own sheep, admitted to having 68 children. "The well-known [Roosevelt] charm had no effect on the old boy. ... Being head of the Moslem world of 400,000,000 million [sic] he was not overly impressed by F. D. R. Our diplomatic success sort of rolled into the cellar here."[408] Apparently, the meeting did not go well. Hopkins' son, Robert, who was the President's photographer for several of the conferences, later wrote his own more detailed reflections of this unique meeting beginning with Saud's arrival on the *Quincy*:

> President Roosevelt sent the destroyer *USS Murphy* to Jidda where the King and his retinue boarded. The captain of the destroyer offered the King his cabin, but the King who was 6'5" tall found it too cramped for him. Bedoin [sic] that he was, he politely declined the offer, saying he preferred to be out on deck under a tent. The king ordered that a tent be brought on board, along with oriental rugs and his throne. These were installed on the foredeck of the ship. A herd of sheep was driven on board, and corralled on the fantail of the destroyer. A

samovar was installed under the powder magazine of the ship, to the captain's consternation. The sleek warship took on the aspect of an exotic royal barge. I watched as the destroyer carefully came along side of the *USS Quincy*, a cruiser which dwarfed the destroyer. The tent had been taken down. The King was nowhere in sight but the three royal princes were standing on the foredeck. Behind them were ten members of the King's bodyguard, described to us as the fiercest warriors selected from various tribes. They were a colorful addition to the scene, armed with sabers and curved daggers. The two ships were lashed together and a catwalk was set up between the two vessels. The King appeared on the upper deck of the destroyer. He was dressed in a black djellaba trimmed in gold. He wore a red and white keffiyeh headdress. He was a striking figure as he walked, ever so slowly, along the narrow catwalk. He suffered from arthritis and used a cane. There was a breathless moment when the two ships moved in opposite directions, threatening to tip the King into the water. The president, wearing his naval cape, received him cordially on deck. Sat between two huge flags of the United Sates and Saudi Arabia, the two men talked for 45 minutes. During the entire time, Colonel William A, Eddy, U. S. Minister to Saudi Arabia, knelt on one knee on the unyielding deck in front of them interpreting their conversation. I was busy taking photographs of the two leaders but it was evident from their demeanor that this was an easy, friendly exchange. The King offered the President a sabre with a bejewelled scabbard and a curved dagger encrusted with jewels. He also offered for Mrs. Roosevelt a pair of diamond earrings and a diamond tiara— adornments I was sure Mrs. Roosevelt would never wear. The President gave the King a signed photograph of himself in a silver frame. I later learned that in their conversation the King mentioned that both he and the President were physically incapacitated, he with arthritis and the President with Polio. He said he envied the President's ability to get around in a wheelchair. At this, the president offered the King one of his folding wheelchairs. There was a short break before lunch. The King retired to a cabin aboard the *Quincy*. I joined my father and the President for a few minutes before they went down below for luncheon with the King and his entourage. The President commented that he was not prepared for such lavish gifts offered by the King and wondered what he could give in exchange. He said that the King had spoken admiringly about the President's airplane, "The Sacred Cow." He particularly liked the feature of the elevator which carried the president up into the plane. The President took this as a hint that the King would welcome this as a gift. "I can't give away the Sacred Cow without Congressional approval," he said, "There has to be another solution." Years later, I learned from Prince Achmed, when he was here with the Saudi exhibit, that the President had sent King Ibn Saud a C-47 airplane, presumable with Congressional approval.[409]

Clearly, the President did enjoy what the elder Hopkins called the "panoply" of the meeting with Ibn Saud.

Although both Roosevelt and Hopkins did suffer from health problems, which were sometimes severe, during this conference, this did not detract from their ability to participate fully in the debates, negotiations, and festivities, scheduled and unscheduled. Hopkins' letters to his wife (one quoted above) reflect his mental acuteness. The problems in his intestinal tract did not affect his concentration. FDR was also ill but mentally sound. Stettinius, who was secretary of state at the time, said of the President, "[t]he stories that his health took a turn for the worse either on the way to Yalta or at the Conference are, to the best of my knowledge, without foundation." The President's ability to participate on fully equal terms with such powerful men as Stalin and Churchill, day after day, "during the grueling give-and-take at the conference table is the best answer to these stories." Hopkins' mind too remained keen and alert.[410]

Roosevelt left Great Bitter Lake on February 14 and sailed through the Suez Canal; at Alexandria Churchill came aboard for lunch. This was the last meeting of these two leaders. On board the *Quincy*, on the way home from Alexandria, Hopkins became too weak to even walk; he could not even leave his cabin. Exhausted from the rigorous schedule of the conference, he decided to fly home rather than remain for the long voyage home on the ship. Hopkins had to inform his boss that he would leave the ship and fly home; he would not remain on board with him. The President was disappointed and even displeased because he had been relying on Hopkins to help him write the speech he was to give to Congress when he returned, reporting on the results of the Yalta Conference. He felt deserted by his friend. Hopkins left without saying his usual warm good bye. He flew to the Mayo Clinic on February 27th; he and the President never met again. FDR died on April 12th. Hopkins was devastated by this loss—both personal and political. He was haunted by the rather cold way in which they had parted after the Yalta Conference. At the funeral he seemed to friends and relatives so despondent, feeling that he had nothing left to live for. But then, later, at a meeting with Robert Sherwood, he said, "God damn it, now we've got to work on our own. ... We've had it too easy all this time, because we knew he was there, and we had the privilege of being able to get to him. ... Well, he isn't there now, and we've got to find a way to do things by ourselves."[411] Hopkins hadn't yet given up. He had a new President to serve.

The death of Roosevelt led to the deterioration of the Western Alliance; Roosevelt fervently believed that he would be able to handle the Russians in the post-war world based on mutual respect. His absence from the equation was fatal. In this case, the personal dynamics was missing in the relationship between Churchill and Stalin. If diplomacy was personal as well as political, Hopkins acted as a catalyst for the Alliance in that he formed both personal and political connections with all three principals: Roosevelt, Churchill, and Stalin.[412]

Although Harry Truman would never take the place of his old boss, Hopkins stepped to his side when he was needed. And Truman did indeed need him to sew up a few ends dangling after Yalta. Halifax sent a telegram to the Prime Minister April 15, 1945 in which he noted that Hopkins had "judged the President's death to have created a completely new situation in which we would be starting from scratch." Halifax wrote "Truman had told Harry that he felt equipped to handle domestic issues but completely ignorant of foreign. ... He was a real country boy." Hopkins knew that Truman's administrative style would be quite different from that of FDR, but he was still willing to work with him. He agreed to give the new president notes on foreign and international policy, anything to help him.[413]

Truman sent Hopkins on what would be his last mission, his second one to Moscow—"to clear the air." This was late May 1945. Bohlen, Harriman, and his wife, Louise, accompanied him. He was to tell Stalin that the United States was fully prepared to carry out the agreements made at Yalta. He wanted to see if the USSR would do the same. He had six sessions during the ten days he spent there. During these meetings, Stalin listed several complaints although he was very courteous to Hopkins. All of Stalin's promises were provisional and, in any case, the West had no way of making him keep any of them. Stalin stonewalled on issue of Poland and on fate of the 16 non-Communist Poles who were arrested. He accused them of shooting Red Army men and insisted that they were going to stand trial. Stalin said that Stanislaw Mikolajczyk, Prime Minister of the Poles in exile in

London, would be able to participate in talks re new government in Poland with two other London Poles. As McJimsey correctly argues, Stalin remained steadfast in using the issue of the formation of the Polish government as a trade for his concessions on the UN Security Council voting rules. At his meeting with Stalin, Hopkins attempted to avoid any real acrimonious disagreement and left the way open for any sign of cooperation between the United States and the Soviet Union. It was the methodology Hopkins had used successfully at Yalta. Hopkins flew home via Berlin and voiced doubts that there could be any real, long-lasting cooperation between the U.S. and the USSR. He had come to the realization that Stalin's aims were in direct conflict with Roosevelt's Four Freedoms. But even so, neither did he want to see a rise of German military power.[414]

On the issue of Russia's ability to veto any discussion that might be critical of USSR, Stalin ordered Gromyko in San Francisco to concede this point and this enabled UN Charter to be adopted. Hopkins also got Stalin to commit to a date for entering the war in the Pacific – August 8. Stalin wanted to keep China weak, and he believed that this could be done by "perpetuating the highly flawed Nationalist regime [rather] than putting the Communists in power." [415]

Hopkins and Churchill remained friends after the war ended; when Churchill was forced out of office after the general elections in 1945, Hopkins was distraught. He wrote to Lord Beaverbrook that he was "greatly dejected that this should happen to him at this time in his life."[416] Hopkins' wartime activities had taken a great toll on him; he was physically exhausted and very ill. Citing his declining health, he resigned from the government and moved to New York

City. He accepted a job with the chairman of the coat and suit industry where he agreed to mediate labor-management conflicts. He received an honorary degree from Oxford and on the recommendation of George Marshall and on September 4th, he was awarded the Distinguished Service Medal from Truman for his courage and contributions to war effort. When President Harry Truman awarded Harry Hopkins the Distinguished Service Medal, he read the citation: Hopkins "lightened the burden of his Commander-in-Chief, and that he attacked with piercing understanding the tremendous problems incident to the vast military operations throughout the world." He was especially pleased about the Oxford honor because this would give him the opportunity to visit with his old friend, late the Prime Minister of Great Britain. When illness prevented Hopkins from traveling to Oxford to receive his honorary degree, Churchill cabled his regret that he could not see his friend again. Friends and relatives had been keeping Churchill apprised of Hopkins deteriorating condition and the Prime Minister rightly feared for his health.

After his last mission—this one to Moscow on behalf of President Truman—Hopkins, tired and ill, had hoped retire and write his memoirs. He wanted to make clear the purpose of the Grand Alliance during "The Good War."[417] He hired Sydney Hyman to help him with this. Hyman had graduated from the University of Chicago and served in the European Theater. Hopkins told Hyman that he wanted nothing destroyed because he wanted Americans to know the whole story. Although much of what Hopkins dictated to Hyman was "rambling and repetitious," it gives some insight into Hopkins' thinking about his career:

I know of no person in his right mind but that he believes if this nation ever had to engage in another war Great Britain would be fighting on our side. I believe that the British have saved our skins twice—once in 1914 and again in 1940. ... This time it was Britain alone that held the fort and they held the fort for us just as much as for themselves, because we would not have had a chance to have licked Hitler had Britain fallen. ... If I were to lay down the most cardinal principle of our foreign policy, it would be that we make absolutely sure that now and forever the United States and Great Britain are going to see eye to eye on major matters of world policy. ... We know that we have been able to fight side by side with the Russians in the greatest war in all History. ... That Russia's interests, so far as we can anticipate them, do not afford an opportunity for a major difference with us in foreign affairs. ... We find the Russians as individuals easy to deal with [and] they like the American people [and] want to maintain friendly relations with us.[418]

He especially wanted to write about his relationship with Churchill. He wanted to set the record straight, about the war, about the Allies, and even about the politics. He told Hyman:

The whole story of Roosevelt—and my story is part of it—is going to come out anyway in the next fifty years. I feel we will both come out with credit. And I don't see any point of trying to edit my past by destroying papers which showed precisely what I did and how I did it. I want people to know that I played politics; I also want them to know why I played politics."[419]

[The irony of this statement from a person who was not a politician is obvious.]

According to contemporary columnist Marquis Childs, Hopkins wanted to write his memoirs in order to defuse the maligners of FDR; he hoped to set straight the record of the New Deal and especially of the Grand Alliance that formed during what we now call "The Good War." Hopkins once said that Roosevelt would not be able to set down an objective account of the war because "the boss never lost a battle. That was his strength. And at times that was his weakness. He just never lost a battle."[420] Biographer, presidential speechwriter and White House insider, Robert Sherwood writes that Hopkins died fearing that there would be "attempts to foul the record ... for selfish reasons." If this were to happen, people might again become disillusioned.[421] For Hopkins this could be very dangerous for the nation. While he was eminently practical, he did have an almost idealistic confidence in the American system of government and in the American people. His relationship with the British Prime Minister was built on this unremitting commitment to the democratic system and especially to the necessity for democratic nations to stand together against fascist aggression. Basic humanitarian assumptions and an unshakable belief in the democratic system formed the foundation of all that he did as President Roosevelt's "right hand man." This is what gave him the inner energy to continue this work even though he had a debilitating illness. Many historians and biographers have either overlooked or underemphasized this part of the Hopkins story.

Hopkins did not anticipate the Cold War and he did not believe that there would be difficulties in maintaining consistent relations with the Soviet Union due to the differences between capitalism and socialism, between democracy and dictatorship. He said that those Americans who said that they didn't care if the Russians or the Germans won the war, who believe that there is no chance for working with the Russians, could cause dangerous rifts between two very powerful nations. The mutually respectful relationship that he had maintained with Stalin surely led Hopkins to believe that the United States could work with the Soviet Union in the future. He was not so naïve as to believe that the east and the west would remain allies, nor did he underestimate the Germans, but he did not foresee the dangerous world that evolved after Yalta. In dictating to Hyman, Hopkins said that such an attitude—not caring if Germany or Russia won the war—could only lead to disaster. He added, "If I were to indicate a country in which the United States, for the next hundred years, had the greatest interest from political and economic points of view, I would name the Republic of China. China will become one of the greatest land powers for many years to come."[422] Here Hopkins certainly exhibits some interesting prescience and one can only wonder where this came from. He was certainly not a fan of Chiang and recognized the failings of the Chinese government and military. But the book he wanted to write, of course, never happened.

Hopkins returned to the hospital in November 1945. There was nothing more that the doctors could do for him and his health rapidly declined. Just a week before he died, Hopkins wrote a letter the Churchill. It was the last: "All I can say about myself at the moment is that I am getting excellent care, while the doctors are struggling over a very bad case of cirrhosis of the liver—not due, I regret to say, from taking too much to alcohol."[423] He died January 29, 1946. His last words were, "You can't beat destiny."[424] He had beaten death on several occasions already and he knew that his time was up. He died with the knowledge that he had done everything humanly possible for his nation as well as the fear that it was sliding into problems that others would have to attempt to solve.

Chapter 10—Conclusion

Americans love the story of a small-town boy who made good, and Hopkins fits perfectly into this scenario. Yet, the Hopkins story has to be much more than an affirmation of the possibilities that this American life offers. From the time he was a teenager, Hopkins began to acquire the qualities that would eventually point him toward public service. His education at Grinnell College where he was steeped in the Social Gospel, his experiences in the Lower East Side ghettoes, his work with the Red Cross during World War I, and his reaction to poverty during the Great Depression, all coalesced into a mind-set ripe for the crises of the mid-twentieth century. The story of Harry Hopkins might be read as part of the Horatio Alger myth of America as the land of opportunity where even the lowest born can achieve the highest pinnacle of power. It might also be read as a story depicting a patriarchal society where men have a privileged place in order to succeed. Hopkins certainly functioned well in this environment; he had the support of accommodating women during his professional life as a social worker: his first wife, Ethel Gross Hopkins, Eleanor Roosevelt, Lorena Hickok, Frances Perkins, and the many women in the New Deal who reported to him. During the Second World War, Hopkins allied himself with powerful men both in the political and military arena who shaped the history of the war and its aftermath. Certainly, absent the Great Depression and

World War II, Hopkins' name might not even appear in accounts of 20ᵗʰ century American history.

There is no question that his friendship with the President drove his career both as his New Deal Administrator and his advisor during the war. But it is important to remember that Hopkins' relationship to Roosevelt did not go back to school years or the Hudson Valley society. Hopkins was not a member of any "old boys" club. They first got to know each other in Albany when Hopkins worked for Governor Roosevelt as TERA administrator. There is no evidence that there were any ties of friendship during this time. Roosevelt was merely his boss. When Hopkins went to Washington, D. C., in 1933, he had no influence with his former boss, now President – he could not even get an appointment to see him. It was Frances Perkins who took his relief plan to Roosevelt. The President liked it, implemented it, and thus began Hopkins' rise to power. It was during the dark years of the Depression that Hopkins began to stand out as a person who got things done, who had little tolerance for those who criticized the unemployed and needy as lazy, who knew how to cut through red tape, and, most importantly, had the administrative skills to manage his projects efficiently and effectively. Roosevelt felt an affinity to this social worker who had joined his administration. To others, he was a spendthrift using other people's money to support those too lazy to work and, furthermore, he was a dangerous man who had shaken hands with Joseph Stalin. Some believed him to be a political threat, even a Rasputin, because he wielded an extraordinary amount of political power, yet had never held an elected office, and had no official title. However, for twelve years, from 1933-1945,

Hopkins was President Roosevelt's trusted advisor, gatekeeper, personal emissary to world leaders, and close confidante.

It might have been his administrative skills, his ability to get things done during crisis years that brought Hopkins to the attention of the president, but there was always a certain charm that attracted those he worked with. His frail body held a fierce loyalty to his country and this reflected on those in Roosevelt's inner circle. Basic humanitarian assumptions and an unshakable belief in the democratic system formed the foundation of all that he did as President Roosevelt's "right hand man." This is what gave him the inner energy to continue this work even though he was ill and suffering.[425]

Hopkins' diplomatic talents peaked during the wartime conferences where the allied powers met to discuss and decide on military strategy. Hopkins understood that Stalin was not to be trusted. Roosevelt and Churchill were fully aware that the Soviet leader had a certain amount of leverage at Yalta. Despite the hostility that simmered just below the surface, each of the Big Three recognized their interdependence.

In the end, the Yalta agreements did not hold; Stalin and the Soviets did not keep their promises. But, the war was won, and this was the primary aim of the Allies. In the aftermath, however, we see a strong-man Russian leader interacting with the American president, Harry Truman, without the tempering effect of a Harry Hopkins. Our relationship with the Soviet Union from 1941 to 1945 was shaped by the exigencies of the war and the expertise of western politicians, military leaders, and diplomats. With the fall of the Soviet Union and the eventual rise of Putin as a Stalin-like dictator—while the world continues to be unstable and vital international alliances are challenged—diplomatic finesse in Washington becomes as critical as ever.

Harry Hopkins was a public servant of the highest sort. If his legacy remains largely unrecognized, his firm belief that, during war and peace, the government must act as the servant of the people and not the reverse, never wavered. He would wish that its citizens would remember that the task of government is to insure the general welfare of the people. Those who have earned the honor to serve in government at any level must understand that this is their first and final responsibility.

About the Author

June Hopkins is Professor Emerita, Georgia Southern University, Armstrong Campus, where she taught history for 17 years. She has a Ph.D. in history from Georgetown University, 1997, with honors.

Her first book, *Harry Hopkins: Sudden Hero, Brash Reformer* (St. Martin's Press, 1999) investigates her grandfather's social work career. (It was issued as a paperback by Palgrave McMillion in January 2009.)

She co-edited *Jewish First Wife, Divorced: The Correspondence of Ethel Gross and Harry Hopkins* (Lexington Books, 2003), with her daughter, Allison Giffen.

She also published "Churchill's Relationship with Harry Hopkins: 'The Main Prop and Anchor of Roosevelt Himself'" in *Finest Hour: The Journal of Winston Churchill*, Autumn, 2013.

June Hopkins, Ph.D.
Bellingham, Washington

Endnotes

---

[1] British Ambassador Viscount Halifax, French Ambassador Bonnet, Secretary of the Navy James Forrestal, Bernard Baruch, Justice Felix Frankfurter, Fleet Admiral Ernest King, Joseph Davies, Henry Morgenthau, Frances Perkins, Senator Claude Pepper, and Mr. and Mrs. Mount Vernon Lewis, the caretakers of the Hopkins' home in Georgetown. Eleanor Roosevelt was in London, laid up with the flu.

[2] Harry Hopkins' Funeral, various newspaper clippings, Personal Family Papers (hereinafter PFP) 9/14.

[3] "John Steinbeck's Memorial to Harry Hopkins Read by Burgess Meredith at the Memorial Services, May 22, 1946," Hopkins Collection I, Box1, Folder 45, Special Collections, Lauinger Library, Georgetown University, Washington, D. C. Hereinafter GUSC.

[4] Sherwood, WHP, xi.

[5] "Hopkins a Power in New Deal, Played a Leading Role in the War," *New York Herald Tribune*, Wednesday, January 30, 1946, p. 22. As the service started, 40,000 garment workers in Manhattan paused at their machines to honor the man who, for a very short time as the chairman of the women's coat and suit industry, had been their advocate. It was a tribute to his continuing efforts to help the laboring classes. PFP, 9/14.

[6] PFP, 9/15.

[7] Ibid.

[8] Christopher O'Sullivan, *Harry Hopkins: FDR's Envoy to Churchill and Stalin* (2014); David L. Roll, *The Hopkins Touch: Harry Hopkins and the Forging of the Alliance to Defeat Hitler* (2013); Michael Fullilove, *Rendezvous with Destiny: How*

Franklin D. Roosevelt and Five Extraordinary Men Took America into the War and into the World, (2013).

[9] Elihu Root was Theodore Roosevelt's secretary of state.

[10] Some famous women followed a career path beginning with settlement work: Eleanor Roosevelt, Julia Lathrop; Florence Kelly, Edith Abbott.

[11] These Widows Pension programs were the forerunners of Title IV of the 1935 Social Security Act, Aid to Dependent Children (ADC, later AFDC, and TANF) the basis of the American Welfare System. Hopkins was on the Committee for Economic Security that wrote the legislation for the Social Security Act.

[12] Hopkins, June. *Harry Hopkins: Sudden Hero, Brash Reformer*. New York: St. Martin's Press, 1999, 128.

[13] Hopkins, *Sudden Hero*, 154-55.

[14] Hopkins, Chapters 3 and 4, passim.

[15] Dwight Tuttle, *Harry Hopkins and Anglo-American-Soviet Relations, 1941-1945* (New York: Garland Press, 1983), p. 43.

[16] Warren F, Kimball, *The Juggler: Franklin Roosevelt as Wartime Statesman* (Princeton: Princeton University Press, 1991), p. 3.

[17] Sherwood, *WHP*, p. 268.

[18] Christopher O'Sullivan, *Harry Hopkins: FDR's Envoy to Churchill and Stalin*. (New York: Rowman and Littlefield, 2015), p. 49.

[19] Kimball, *The Juggler*, p. 3.

[20] Tuttle, p. 97.

[21] PFP, 9/19.4, p. 1.

[22] Sherwood, *WHP*, p. 81.

[23] Sherwood, *WHP*, p. 121.

[24] Tuttle, pp. 26-29.

[25] Memo Jan. 11, 1941, Robert Hopkins Papers I, Bi, F 14, GUSC.

[26] Sherwood, *WHP*, pp. 118-19; Halsted MS, Chapter 8, passim.

[27] See Halsted Ms.

[28] Robert E. Sherwood, *Roosevelt and Hopkins: An Intimate History* (New York: Harper & Brothers, 1948), pp. 2-3. Dwight Tuttle agrees with the assessment that the relationship between the two was based on Hopkins' unfailing loyalty to the president. (Tuttle, *Harry Hopkins*, p. 30.)

[29] Quoted in Tuttle, p. 33.

[30] Biographer Tuttle overstates Hopkins political ambition at Grinnell College where he was more admired for his ability on the basketball court than in the collegiate political arena. He correctly describes Hopkins in Washington as a liberal reformer. See pp. 26-29.

[31] Stoler, *Allies in War*, xx.

[32] Kimball, *The Juggler*, p. 27.

[33] Fraser Harbutt, "Churchill, Hopkins, and the 'Other' Americans: An Alternative Perspective on Anglo-American Relations, 1941-1945," *The International History Review*, Vol. 8, No. 2 (May, 1966), p. 237

[34] Sherwood, *WHP*, 158.

[35] Turner Catledge, "It's Send for Harry," *The New York Times Magazine*, March 16, 1941, p. 6. PFP, 9/61.

[36] As quoted in Cole C. Kingseed, "The Juggler and the Supreme Commander," *Military Review*, 76, No. 6 (1996), p. 78. See also Kimball, *The Juggler*; John Meacham, *Franklin and Winston: An Intimate Portrait of an Epic Friendship* (New York: Random House, 2003), p. xx.

[37] Dr. James Halstead and Diana Hopkins Baxter Halsted, unpublished manuscript. In author's possession. Hereinafter Halsted MS. Ch. 10, p. 19. This is what Hopkins was worried about before the Atlantic Conference.

[38] Dictation by Harry Hopkins, July 20, 1945, Hopkins I, Box 57 Folder 12; "What Victory Will Bring Us" by Harry Hopkins, November 4, 1943, , GUSC Hopkins Papers I, Box 57, Folder 4.]

[39] John Charmley, "Churchill and the American Alliance," Sixth Series (*Transactions of the Royal Historical Society*, 2001), pp. 356-58.

[40] Charmley, pp. 356-58.

[41] Fraser Harbutt, "Churchill, Hopkins, and the 'Other' Americans: An Alternative Perspective on Anglo-American Relations, 1941-1945," *The International History Review*, Vol. 8, No. 2 (May, 1966), p. 237; Francis L. Loewenheim, Harold D. Langley, and Manfred Jonas, eds. *Roosevelt and Churchill: Their Secret Wartime Correspondence* (New York: E. P. Dutton & Co., Inc., 1975), p. 403.

[42] Timothy Snyder, *On Tyranny: Twenty Lessons from the Twentieth Century* (New York: Tim Duggan Books, 2017), p. 125.

[43] Queen Consort of King George VI, she is referred to as Queen Mother to avoid confusion with her daughter Queen Elizabeth II.

[44] *The New York Times*, April 24, 1938, Rotogravure Section, PFP, 9/74.

[45] Sherwood, *WHP*, p. 21.

[46] McJimsey, pp. 126-27.

[47] Sherwood, *Roosevelt and Hopkins*, pp. 180-81.

[48] Sherwood *WHP*, pp. 120, 180-81.

[49] Sherwood, *WHP*, pp. 111-12.

[50] Lou Jagerman, Interview, November 2019

[51] By 1943 both Roosevelt and Churchill were in a bind. They were anxious to keep Stalin from leaving the Alliance because the Red Army was so vital to the war effort. So, neither western leader was willing to accuse the Soviets of the shootings during either the Teheran Conference or the Yalta Conference. It was only in 1989 that the truth came out; Soviet leader Mikhail Gorbachov admitted that the Soviets had murdered tens of thousands of Poles at Katyn and several other places.

[52] Stoler, Allies in War, p. 12-13.

[53] Sherwood, Roosevelt and Hopkins, p. 142.

[54] Sherwood, Roosevelt and Hopkins, p. 141.

[55] Robert Hopkins Correspondence, Doc. 7, p. 9. A collection in author's possession. Hereinafter RHC.

[56] This was the first of several wartime missions that Hopkins made at the behest of Roosevelt.

[57] Sherwood, WHP, pp. 97-99.

[58] Sherwood, WHP, p. 135. The (unknown) correspondent who sent the poem to Roosevelt explained that "Amerikay" was a pronunciation common to both Abraham Lincoln and Jefferson Davis.

[59] Robert Hopkins, "Councils of War," p. 9. PFP, 9/18.

[60] Harry and Barbara Hopkins first lived in Rock Creek Park when they married in 1931 and then moved to N Street in Georgetown. Harry and his daughter Diana stayed there when Barbara died in 1937. There was a direct line installed to the White House. In May 1940, Harry and Diana moved to the White House. The article said that presidents lead very lonely lives but that FDR had found "a friend, creative and complex." Sunday News, July 26, 1942, p. 49. PFP, 9/48.

[61] McJimsey, Harry Hopkins, p. 129

[62] Warren F. Kimball, Forged in War: Roosevelt, Churchill and the Second World War (New York: Morrow, 1997), p. 77.

[63] Sherwood, WHP, p. 211. Drummond and Perry, Look (6/27/44) p. 21; PFP, 9/39

[64] Kimball, The Juggler, p. 5.

[65] Sherwood, WHP, pp. 204-06.

[66] Sherwood, WHP, pp. 144, 202; Warren Kimball, Forged in War: Churchill, Roosevelt and the Second World War (London: HarperCollins, 1997), pp. 77-78. Kimball describes Hopkins' position during the years that Hopkins lived at the White House, from 1941 through 1943, as a national security advisor decades before the position was installed, and with only a skeleton staff.

[67] Fraser Harbutt. "Churchill, Hopkins, and the 'Other'

Americans", p. 237.

[68] Harbutt, "Churchill, Hopkins, and the 'Other' Americans," pp. 237, 239, 244

[69] Sherwood, *WHP*, p. 145.

[70] Quoted in Sherwood, *WHP*, p. 148.

[71] RHC, Doc. 9, pp. 11-14. There is a formality to this letter that is typical of Hopkins' correspondences with his sons, although sometimes he signed letters, "Dad". In 1940 the two eldest were old enough to enlist and the youngest, Stephen, was 15 and joined the Marines in 1943; he was killed in the Pacific war just as he turned 18. The eldest, David, joined the Navy and served in the Pacific on an aircraft carrier; Robert joined the Army Signal Corps and served in the European Theater; both survived.

[72] Tuttle, p. 55.

[73] Robert Hopkins, "World War II: From Alpha to Omega," p.p. 1-9. PFP.

[74] Sherwood, *WHP*, p. 169.

[75] PFP, 9/70 and 9/70.1; McJimsey, p. 129.

[76] Sherwood, *WHP*, p. 179; McJimsey, p. 130.

[77] Sherwood, *WHP*, p. 244.

[78] Ibid.

[79] Kimball, *Forged in War*, p. 70

[80] Kimball, Warred, ed, "Churchill & Roosevelt: The Complete Correspondence. Vol. I, Alliance Emerging. (London: Colins, 1984), pp. 42-43, 51, 52, 59, 60. Emphasis in original.

[81] Sherwood, *WHP*, p. 223.

[82] Kimball, *Forger in War*, p. 71

[83] Sherwood, *Roosevelt and Hopkins*, p. 224.

[84] Sherwood, WHP, p. 225; McJimsey, pp. 133-34.

[85] Sherwood, WHP, pp. 224-27.

[86] Fullilove, 112-13.

[87] Tuttle, p. 53; O'Sulivan, p. 52; McJmsey, *The Presidency*, p. 210.

[88] Marquis Childs, *Saturday Evening Post,* April 19, 1941, "The President's Best Friend," PFP, 8/9. Kimball, *Forged in War,* p.78.

[89] Frank Costigliola, *Roosevelt's Lost Alliances: How Personal Politics Helped Start the Cold War* (Princeton: Princeton Univ. Press, reprint, 2013), 101-03.

[90] Costigliola, 98.

[91] McJimsey, *The Presidency of Franklin Roosevelt,* pp. 201-202.

[92] Tuttle, p. 7.

[93] Sherwood, *Roosevelt and Hopkins,* p. 231; McJimsey, p, 134.

[94] Fullilove, p. 112.

[95] Costigliola, pp. 101-103, 109.

[96] Harbutt, , p. 236.

[97] Sherwood, *Roosevelt and Hopkins,* p. 232.

[98] Sherwood, *WHP,* p. 288.

[99] Sherwood, *WHP,* 234-35.

[100] Sherwood *WHP. P.* 237.

[101] Halsted MS, Chapter 10, p. 2; Churchill 1950, 402.

[102] Sherwood, *WHP,* pp. 237-39; Costigliola, p. 104-0p6.

[103] Winston S. Churchill *Memoirs of the Second World War* (Boston: Houghton Mifflin, abridged version, 1959), 401-02.

[104] Churchill, *Memoirs,* pp. 402-03; Sherwood, WHP, p. 237

[105] Sherwood, *Roosevelt and Hopkins,* pp. 238-43; Harbutt, "Churchill, Hopkins, and the 'Other' Americans," p. 239.

[106] Sherwood, *WHP* 237; Costigliola, 104; According to a New Yorker "Off the Record" article, Churchill responded to Hopkins with the "smile of a relieved grandson of the seventh Duke of Marlborough and pulled out a fresh cigar." Robert Hopkins Papers, 3, Box 20, File 32, GUSC.

[107] McJimsey, *The Presidency of Franklin Roosevelt,* p.204.

[108] Sherwood, *WHP* 261.

[109] Halsted MS, Ch. 10, passim.

[110] See Sherwood and Halsted MS, Ch. 10. .

[111] Sherwood, *WHP,* p. 248.

[112] Hopkins Diary, January 30, 1941, pp. 3-4. PFP, 9/68.1.

[113] Ronald Lewin, *Churchill as Warlord* (New York: Stein and Day, 1973) p. 63.

[114] *New York Journal American*, January 17, 1941, PFP, 9/65.4.

[115] Sherwood, *WHP*, 268, 288.

[116] Sherwood, *WHP*, p. 268; McJimsey, p. 150.

[117] Harbutt, "Churchill, Hopkins and the 'Other' Americans, p. 241.

[118] Tuttle, p. 72.

[119] Sherwood, *Roosevelt and Hopkins*, p. 251.

[120] Sherwood, *WHP*, pp. 640-42; Sherwood, *Roosevelt and Hopkins*, p. 268.

[121] McJimsey, 148.

[122] "Nazi Line Coast for Gas Blitz," *Daily News*, February 17, 1941. PFP, 9/65.3.

[123] PFP, 9/67, p. 2.

[124] Quoted in Dwight Tuttle, *Harry L. Hopkins and Anglo-Soviet Relations, 1941-1945* (New York: Garland Publishing, Inc., 1993), p. 42-43.

[125] Lewin, p. 63.

[126] Lewin, p. 64.

[127] Raymond Gram Swing, *Look* article, 1941 (just after HLH returned from Great Britain), "The World's Most Important Contact Man," Robert Hopkins, Box 7, F. 3, GUSC.

[128] McJimsey, *The Presidency*, p. 205.

[129] McJimsey, *Harry Hopkins*, pp. 148-49.

[130] Tuttle, p. 71.

[131] Tuttle, pp. 76-78.

[132] Hopkins had let his wife divorce him for the sake of propriety. He had fallen in love with another woman, Barbara Duncan, and did not want to continue in his marriage to Ethel.

[133] Allison Giffen and June Hopkins, eds. *"Jewish First Wife, Divorced: The Correspondence of Ethel Gross and Harry Hopkins* (New York: Lexington Books, 2003), pp. 251-55.

[134] Sherwood, WHP, pp. 212, 166; Warren Kimball, ed. *Churchill and Roosevelt: The Complete Correspondence, Vol. I Alliance Emerging* (London: William Collins and Son, 1984), p. 148.

[135] Sherwood, *WHP*, p. 265; Sherwood, *Roosevelt and Hopkins*, pp. 257 and 265.

[136] McJimsey, p. 148-49.

[137] Churchill, Memoirs, "The Grand Alliance" (New York: Houghton & Mifflin, 1950), p 23.

[138] Fullilove, p. 150.

[139] Sherwood, WHP, pp. 761-62.

[140] Ministry of Foreign Affairs, *Correspondence between the Chairman of the Council of Ministers of the U.S.S.R. and the Presidents of the U.S.A, and the Prime Ministers of Great Britain during the Great Patriotic War of 1941-1945* (Moscow: Foreign Languages Publishing House: 1957), p. 11.

[141] Lewin, p. 77-78; Churchill, *Memoirs*, abridged, pp. 460-62, 470.

[142] "The Stalin Hitler Grudge Fight, p. 4. See Kimball, *Forged in War*, pp. 87-90.

[143] Lewin, pp. 77-78.

[144] Churchill, *Memoirs*, p. 460-61, 470.

[145] Sherwood, R and H, p. 305.

[146] Kimball, *Forged in War*, p. 90-91; Lewin, p. 77. Churchill embraced the sentiment, "the enemy of my enemy is my friend."

[147] Fullilove, p. 280-81; Sherwood *WHP*, 302-03.

[148] Sherwood, R and H, pp. 304-305.

[149] Sherwood, R and H, pp 210-311.

[150] Tuttle, pp. 86-88.

[151] Sherwood, R and H, p. 311,

[152] Sherwood, *WHP*, pp. 351, 362.

[153] First at Teheran in November 1943 and then at Yalta in February of 1945.

[154] Sherwood, *WHP*, pp. 306-09.

[155] McJimsey, p. 190.

[156] Sherwood, *WHP*, p. 306, Kimball, *Correspondences*, p. 239.

[157] Kimball, *The Juggler*, p. 29.

[158] Tuttle, p. 96.

[159] Churchill, *Memoirs*, abridgement, p.487-89.

[160] Sherwood, *WHP*, p. 318.

[161] Kimball, *The Juggler*, p.p 32-33, and note 49, and *Forged in War*, p. 90; Tuttle, pp. 96-97; Sherwood, *WHP*, pp. 317-318; Fullilove, p. 281.

[162] Churchill Archives, CHAR/20/41/63.

[163] Ambassador to the Soviet Union in 1941, Adolph Steinhardt, and his staff later evacuated to Kuybushev after the German attack on Russia. The only diplomat left was Second Secretary Llewellyn E. Thompson.

[164] Sherwood, *WHP*, p. 318.

[165] Quoted in McJimsey, p. 181-82; Hopkins flew on an American made PBY "flying boat" from Invergorden, Scotland, to Archangel, a route recently opened by the RAF Coastal Command. Wills, pp. 25-26.

[166] Sherwood, *WHP*, p. 321.

[167] Fullilove, pp. 284-85.

[168] Halsted MS, Chapter 10, p. 15.

[169] Fullilove, p. 287-90.

[170] Sherwood, WHP, pp. 325-327.

[171] McJimsey, p. 184; Fullilove, p. 292.

[172] Sherwood, WHP, p. 328.

[173] Sherwood, *WHP*, pp. 322.

[174] Sherwood, *WHP*, pp. 321-22.

[175] Quoted in McJimsey, p. 183.

[176] Sherwood, *WHP*, p. 329; McJimsey, p. 184.

[177] Fullilove, p. 283; see Chapter 7, pp. 279-312 "Uncle Joe's Favorite" for an excellent and very detailed account of Hopkins' July 30 to August 1 meetings with Stalin.

[178] "The Stalin-Hitler Grudge Fight," p. 20, PFP 9/55

[179] Sherwood, *WHP*, 335-36.

[180] Matthew B. Wills, Wartime Missions of Harry L. Hopkins (Bloomington, Ind.: Author House, 2004), pp. 31-37.

[181] Sherwood, *WHP*, p. 343.

[182] "The Stalin-Hitler Grudge Fight," p. 2.

[183] Wills, p. 37; Halsted MS, Ch. 10, pp. 15-16.

[184] Sherwood, *WHP*, p. 323; Tuttle, p. 104.

[185] Tuttle, p. 107.

[186] *Journal American* (July 30, 1941) and *The Sun* (July 30, 1941), PFP, 9/60.1.

[187] Sherwood, *WHP*, pp. 731-33."

[188] *Daily Worker*, August 1, 1941, p. 1, PFP, 9/58, pp. 2-4.

[189] Leonard Lyons, "They Told Me," *The Los Angeles Times, This Week*, January 28, 1945, p. 4.

[190] Halsted MS, Chapter 10, p. 15.

[191] "The Stalin-Hitler Grudge Fight," pp. 21-23, PP 9/55; *The Daily Worker*, August 1, 1941, PFP, 9/58.

[192] Loewenheim, et al, Letter August 5, 1941, p. 153.

[193] Theodore A. Wilson, *The First Summit* (Lawrence: Univ. of Kansas Press: 1991), pp. 3-6.

[194] Sherwood, *WHP*, p. 350.

[195] Churchill Archives 20/41/02.

[196] Letter to Lewis Hopkins from Harry Hopkins, 9th August, 1941, aboard H.M.S. Prince of Wales. PFP, 9.56.

[197] Letter to Harry Hopkins, July 21st, 1941, from Lyndon B. Johnson. PFP, 9.62.

[198] H. V. Morton, *Atlantic Meeting: An Account of Mr. Churchill's Voyage in H.M.S.* Prince of Wales, *in August, 1941, and the conference with President Roosevelt Which Resulted in the Atlantic* Charter (New York: Dodd, Mead, 1943), p. 62.

[199] Fullilove, p. 320. Quoted on p. 322.

[200] Churchill, p. 410.

[201] Morton, p. 155.

[202] Tuttle, pp. 110-11.

[203] Morton, 90.

[204] The two had met in 1918 in London when Roosevelt was under-secretary of the navy under Woodrow Wilson and Churchill was First Lord of the Admiralty. He was somewhat awed by Churchill, but the Prime Minister did not remember meeting him.

[205] Sherwood, *WHP*, pp. 361-62. The Ottawa Agreements ensured trade and tariff concessions to the Dominions.

[206] Kimball, *The Juggler*, p. 43.

[207] O'Sullivan, p. 55.

[208] Sherwood, *WHP*, p. 355.

[209] Sherwood, *WHP*, p. 362.

[210] Sherwood, *WHP*, p. 364.

[211] Sherwood, *WHP*, p. 377.

[212] Kimball, *Forged in War*, p. 98-99; Fullilove, p.p. 327-30.

[213] PFP, 9/62.2

[214] Churchill Archives 20/42/35

[215] Fullilove, p. 335-36; Kimball, *The Juggler*, p. 39.

[216] Sherwood, *WHP*, p. 282.

[217] Sherwood, *WHP*, pp. 267-68, 288.

[218] Sherwood, *WHP*, p. 269.

[219] Harbutt, "Churchill, Hopkins, and the 'Other' Americans, p. 239.

[220] Harbutt, "Churchill, Hopkins, and the 'Other' Americans," p. 241.

[221] Fullilove, p. 340; Sherwood, *Roosevelt and Hopkins*, pp. 430-31. The previous day, December 6, after having read some decoded Japanese cables, Hopkins had remarked to Roosevelt that since war with the Japanese was inevitable, "it was too bad that we could not strike the first blow and prevent any sort of surprise." Roosevelt replied, "No we can't do that. We are a democracy and a peaceful people." Sherwood, *Roosevelt and Hopkins*, p. 427.

[222] Churchill, *Memoirs*, p. 506.

[223] Sherwood, *WHP*, p. 264.

[224] Harbutt, "Churchill, Hopkins and the' Other' Americans," pp. 242, 245, 247. Harbutt correctly points out Hopkins' effectiveness by assuring Churchill that Britain would get a sufficient amount of Lend Lease material after Pearl Harbor; in calming the waters when the Free French seized Saint Pierre and Miquelon; and in persuading Churchill to accept the CCOS.

[225] Fraser Harbutt, *Yalta 1945: Europe and America at the Crossroads* (New York: Cambridge University Press, 2010), p. 139.

[226] Jonathan Fenby, *The Inside Story of How Roosevelt, Stalin & Churchill Won One War and Began Another* (New York: Simon and Schuster, 2006), p. 4.

[227] Harbutt, *Yalta,* pp. ix-xx; Martin Folly, "'A Long, Slow and Painful Road": The Anglo-American Alliance and the Issue of Co-operation with the USSR from Teheran to D-Day, *Diplomacy & Statecraft,* 23 (2012), p. 472.

[228] Sherwood, *WHP,* p. xv.

[229] Sherwood, *WHP,* p. 302. All three were regarded by the Allies as collaborators.

[230] Sherwood, *WHP,* pp. 369-79.

[231] Many of these powerful British officials stayed at the White House, causing untold disruptions to the Roosevelt family for the Christmas holidays.

[232] Tuttle, p. 125.

[233] Sherwood, *WHP,* pp. 446-48.

[234] Sherwood, WHP, pp. 470, 479.

[235] David J. Bercuson and Holger H. Herwig, *One Christmas in Washington: The Secret Meeting Between Roosevelt and Churchill That Changed the World* (New York: The Overlook Press, 2005), pp. 224-25.

[236] Bercuson and Herwig, pp. 219-222; see also Tuttle, pp. 128-30.

[237] Sherwood, *WHP,* pp. 450-59; Sherwood, *Roosevelt and Hopkins,* pp. 446-55; Tuttle, pp. 128-31.

238 Tuttle, 126-28. Hopkins also convinced Churchill to accept Roosevelt's proposal for a unified command for Allied troops under General Sir Archibald Wavell. p. 130-31; Harbutt writes that Hopkins had forewarned Churchill about FDR's preference for the North African campaign in 1942, which helped the PM plan for Torch. Harbutt, Churchill, Hopkins, and the 'Other' Americans," p, 244.

239 Tuttle, p. 131. Tuttle does not make the connection, but this demonstrates that Hopkins could say things to the Prime Minister that the President could not or should not say.

240 Tuttle, p. 125. If Hopkins "downplayed fears" about what would happen if the Red Army reached Berlin first, it did not "betray an insecurity about our own political system," as Tuttle claims. Hopkins became convinced that Stalin had such complete control over the Soviet Union and such hatred of Hitler that he would never abandon the fight. It was Hopkins unwavering faith in democracies that led him t suggest that civil liberties might even emerge in the post-war Soviet Union.

241 Sherwood, *WHP*, pp. 408-09.

242 Earle Rice, Jr., Chapter 2, "Operation Overlord: Planning and Preparing," *Normandy*, 18, U. S. Facts on File.

243 Charles Wilson (Lord Moran). *Churchill: Taken from the Diaries of Lord Moran* (Boston: Houghton Mifflin Company, 1966), p. 37

244 Jon Meacham, "The Winding Road to D-Day," *Time*, 183, No. 23 (June 6, 2014), p. 6.

245 Vyacheslav Molotov, *Molotov Remembers*, pp. 46-47, PFP, 9/64, folder 1. Molotov wrote that the Soviets signed the Declaration on the Liberation of Europe because "it was to our benefit" and claimed that the Allies were trying to impose a bourgeois government on Poland that would certainly have been an agent of imperialism. The Soviets

were only interested in Poland as "an independent but not hostile nation." pp. 51-53.

[246] Letters October 17-29, 1942, Robert Hopkins Correspondence, pp. 40-53, docs. 32-56 in author's possession. The incidents are related in Robert Hopkins MS "World War II: From Alpha to Omega," 1998, pp. 20-28, PFP 9/5.

[247] Churchill Archives, 20/77/56, July 2, 1942.

[248] Sherwood, *WHP*, pp. 731-733.

[249] Quoted in Wills, p. 39.

[250] By early June General Edwin Rommel was threatening Tobruk, which fell on the 21st.

[251] Churchill Archives. 20/78/71

[252] Wills, p. 41.

[253] Sherwood, pp. 611-615; Loewenheim, et al. p. 87.

[254] Wills, pp. 43-45.

[255] Hopkins told Churchill first about his coming marriage to Louise Macy when he was at the British Embassy for a dinner, and then he told FDR.

[256] Sherwood, *Roosevelt and Hopkins*, pp. 612-614. This was just after the Marshall-Hopkins-King meeting in London in mid-July with Churchill to discuss military strategy for the rest of 1942. Churchill wrote Roosevelt that he was very pleased with the results of the "strenuous week" and doubted "if success would have been achieved without Harry's invaluable aid." Churchill referred to them as "the three musketeers. Loewenheim, et al. letter July 17, 1942, p. 225, 227.

[257] Draft of an article by Louis de Villefosse, for *Contretemps*. PFP 9/43. He was a Frenchman who wrote an article in 1979 in French on the Second World War, referencing a visit to Robert Hopkins' Georgetown home, which was translated by Robert Hopkins. p. 10; Kimball, *Correspondence*, Vol. I, p. 165.

[258] Warren Kimball, *Forged in War*, p. 18.

[259] Churchill Archives, 20/80/123. Oliver Lyttelton was Minister of Production.

[260] Churchill Archives 20/81/52

[261] Kimball, Forged in War, p. 18; See Sherwood, *Roosevelt and Hopkins*, pp. 180-81.

[262] François Darlan was assassinated in 1942 by a monarchist.

[263] Fenby, pp. 159-161.

[264] Churchill Archives 20/80/73, 20/80/74.

[265] Sherwood, *WHP*, 653.

[266] McJimsey, p. 260; Sherwood, *WHP*, 653.

[267] Charles Wilson (Lord Moran) *Churchill: Taken from the Diaries of Lord Moran* (Boston: Houghton Mifflin, 1966), p. 86.

[268] Kimball, *The Juggler*, p.70.

[269] *Los Angeles Times*, January 27, 1943, Section B. PFP 9/46.

[270] Robert Hopkins, *Witness to History: Recollections of a WWII Photographer* (Seattle: Castle Pacific Publishing, 2002), p. 44.

[271] Rice, Jr. "Chapter 2.

[272] Sherwood, *WHP*, pp. 692-93.

[273] See General Jacob E. Smart, "The Casablanca Conference, January 1943," (*Air Power History* 46 (Fall, 1999). Stoler, *Allies in War*, pp. 90-91 and 129, argues that Roosevelt and Churchill had already agreed upon this policy before the conference when the foreign ministers, Eden and Hull, met in Moscow in October; unconditional surrender would be the only way for the Allies to wipe out fascism.

[274] McJimsey writes that Hopkins may not have expected Roosevelt's announcement and probably did not fully understand the import of the decision and how it might affect world peace after the war. p. 278-80. Sherwood, I, p. 693; See Kimball, *Forged in War*, p. 188-91, for speculation as to the effects of the Allied demand for unconditional surrender.

[275] See Giffen and Hopkins, pp. 259-60. Hopkins wrote a letter to his ex-wife on February 2, 1943, describing their son's appearance at the Casablanca Conference

[276] Robert Hopkins, "Roosevelt, Churchill, and Stalin: Councils of War and Peace, 1943-1945, PFP, 9/18, p. 2.

[277] An example of Robert's access to the President because of his father is an incident that happened in late November 1941. He had joined the President, his father, and Missy LeHand, the President's private secretary, for a casual dinner in the Oval Office. When Robert realized that it was too late for him to get back to Fort Dix if he were to hitchhike, he asked his father for five dollars bus fare. When Hopkins said he didn't have it, the President said, "I'll lend five dollars." When Robert demurred, the President insisted. He also gave him a card with the presidential seal embossed in gold, saying, "Let me give you this in case you don't arrive in time for revile.". On the card he wrote, "November 30, 1941, To Whom it May Concern: Private Robert Hopkins is to be excused from revile because he has been in consultation with the Commander-in-Chief. Signed Franklin D. Roosevelt." Just before he left, Robert, concerned about his father's health, asked the President to take him on a vacation. The President promised to do this, "as soon as the Japanese situation is settled." One week later, the Japanese attacked Pearl Harbor. Robert Hopkins, "Councils of War," PFP, 9/18, p. 14.

[278] Robert Hopkins, "From Alpha to Omega," PFP, 9/6, p. 45.

[279] Moran, p. 89.

[280] Robert Hopkins, pp. 43-53; Sherwood, pp. 692-93; Moran, p. 89.

[281] Sherwood, p. 690.

[282] de Villefosse. PFP 9/43, p. 2. Frenchman Louis de Villefosse wrote in 1979, that it was largely due to Hopkins that the Soviet Union did not collapse. Hopkins was "artisan of the operation" to fly to Moscow, meet with Stalin, and

promise the dictator that America would do all it could to support Russia against the Germans. Stalin gave Hopkins a silver snuff box as a thank you.

283 Villefosse, pp. 8-9.

284 Tuttle, pp. 133-34. Hull had already been upset by the President favoring his undersecretary and frequently sending Sumner Welles for important mission instead of himself. By this time he was likely easily upset.

285 O'Sullivan, p. 59.

286 Kimball, The *Juggler*, pp. 71-72.

287 See Kimball, *The Juggler*, pp. 80-81; Richard Raskin, "*Casablanca* and Foreign Policy," *Film History*, Vol. 4, 1990, pp. 153-164. See Darlan Deal. It is hard to imagine that Warner Bros. had this in mind when making the movie; it is much easier to imagine Roosevelt chuckling as he showed the film to his guests.

288 Sherwood, *WHP*, pp. 727-28.

289 Sherwood, *WHP*, 729,

290 Tuttle, pp. 202-05. John Charmley claims that the British paid much too much for America's support, that concessions such as the "destroyers for bases deal" amounted to "extortion." It was a mistake for Churchill to side with the Americans against the French. "Churchill and the American Alliance." p. 358. Charmley, however, discounts the nature of the "Special Relationship" and the mutual need of both leaders who, of course, could not wage the war without each other. Martin Folly writes that Churchill and Roosevelt could agree on military strategy to a larger degree than they could on what could be an effective political policy toward the Soviets after the war. Hopkins regarded economic "carrots" as a way to control Stalin and ensure US-Soviet cooperation after the war. "A Long, Slow and Painful Road," p. 474. It is also important to note that after Teheran, Hopkins' illness kept him out of

commission for several months. See CHAR 20/142A/74, 76, 79.

[291] Moran, p. 90.

[292] Robert Hopkins Correspondence, Doc. 66, p. 99. In author's possession.

[293] Sherwood, *WHP*, pp. 742-46.

[294] David Roll, *The Hopkins Touch: Harry Hopkins and the Forging of the Alliance to Defeat Hitler* (Oxford: Oxford University Press, 2013), pp. 284-291. Dwight Tuttle writes that at the First Quebec Conference (Quadrant) Hopkins argued against Churchill's caveat that Overlord could not be launched until there were fewer than twelve German divisions in northern France saying that the PM needed to be more flexible. Tuttle, pp. 208-09.

[295] Ibid. Hopkins relationship with Stalin has been the topic of much investigation in recent years. See Ronald Radosh's review of Diane West's *American Betrayal: The Secret Assault on Our Nation's Character. Frontgate*, August 6, 1913. Radosh unequivocally refutes West's allegation that Hopkins was a secret Soviet agent during the war years (Agent 19) and that the Roosevelt government was "occupied" by Communists.

[296] Sherwood, *WHP*, pp. 756, 774.

[297] Mark A. Stoler, *Allies in War: Britain and America Against the Axis Powers 1940-1945* (London: Hodder Arnold, 2005), p. 127. Stoler argues that fear of Soviets "counterbalanced their growing differences and helped keep them closely aligned." By this time the British were certainly junior partners in the triumvirate. While the agreement between Roosevelt and Churchill not to share atomic secrets with the Soviets certainly reflected the Western Allies' distrust in Stalin's postwar intentions and their desire to limit the communist threat, they still needed the Red Army. At the Teheran Conference, FDR cozied up to Stalin much to the annoyance of Churchill and probably led to a temporary weakening of

the Special Relationship with power continuing to shift to the Americans.

[298] Sherwood, *WHP*, pp. 654-58.

[299] Roosevelt and Hopkins sailed to Cairo on the *USS Iowa*; the *USS William D. Porter* accidently sent a live torpedo to the Iowa, which was able to avoid a hit. PFP 9/42.1.

[300] W. Averell Harriman and Elie Abel, *Special Envoy to Churchill and Stalin*, 1941-1946 (New York: Random House, 1975), p. 258.

[301] "Extracts from Diary at the Time of the Conferences at Cairo and Teheran by Robert Hopkins," pp. 139-41,The Robert Hopkins Collection, Georgetown University Lauinger Library Special Collection, Washington, D.C. [hereinafter "Excerpts."]

[302] Robert Hopkins, "From Alpha to Omega," p. 86-87, unpublished manuscript, PFP, 9/5.

[303] "Excerpts," p. 143; "From Alpha to Omega," p. 88.

[304] Ronald Ian Heiferman, *The Cairo Conference of 1943* (Jefferson, N. C.: McFarland, 2011), pp. 4-18.

[305] The Burma Road was essential for transporting munitions to the Chinese army; when the Japanese bombed it making it severely hindered the Chinese efforts t fight the Japanese.

[306] Sherwood, *WHP*, 657-58. In his *Allies in War*, Stoler argues that Madame Chiang merely revealed her "vanity and arrogance" during her trip to the States. p. 181.

[307] "Memorandum for the President, April 4, 1942," Box 39, #12, Map Room Papers, FDR Library, Hyde Park, New York.

[308] Sherwood, *WHP*, 704

[309] "Excerpts," p. 143.

[310] Madame Chiang spoke perfect English and was a graduate of Wellesley College.

[311] Heiferman, pp. 70-116 passim.

[312] Stoler, *Allies in War*, p. 135.

[313] Sherwood, *WHP*, p. 769.

[314] Fenby, p. 320.

[315] Sherwood, *WHP*, 766-67.

[316] Moran, p. 141.

[277] Churchill Archives, 20/125/54.

[318] John R. Miller, "The Chiang-Stilwell Conflict, 1942-1944(43 *Military Affairs*), p. 60. The conflict between Chiang and Stillwell continued until Stillwell just recommended removing Chiang as Allied Commander. FDR agreed. Consequently, Chiang demanded Stilwell's removal and because China was still crucial to the war effort in the Pacific, General Albert C. Wedemeyer replaced Stilwell in October 1944.

[319] Keith Eubank, *Summit at Teheran: The Untold Story* (New York: William Morrow & Co., 1985), p. 254.

[320] Sherwood, *WHP*, 783-84

[321] Churchill Archives, CHAR 20/121/44.

[322] Sherwood, *WHP*, p. 761-62; Churchill Archives, CHAR 20/20/56.

[323] Harbutt, "Churchill, Hopkins and the 'Other' Americans," p. 251.

[324] Robert Hopkins, *Witness*, p. 88. In the midst of the war, Hopkins noticed a piece that E. B. White had written in the New Yorker on the meaning of democracy, and he passed it on the President. "Democracy is the recurrent suspicion that more than half of the people are right more than half the time." And then putting it into American terms, "Democracy is a letter to the editor ... the score at the beginning of the ninth ... the mustard on the hot dog and the cream in rationed coffee." Meacham, pp. 368-69. The President loved it.

[325] Moran, pp. 142-43. Apparently, Hopkins could become "quite fierce" with Moran, something he would never do with Churchill or Roosevelt.

[326] Stoler, *Allies in War*, pp. 139-42. According to Stoler, the tenor at this conference became increasingly tense. The President might have been simply acting as the "Juggler" in

this instance, certainly ingratiating Stalin at the expense of Churchill, but for important strategic reasons.

[327] Eubank, p. 239.

[328] Sherwood, *WHP*, 776.

[329] *Molotov Remembers*, 46-47; PFP, 9.64.0, folder 1.

[330] Robert Hopkins Diary, PFP, 13/27; Robert Hopkins, *Witness*, p. 93-94.

[331] O'Sullivan, pp. 90-91.

[332] Fenby, p. 232.

[333] Sherwood, *WHP*, p. 314.

[334] O'Sullivan, p. 91.

[335] Churchill Archives, CHAR 20/154/24.

[336] Churchill Archives, CHAR 20/154/34.

[337] O'Sullivan, p. 92.

[338] Stoler, *Allies in War*, p. 143.

[339] Fenby, p. 232.

[340] Churchill Archives, CHAR 20/142A/22.

[341] Churchill Archives CHAR 20/142A/80.

[342] Sherwood, *WHP*, 805-06.

[343] Churchill Archives, CHAR 20/142A/122.

[344] Churchill Archives, CHAR 20/168/93.

[345] Halsted, MS, Chapter 13, passim.

[346] Sherwood, *R&H*, pp. 521-22.

[347] Churchill, *Triumph and Tragedy*, p. 142; Roll, p. 343-44; O'Sullivan, p. 12.

[349] Stoler, *Allies in War*, p. 194. Stoler claims that the Second Quebec Conference marked the last time that "Churchill could claim any sort of equality with the Americans." p. 170. See also Kimball, *Forged in War*, pp. 274-79. Hull and Eden knew that a strong Germany would be a useful bulwark against the spread of Soviet influence in postwar Europe and objected to the Morgenthau Plan.

[350] Sherwood, *WHP*, p. 824.

[351] Robert Hopkins, p. 103.

[352] Churchill Archives, CHAR 20/197B/196).

[353] Sherwood, *WHP*, p. 825; Halsted MS, Chapter 14, p. 19.

[354] Halsted MS, Chapter 14, p. 22.

[355] Stoler, *Allies in War*, p. 187-89; "The Churchill-Stalin 'Percentages' Agreement on the Balkans, Moscow, October 1944, *The American Historical Review*, 1978, p. 368, from Stoler.

[356] Stoler, *Allies in War*, p. 188.

[357] Sherwood, *WHP*, p. 826. Warren Kimball explains the power politics that underlay the percentages deal in *The Juggler*, p. 163-65. A somewhat desperate Churchill, in the absence of the President, in a one-on-one with Stalin sought to protect British interest in Greece and Yugoslavia by relenting on Poland.

[358] Kimball, *The Juggler*, pp. 160-62.

[359] O'Sullivan suggests that WSC withheld information in his messages to Hopkins about Tolstoy; he did not mention the Percentages Deal. But, Hopkins knew the PM well enough to know that "vital information was deliberately left out of Churchill's reports to Washington." p. 114; Churchill, *Triumph and Tragedy*, p. 264.

[360] The angry draft was sent to Hopkins instead. Kimball, *The Juggler*, p. 165; Stoler, *Allies in War*, pp. 188-89; Wills, pp. 19-20. Neither Kimball nor Stoler note Hopkins' interventions. See Sir Robin Renwick, *Fighting with the Allies: America and Britain in Peace and at War* (New York: Random House, 1996), pp. 99-100. Two years later, as Churchill wrote, the United States president, with public opinion on its side, was actively against Communist insurrection in Greece.

[361] Churchill, *Memoirs*, p. 911.

[362] Churchill Archives, CHAR 20/174/101 and 109.

[363] Halsted MS, Chapter 14, p. 4.

[364] Quoted in Kimball, *Forged in War*, p. 264.

[365] Churchill Archives, CHAR 20/169/74-76. Operation Anvil, later named Dragoon, were centered in southern France in preparation for support Operation Overlord.

[366] Churchill Archives, CHAR 20/169/87.

[367] McJimsey, pp. 291-93.

[368] Sherwood, *WHP*, pp. 744-45. Mark Stoler, *Allies in War,* argues that FDR was very realistic as to the power that the Soviet Union and Stalin would have after the war was over but felt that his "personal charm" could mitigate any negative effect that this would have. p. 140. At the same time, British power was on the wane. Churchill realized this at Teheran when the President often ignored the Prime Minister, once laughing at him with Stalin. Stoler, *Allies in War*, p. 142. Hopkins seemingly either understood this as his boss's strategy in trying mightily to engage Stalin or as a real change in the balance of power in the Grand Alliance, or both. He clearly knew that the Red Army was the key to defeating the Axis powers and that Stalin exercised total control of the Soviet Union and the army.

[369] Villefosse, p. 11; Sherwood, *Roosevelt and Hopkins*, p. 167.

[370] Halsted MS, Chapter 14, p. 5

[371] Churchill Archives, 20/177/88 and 23.

[372] Halsted MS, Chapter 14, p. 7; Sherwood, *Roosevelt and Hopkins*, p. 847.

[373] Jean Lacoutre, *De Gaulle, The Ruler, 1945-1970* (New York: W. W. Norton, 1991), pp. 55-57.

[374] Villefosse, p. 11; McJimsey, pp. 361-63; Sherwood, *Roosevelt and Hopkins*, p. 847.

[375] Sherwood, *Roosevelt and Hopkins*, p. 849.

[376] McJimsey, p. 360.

[377] Robert Hopkins Collection, Georgetown University Library Special Collections, Box 6, F2. There are many iterations of this "lemon tree" story but this one seems to be believable since Robert Hopkins related it himself and he was there.

[378] McJimsey, pp. 364-65.

[379] S, M. Plokhy, *Yalta: The Price of Peace* (New York: Penguin Books, 2010). p. 179.

[380] During this session only military issues were discussed.

[381] Robert Hopkins notes, PFP, 9/27. The photographers were not admitted to any of the meetings but were able to photograph the leaders at dinners and at what we now call photo-ops. He noted that there was plenty of caviar at the conference, even for breakfast, followed always by herring, bread, fruit and tea. However, the American delegation of 258 souls, devoured coffee, eggs, toast and orange juice for breakfast prepared by the mess boys from the Presidential yacht, Potomac.

[382] Hopkins stayed on the ground floor in quarters near the President, likely in consideration of his physical condition. Nevertheless, the room was apparently "bedeviled by bedbugs." PFP 6/2.

[383] McJimsey, pp. 365-67.

[384] Moran, p. 241. Roosevelt was ill during the Yalta Conference, and so was Hopkins. But Allied victory was all but assured by this time.

[385] Plokhy, pp. 92-101.

[386] Plokhy, pp. 17-18, 77. Stoler, in *Allies in War*, writes that neither Roosevelt nor Churchill "gave away anything at the conference that they actually possessed." To accuse them of giving away Eastern Europe makes the mistake of judging them by present standards, of being "present minded." p. 193.

[387] McJimsey, p. 366.

[388] Plokhy, p. 155,

[389] Plokhy, p. 156.

[390] McJimsey, p. 367.

[391] James Gaut Ragsdale, "Yalta (1945): Did Roosevelt Sell Out Poland?" (*The Florida Communication Journal*, XVIII, 1990), pp. 16-20; Churchill, *Memoirs*, p. 927.

392 Plokhy, 244.

393 McJimsey, p. 363-64; see also Sherwood, *Roosevelt and Hopkins*, pp. 850-56.

394 McJimsey, p. 365.

395 McJimsey, p. 365.

396 McJimsey, p. 366.

397 McJimsey, p. 367.

398 McJimsey, p. 369; Sherwood, *Roosevelt and Hopkins*, pp. 857-861.

399 Halsted MS. Chapter 14, p. 10.

400 Halsted MS, Chapter 14, p. 14.

401 Sherwood, *Roosevelt and Hopkins*, p. 870.

402 Churchill, *Memoirs*, p. 929.

403 Stoler, *Allies in War*, p. 194; Sherwood, *Roosevelt and Hopkins*, p. 870.

404 London Poles had instigated the Warsaw Uprising and the Soviets refused to help while the Germans slaughtered them, determined to establish a Communist government there. In addition, the Katyn Forest Massacre of Polish soldiers by the Russians was overlooked by the Americans and British, and U.S. policy was conciliatory toward the Soviets over Poland. McJimsey, p. 356.

405 Plokhy, pp. 15-25; see Sherwood, *Roosevelt and Hopkins*, pp. 864-65 for outcomes at Yalta.

406 Sherwood, *Roosevelt and Hopkins*, p. 871.

407 Sherwood, *Roosevelt and Hopkins*, p. 872.

408 Halsted MS. Chapter 14, p. 16.

409 Robert Hopkins, "The Meeting Between President Franklin D. Roosevelt and King Ibn Saud, Great Bitter Lake in the Suez Canal, February 14, 1945," PFP, 9/26.

410 Halsted MS. Chapter 14, p. 19.

411 Sherwood, *Roosevelt and Hopkins*, p. 881; Churchill, *Memoirs of the Second World War*, abridgement, p, 945-46. Churchill had originally planned on attending Roosevelt's funeral and afterwards he would meet with President

Truman. However, he yielded to pressure from friends and did not make the trip. He seems to regret not meeting the new President more than actually saying goodbye to his old friend. He even mildly criticizes FDR for not having informed Truman fully about matters of state.

[412] Costigliola, p. 3.

[413] Churchill Archives, CHAR 20/214/138-139.

[414] McJimsey, pp. 387-89.

[415] Fenby, pp. 404-05. Roosevelt's State of the Union speech in 1941 proposed the Four Freedoms. Freedom of speech. Freedom of worship. Freedom from want.

[416] McJimsey, p. 393.

[417] Marquis Childs, the *Los Angeles Times*, January 31, 1946; "Hopkins Finished Most of Memoirs," *The New York Times*, Saturday, February 2, 1946. PFP, 9/15.

[418] Sherwood, *Roosevelt and Hopkins*, p. 922.

[419] Sherwood, *Roosevelt and Hopkins*, pp. 920-27.

[420] Marquis Childs, the *Los Angeles Times*, January 31, 1946; "Hopkins Finished Most of Memoirs," *The New York Times*, Saturday, February 2, 1946. PFP, 9/15. Of course, Hopkins never did write his memoirs.

[421] Sherwood, *WHP*, p. 923.

[422] Sherwood, *Roosevelt and Hopkins*, p. 922-23.

[423] Halsted MS, Chapter 15, p. 15. Scholars have often asked how Hopkins could have accomplished so much with all the illnesses that plagued him. Dr. James Halsted suggests that people with severe illness often have the moral energy to sustain "an unswerving commitment to their calling." Halsted MS, Introduction, p. 2.

[424] Halsted, Chapter 15, p. 27; Sherwood, *Roosevelt and Hopkins*, p. 931.

[425] Women were attracted to him and he did have several flings. Actress Dorothy Hale committed suicide after he publicly declared that they were not engaged. Clare Booth

Luce, no fan of his politics, wondered what made a woman do such a thing over such a man. Costigliola, p. 78.

Made in United States
Troutdale, OR
08/28/2023

12434296R00166